NELSON'S
BATTLES

Nelson's Battles

The Art of Victory in the Age of Sail

Nicholas Tracy

Other works by the author

Manila Ransomed, Exeter: University Press, 1995

Canada's Naval Strategy, Security Occasional Paper No.1, Dalhousie University Centre for Foreign Policy Studies, 1995

A Cruising Guide to the Bay of Fundy and the St John River, Frederiction: Goose Lane, 1992

Attack on Maritime Trade, London: Macmillan, 1991

Naval Warfare in the Age of Sail, (ed), London: Conway Maritime Press, 1990

Navies,Deterrence and American Independence, University of British Columbia Press, 1988

Copyright © Nicholas Tracy 1996

First published in Great Britain in 1996 by Chatham Publishing, an imprint of Gerald Duckworth & Co Ltd

This Edition published 2001 by Caxton Editions, an imprint of The Caxton Publishing Group

ISBN 1 84067 3575

British Library Cataloguing in Publication Data
A catalogue record for this book is available from the British Library

The author and publisher acknowledge the assistance of the National Maritime Museum, London, in the supply of illustrations.

Battle plans drawn by Sarah Petite
Designed and typeset by Tony Hart, Isle of Wight
Printed and bound by C.T.P.S.

CONTENTS

FOREWORD

HORATIO NELSON exercises an enduring fascination. Put in today's terms, he is the stuff of which tabloid headlines are made, combining heroism, charisma and tactical genius with very human faults, including what may be regarded as a loose approach to 'traditional family values'. As the bicentenary of Trafalgar approaches, the one naval hero whose name remains generally familiar will doubtless become once again a household word.

Dr Tracy's book is not a 'mere biography', nor is it hagiography. *Nelson's Battles* is the vehicle for a study of the nature and conduct of war at sea during the first true 'World War' and it will stand as a most useful reference work for anyone who wishes to look beyond the man and his achievements. It is also an eminently suitable book for the lay reader or beginner in naval history, for scholarship is combined with a deft narrative style and nicely chosen contemporary comments by aquaintances and participants in the battles.

It is sometimes difficult to remember in these days of rapid change, 200 years after Nelson's battles, that the essentials of sea warfare had not changed a great deal during the 200 years which preceded them. Wooden ships were still propelled by scarcely predictable natural forces, the main weapon was still loaded from the same awkward direction (and engagement ranges were, if anything, rather shorter), while the commanders' control of fleet engagements were as limited as their communications. Yet Nelson's generation brought something different and transformed the formal, stately but often sterile dance of a battle under sail into a shocking brawl. These captains had what might nowadays be known as the 'killer instinct' and, loosed from the shackles of the rigid line by admirals such as Nelson and his mentor, John Jervis, they probed for and exploited weakness with a ferocity which they transmitted to their officers and men and which repeadedly overwhelmed their opponents.

For a captain of a ship of the line serving with a main fleet opportunity came seldom—there were barely a dozen major actions between 1793 and 1805—but not just promotion and prize money beckoned those who distinguished themselves: perhaps for the first time in an external war, there was the genuine dislike of an enemy for the sake of his ideology. Nelson acted as a touchstone, for service alongside and later under his command seldom attracted anything but success—the Tenerife and Boulogne enterprises were notable exceptions. Altogether, over a hundred captains served with or for him in eleven actions afloat, three of these—Thomas Fremantle, Robert Miller and Thomas Foley—serving with him on five occasions. Some of them, like Philip Durham, Henry Digby and James Gore, had already distinguished themselves in a dozen successful actions apiece in the nursey of great seamen, the continuous blockade of the coast of France, before promotion to 74s and allocation to Nelson's command.

Whether these men were familiar with his ways or they came to him as accomplished fighting seamen, Nelson provided inspiration and leadership which filtered down to the lower deck, where prize money and promotion counted for little and ideology was limited to the efforts of the United Irishmen to provoke mutiny. The disturbances which affected the Mediterranean Fleet did not affect the outcome of the Tenerife expedition and the battle of the Nile was won by a squadron including four ships which had, at the least, displayed what St Vincent described as 'ill humour' just a year before. Mutiny, the evils of 'the Press' and the social shortcomings of life between decks make more attractive popular reading than the seamanship and gunnery drills instilled into the ordinary sailors to create and perpetuate such a fearsome fighting machine.

His premature death, during the battle which is often regarded as England's finest nineteenth-century hour, turned high competence and charisma into legend. In the years after his death, Nelson came to represent, to the general public, the general superiority, if not invincibility, of the Royal Navy and its men—in which the sense of pride was so strong that one well-known tragedian could get away with dancing the hornpipe in 'King Lear' because in his salad days he had been a sailor under Nelson at the Nile, Copenhagen and Trafalgar!

How the hero would have fared in the post-Trafalgar era of undeniable maritime superiority stands open to question, but this is not something which Nicholas Tracy attempts to guess. The man should be remembered by his battles and these are worthily described.

David Brown

Part I

NELSON AND SEA POWER

Vice Admiral Horatio Nelson (1758-1805), painted in 1801 by Sir William Beechey (1753-1839). (National Maritime Museum, London: BHC 2892)

VICE ADMIRAL Horatio Lord Nelson was a hero from the time of his first great victory at the battle of the Nile in 1798. He was mobbed wherever he went, and showered with titles and orders of chivalry by the powerful, presentation swords by his brother officers, and gifts of money by Parliament and the East India Company. He is probably the only admiral whose name is known to the general public, and not only in Britain. Hero status was richly deserved and arduously earned. He was, and continues to be, honoured by the Royal Navy because he was a master of his profession. He set the highest standards for performance, and his consummate leadership transformed the way the profession went about its business. In 1797, in justification for the receipt of a pension, he wrote

> That, during the present war, your Memorialist has been in four actions with the fleets of the enemy, viz. on the 13th and 14th of March 1795; on the 13th July 1795; and on the 14th of February 1797; in three actions with frigates; in six engagements against batteries; in ten actions in boats employed in cutting out of harbours; in destroying vessels, and in taking three towns. Your Memorialist has also served on shore with the army four months, and commanded the batteries at the sieges of Bastia and Calvi. That during the war, he has assisted at the capture of seven sail of the line, six frigates, four corvettes, and eleven privateers of different sizes; and taken and destroyed near fifty sail of merchant vessels; and your Memorialist has actually been engaged against the enemy upwards of ONE HUNDRED AND TWENTY TIMES. In which service your Memorialist has lost his right eye and arm, and been severely wounded and bruised in his body. All of which services and wounds your memorialist must humbly submit to your Majesty's most gracious consideration.[1]

In the next eight years he was to fight and win his three great victories at the Nile, Copenhagen, and Trafalgar. He was devoted to his duty to a degree which may be hard for the late twentieth century to understand. His devotion to his friends, and they to him, awake easier echoes and ensure his continuing popularity.

Over one hundred years after his death, the Admiralty thought it important at the eve of the First World War to order a study of the tactics Nelson had employed at Trafalgar.[2] The Admiral's art was developing faster during Nelson's early years than at any time since the mid-seventeenth century when the line of battle was first introduced. The Seven Years War and the War of the American Revolution stimulated the development of new ideas about the most effective use of naval materiel, making tactics more technical, but also more flexible. Experience, developments in ship design and signalling, and the perfection of drill, transformed naval methods. Nelson became a master of them.

His victories, however, were not simply the fruits of technical prowess. No less important was his ability to judge the capacity of his enemy, and most important of all was his ability to lead his men. Writing to congratulate Nelson after his victory in the battle of the Nile, Admiral Lord Howe, who had himself done so much to develop British naval tactics and team work, remarked on the 'singular' success in which 'every Captain distinguished himself'. Nelson himself referred to them as a 'band of brothers', and the Nelsonic band of brothers remains a model for command relationships in a service which has to its cost not always followed the standard set in Nelson's great cabin. His capacity to make decisive moves which produced unprecedented results, based on his understanding of the strengths and weaknesses of his enemy and of his own fleet, became known as 'the Nelson Touch'. Nelson had an all but unique capacity to infuse the same spirit into others as inspired his own actions.

Throughout his service life Nelson continued to evoke the warmest loyalty from subordinates by his own commitment to them. George Duff, captain of the *Mars*, had not previously met Nelson before the latter assumed command of the force assembled off Cadiz in October 1805. He was invited to dine with

Nelson on board *Victory*, and reported to his wife that 'He certainly is the pleasantest admiral I ever served under.' A few days later he added: 'He is so good and pleasant a man, that we all wish to do what he likes, without any kind of orders. I have been myself very lucky with most of my admirals, but I really think the present the pleasantest I have ever met with.'[3]

Edward Berry, captain of Nelson's flagship at the battle of the Nile in 1798, sent a 'Narrative' to *The Naval Chronicle* which contains the following account of Nelson's method. Nelson, he wrote, had the 'highest opinion of, and placed the firmest reliance on the valour and conduct of every captain in his squadron'. Whenever the weather permitted, he signalled for his captains to come over to the *Vanguard*, where he described to them his 'ideas of the different and best modes of attack, and such plans as he proposed to

Nelson receiving the surrender of the San Nicolas, *by Richard Westall (1765-1836).* (National Maritime Museum, London: BHC 2909)

1. To the King's most excellent Majesty, the Memorial of Sir Horatio Nelson, October 1797, *NC* 1 (1797) p29.

2. See: *Evidence Relating to the Tactics Employed by Nelson at the Battle of Trafalgar*, Report of a Committee Appointed by the Admiralty, Great Britain, Cd. 7120, 1913.

3. Duff to his wife, Sophia,– and 10 October 1805; DLN VII pp70n and 71n.

4. Edward Berry, *Engagement of the Nile, An Authentic Narrative of the Proceedings of His Majesty's Squadron under the Command of Rear Admiral Sir Horatio Nelson, from its Sailing from Gibraltar to the conclusion of The Glorious Battle of the Nile*, drawn up from the minutes by an Officer of Rank in the Squadron [Edward Berry]. To which is added, Lord Nelson's official dispatches, and an intercepted letter from Rear Admiral Genteaume, giving an account of the engagement. *NC* 1, pp50–51; republished at Quebec by John Neilson, Mountain Street, 1799.

5. George L Browne to his parents, 4 December 1805, *Logs* II p195.

6. 'The Friend', Essay V, *Coleridge* I p512.

7. To Dr Alexander Carlyle, 24 August 1801, *Collingwood* #69, p130.

8. Robert Southey, *Life of Nelson*, (first published 1813) London: Constable & Co, 1916 pp36–7. See Note by Oliver Warner, *The Mariner's Mirror*, Vol. 50 (1964) pp57–9.

9. 10 March 1795, James Stanier Clarke, and John M'Arthur, *Life of Admiral Lord Nelson K.B. from his Lordships Manuscripts*, (1840) II pp266–67, and DLN II p17.

10. Colonel Stewart's Narrative, DLN IV p308.

11. 'Extract of a Letter from the Master of his Majesty's Ship *Bellona*, dated 19th April 1801', *NC* 5 p452, reprinted in DLN IV p344.

execute upon falling in with the enemy, whatever their position or situation might be by day or by night'. He had prepared a plan for every eventuality, and made his captains 'thoroughly acquainted' with them all. The result was that 'upon surveying the situation of the enemy, they could ascertain with precision what were the ideas and intention of their commander, without the aid of any further instructions'. This careful preparation made signalling almost unnecessary, and saved time. 'The attention of every captain could almost undistractedly be paid to the conduct of his own particular ship.'[4] Lieutenant George Browne of the *Victory*, writing to his parents six weeks after the Battle of Trafalgar in 1805, virtually reiterated Berry's assessment: 'the frequent communications he [Lord Nelson] had with his Admirals and captains put them in possession of all his plans, so that his mode of attack was well known to every officer of the fleet'.[5]

Samuel Taylor Coleridge, who spent some time as secretary to Alexander Ball who was one of Nelson's captains at the Nile and later Governor of Malta, wrote that Nelson was as capable of learning from others as he was of teaching. He

collected, as it passed by him, whatever could add to his own stores, appropriated what he could assimilate, and levied subsidies of knowledge from all the accidents of social life and familiar intercourse. Even at the jovial board, and in the height of unrestrained merriment, a casual suggestion, that flashed a new light on his mind, changed the boon companion into the hero and the man of genius; and with the most graceful transition he would make his company as serious as himself.[6]

Cuthbert Collingwood was Nelson's friend from the time they served together as lieutenants in the West Indies, although their personalities were very different. In comments to a friend about Nelson's method, he expressed a belief that it was not a matter of careful planning in a narrow sense. In Collingwood's

opinion, it was Nelson's habit of tactical analysis, flexibility of mind, and rapport with his officers, which enabled him to make deft responses. 'Without much previous preparation or plan', Collingwood wrote, 'he has the facility of discovering advantages as they arise, and the good judgment to turn them to his use. An enemy that commits a false step in his view is ruined, and it comes on him with an impetuosity that gives him no time to recover.'[7] Nelson was implacably committed to one object: the annihilation of the French fleet. He constantly worked over his strategic and tactical ideas, without ever losing his flexibility, and was ever ready to pursue his enemy to the end of the earth. At the Nile there was no time for last-minute detailed instructions, unless the element of surprise were to be lost. Everything depended upon the capacity of his captains to interpret the tactical ideas Nelson had discussed with them. When there was time to issue more detailed and particular tactical instructions, however, as there was at Copenhagen, Nelson was careful to do so.

Behind Nelson's ability to take his officers so completely into his confidence was his own devotion to duty, and his humanity. According to the contemporary biography of Robert Southey, Nelson as a young man, returning from the East Indies an invalid, depressed, and worried about his future without important connections in the Admiralty or at Court, suddenly caught the idea that his patron should be his 'King and Country'. 'Well then,' I exclaimed, 'I will be a hero, and confiding in Providence, I will brave every danger.'[8] He was as good as his word, and acquired a reputation for seeking danger. He once wrote to his wife: 'A glorious death is to be envied; and if anything happens to me, recollect that death is a debt we all must pay, and whether now, or a few years hence, can be but of little consequence.'[9] At the battle of Copenhagen he cheerfully remarked to Colonel Stewart, who wrote the most important eyewitness account of the battle, that 'It is warm work and this day may be the last to us at any moment. But mark you!' he added, 'I would not be elsewhere for thousands.'[10] However, his own euphoria did not blind him to the need to sustain the morale of others.

His concern for the public service, and determination to ensure that the task in hand was properly done, could be illustrated by many instances. A powerful example of his commitment is provided by the account given by Alexander Briarly, Master of the *Bellona*. After the battle of Copenhagen, when Nelson was left behind to conduct diplomacy with the Crown Prince's officers, the Commander-in-Chief, Admiral Sir Hyde Parker, sent a message to him that the Swedish fleet was reported to be at sea. Nelson immediately

ordered a boat to be manned, and without even waiting for a boat cloak (though you must suppose the weather pretty sharp here at this season of the year) and having to row about 24 miles with the wind and current against him, jumped into her and ordered me to go with him, I having been on board to remain till she had got over the Grounds [the shoals south of Copenhagen].

All I had ever seen or heard of him could not half so clearly prove to me the singular and unbounded zeal of this truly great man.

His anxiety in the boat for nearly six hours (lest the Fleet should have sailed before he got on board one of them, and lest we should not catch the Swedish squadron) is beyond all conception.[11]

His humanity transformed his demanding sense of duty. Prince William Henry, son of King George III, described his meeting with Nelson onboard Admiral Lord Hood's flagship at New York in 1781.

Captain Nelson, of the *Albemarle*, came in his barge alongside, who appeared to be the merest boy of a Captain I ever beheld: and his dress was worthy of attention. He had on a full laced uniform: his lank unpowdered hair was tied in a stiff Hessian tail, of an extraordinary length; the old fashioned flaps of his waistcoat added to the general quaintness of his figure, and produced an appearance which particularly attracted my

notice; for I had never seen anything like it before, nor could I imagine who he was, nor what he came about. My doubts were, however, removed when Lord Hood introduced me to him. There was something irresistibly pleasing in his address and conver-

'Frigate Becalmed', by Charles Brooking. Brooking lived only thirty-six years, dying in 1759, and his short life was made miserable by ruthless dealers who exploited his poverty. Unquestionably, however, he knew ships and the sea. The title given to this picture is puzzling because the ship is a two-decker, whereas the term 'frigate' was usually applied to single-decked ships like Nelson's Boreas. *Brooking's painstaking detail of the rigging gives a good impression of the journey the young midshipmen had to make to the masthead. (British Museum: BM 1875.8.14.949).*

sation; and an enthusiasm, when speaking on professional subjects, that showed he was no common being. . . . I found him warmly attached to my Father, and singularly humane: he had the honour of the King's service, and the independence of the British Navy, particularly at heart.[12]

Unfortunately, Nelson's devotion to the royal family was extended to the dissipated and undisciplined prince, and earned him no regard from King George.

Lady Hughes, who travelled to the West Indies in the *Boreas* under Nelson's command, provided a vivid account which was published by Southey. There were thirty young midshipmen onboard, and some of them were naturally timid. Nelson apparently never rebuked them. He

Frances Nelson, Horatio's wife. (National Maritime Museum, London: BHC 2883)

always wished to show them he desired nothing of them that he would not instantly do himself: and I have known him say– 'Well, Sir, I am going a race to the masthead, and beg I may meet you there.' No denial could be given to such a wish, and the poor fellow instantly began his march. His Lordship never took the least notice with what alacrity it was done, but when he met at the top, instantly began speaking in the most cheerfull manner, and saying how much a person was to be pitied who could fancy there was any danger, or even anything disagreeable, in the attempt. After this excellent example, I have seen the timid youth lead another, and rehearse his Captain's words.[13]

When on the West Indies Station, Nelson was discovered by John Herbert, the President of the Nevis, under a table playing with the young son of his widowed niece Fanny. Nelson was introduced to Fanny, and they soon married.

His attitude to subordinates was both firm and considerate. As a young man he had been impressed by the First Lieutenant of the *Carcass*, on which ship he sailed on a voyage north of Spitzbergen, who, whatever the dangers or difficulties, 'never was heard...to enforce his commands with oath, or to call a sailor by any other than his usual name.'[14] As a young captain in the West Indies he was reprimanded by the Admiralty for pardoning a sailor who had been condemned to death for desertion, and discharging him from the service. He went to considerable trouble to establish a plea of insanity for another of his men who murdered a prostitute. During the early years of the French Revolution, while he was unemployed, he became actively concerned by the agitators preaching social revolt in his native Norfolk, but when he considered how hard was the lot of the poor labourers he felt indignation that the landlords had not long before increased their wages to keep pace with rising costs. On the other hand, he did not shrink from inflicting the tough punishments which were such a feature of naval life.

Towards his superiors whom he thought deficient in their duty he was resolute. His efforts to ensure that officers did not abuse their authority to enrich themselves during his service in the West Indies did not endear himself to the Admiralty and may explain the five years he was unemployed before the outbreak of war with France in 1793. He always sought the annihilation of his enemy, and was intolerant of commanders with lower standards. When in 1795 he commanded the 64-gun ship, *Agamemnon*, in action under the command of Admiral Hotham and captured a French 80-gun ship, *Ça Ira*, he was bitter about the failure to pursue the defeated enemy. Fourteen British ships had taken on seventeen French, and captured only two. In indignation Nelson wrote his wife:

> had we taken ten Sail, and allowed the eleventh to escape, when it had been possible to have got at her, I could never have called it well done . . . We should have had such a day as I believe, the annals of England never produced . . . Nothing can stop the courage of English seamen.[15]

When one of the captains who commanded a ship at the battle of Camperdown in 1797 was court-martialed for misconduct, Nelson commented to Captain Bertie, who was one of the members of the court, that he wanted officers going into battle to have in mind that the chance of being shot by the enemy if they did their duty was less than the certainty of being shot by their friends if they failed in it.[16] However, the mellowing effect of experience increased his willingness to comprehend the limitations of others. He was to be more sympathetic with Vice Admiral Sir Robert Calder, who, in the campaign leading to Trafalgar, conducted a battle against the odds with technical skill but broke off the engagement without seeking annihilating results.

Nelson rightly regarded the spirit and ability of his officers and men as more important than the materiel strength of the fleets placed under his command. Writing to Lord Melville in support of one of his captains who had been censured and broken by a Court Martial for wrecking his ship, he said that he did not 'regret the loss of the *Raven* compared to the value of Captain Layman's services, which are a National loss'.[17]

Writing to an old friend during the long blockade of Toulon in 1804, Nelson commented that

> The great thing in all Military Service is health; and you will agree with me, that it is easier for an Officer to keep men healthy, than for a Physician to cure them. . . . I have, by changing the cruizing ground, not allowed the sameness of prospect to satiate the mind–sometimes by looking at Toulon, Ville Franche, Barcelona and Rosas; then running round Minorca, Majorca, Sardinia and Corsica; and two or three times anchoring for a few days, and sending a Ship to the last place for *onions*, which I find the best thing that can be give to Seamen; having always good mutton for the sick & cattle when we can get them, and plenty of fresh water.

Admiral Cornwallis, he complained, who commanded the Channel Fleet blockading Brest

> has great merit for his perservering cruise, but he has everything sent him: we have nothing; We seem forgotten by the great folks at home.[18]

The burden of contracting locally for supplies, and of corresponding with the surgeons at Gibraltar to ensure that his men in hospital were properly cared for, he resolutely shouldered. Ball observed that Nelson

> looked at everything, not merely in its possible relation to the Naval Service in general, but in its immediate Bearings on his own Squadron; to his officers, his men, to the particular ships themselves, his affections were as strong and ardent as those of a Lover. Hence, though his temper was constitutionally irritable and uneven, yet never

12. Minutes of a Conversation with the Duke of Clarence at Bushey Park, Clarke and M'Arthur, (1840) I p 53; DLN I p70.

13. Lady Hughes to Mr Matcham, 24 June 1906 (Nelson Papers) DLN I pp124–25.

14. John Baird. Quoted in Tom Pocock, *Horatio Nelson*, London: Bodley Head, 1987 p23.

15. To Mrs Nelson, 1 April 1795, Clark and McArthur (1840) i p304; DLN II p26

16. 4 January 1798, DLN III pp1–2.

17. 10 March 1805, *NC* vol 38 p 18; DLN IV p353.

18. To Dr Moseley, 11 March 1804, DLN V p437–38.

was a Commander so enthusiastically loved by men of all ranks, from the Captain of the Fleet to the youngest Ship-boy. Hence too the unexampled Harmony which reigned in his Fleet year after year, under circumstances that might well have undermined the patience of the best balanced Dispositions, much more of men with the impetuous character of British Sailors.[19]

It is hardly surprising that he inspired devotion amongst his men. In a boat action at Cadiz he had his life saved three times by his coxswain who even interposed his hand to ward off a sword blow aimed at Nelson's head. A sailor writing home after Trafalgar said

I never set eyes on him, for which I am both sorry and glad, for to be sure I should like to have seen him, but then, all the men in our ship who have seen him are such soft toads, they have done nothing but Blast their Eyes and cry ever since he was killed. God bless you! chaps that fought like the Devil sit down and cry like a wench.[20]

Nelson's sense of the theatrical, while entirely natural to him, was also a useful tool of leadership. Like several other well-known commanders, he wore distinctive headgear: he wore his cocked hat worn in line with his shoulders which was not the contemporary fashion. His taste for the gaudy stars of chivalry helped to identify him to sailors who would not otherwise have recognised him.

William Beatty, Nelson's personal physician during the Trafalgar campaign, wrote that Nelson's habits of life were abstemious, and yet very open.

His Lordship used a great deal of exercise, generally walking on deck six or seven hours in the day. He always rose early, for the most part shortly after daybreak. He breakfasted in summer about six, and at seven in winter: and if not occupied in reading or writing despatches, or examining into the details of the Fleet, he walked on the quarter-deck the greater part of the forenoon; going down to his cabin occasionally to commit to paper such incidents or reflections as occurred to him during that time, and as might be hereafter useful to the service of his country. He dined generally about half-past two o'clock. At his table there were seldom less than eight or nine persons, consisting of the different Officers of the Ship: and when the weather and the service permitted, he very often had several of the Admirals and Captains in the Fleet to dine with him; who were mostly invited by signal, the rotation of seniority being commonly observed by his Lordship in these invitations. At dinner he was alike affable and attentive to every one: he ate very sparingly himself, the liver and wing of a fowl, and a small plate of macaroni, in general composing his meal, during which he occasionally took a glass of champagne. He never exceeded four glasses of wine after dinner, and seldom drank three; and even those were diluted with either Bristol or common water.

Few men subject to the vicissitudes of a Naval life, equalled his Lordship in an habitual systematic mode of living. He possessed such a wonderful activity of mind, as even prevented him from taking ordinary repose, seldom enjoying two hours of uninterrupted sleep; and on several occasions he did not quit the deck during the whole night. At these times he took no pains to protect himself from the effects of wet, or the night air; wearing only a thin great coat: and he has frequently, after having his clothes wet through with rain, refused to have them changed, saying that the leather waistcoat which he wore over his flannel one would secure him from complaint. He seldom wore boots, and was consequently very liable to have his feet wet.[21]

One of Nelson's many biographers, Oliver Warner, remarked that 'with the Battle of the Nile, such a light fell upon Nelson as might have distressed a man of another stamp. He welcomed it. He loved being a hero'.

19. 'The Friend', *Coleridge* II p364.

20. Warner p356.

21. Sir William Beatty, *The Authentic Narrative of the Death of Lord Nelson*, London: Cadell & Davies, 1807; DLN VII pp260–62.

22. Warner pp12--13.

23. 19 April 1799, *Keith* p37.

24. Collingwood to Spencer-Stanhope, 2 November 1805, Add MSS 52780.

25. Note of a conversation with Wellington, 1 October 1834, *Croker*, II p233.

Twin ardours burnt in him. One was for fame: the other for Emma Hamilton. Through his admiration for Lady Hamilton, Nelson made himself, at times, ridiculous. The evidence is overwhelming, some of it forced from reluctant friends.[22]

There is no denying that following his victory, the experience of adulation in so dissipated a court as that of Naples, and the constant attention of Sir William Hamilton's beautiful and forceful wife Emma, went to Nelson's head. For some months he neglected his duty, and exercised irresponsibly the latitude for ignoring orders which he allowed himself with such good results at the battles of Cape St Vincent, and Copenhagen, and which he was willing that his subordinates exercise when they were well placed to interpret his general intention. The Commander-in-Chief Mediterranean, Admiral Lord Keith, wrote to his sister that Nelson at Palermo was 'cutting the most absurd figure possible for folly and vanity'.[23] Eventually, he was ordered home. Writing shortly after his death, Collingwood admitted that Nelson 'liked fame, and was open to flattery, so that people sometimes got about him who were unworthy of him'. But, he concluded, Nelson was 'a loss to his country that cannot easily be replaced'.[24]

In extenuation, it should be noted that the psychological strain was so great for Nelson in the days before the Nile battle, and later before Copenhagen, and when he sailed on what was to be his last campaign, that he experienced tormenting physical pain. If he had been brought straight back to England for a period of leave with his family after the Nile he might have dealt with the inevitable reaction with better balance. There is also reason to suspect that the head wound he received at the Nile affected his judgment.

Arthur Wellesley, the future Duke of Wellington, only met Nelson once, in September 1805 shortly before Nelson sailed on his last campaign. At first Nelson did not know who Wellesley was, and paraded all the foolish affectation of which he was capable. When he discovered Wellington's identity, however, he entirely changed his manner.

All that I had thought a charlatan style had vanished, and he talked of the state of the country and of the aspect and probabilities of affairs on the continent with a good sense, and a knowledge of subjects both at home and abroad, that surprised me equally and more agreeably than the first part of our interview had done; in fact, he talked like an officer and a statesman. . . . I don't know that I ever had a conversation that interested me more.[25]

Lady Emma Hamilton (c1761-1815) as Ariadne, by George Romney (1734-1802). (National Maritime Museum, London: BHC 2736)

His character was inconsistent, but most who knew him were able to come to terms with the vagaries, and the common man responded to him with whole-hearted devotion.

He was loyal to his family, but in the end he deserted his wife for Emma Hamilton. Fanny was a quiet and dignified woman who was devoted to Horatio, and remained close to his father for the rest of his life.[26] She had a reputation even before she met Nelson for being a sympathetic listener to 'difficult' people, and Nelson's flag-captain at Trafalgar, Thomas Masterman Hardy, regarded her as the best of women. He deprecated his friend's conduct. Fanny, however, was not one to feed his vanity, and her solicitude for his safety provoked him. She was made desperately unhappy by her husband's betrayal, and good society in England did not exonerate him. The King all but snubbed him, and there was never any possibility that Emma would be accepted at court.

Emma was boisterous, more than a little vulgar, and incapable of any sympathy for her displaced rival, but she filled a need. She was a woman who is more easily respected in the late twentieth century than in her own. A blacksmith's daughter who had been taken up by a succession of 'protectors' because of her beauty and vivacity, she had eventually been passed on to Sir William Hamilton by his nephew. She made the best of her vicissitudes, and retained an affection for all her lovers. Sir William was a remarkable man who used his post as Envoy to the Court of Naples to study antiquities and natural history. He eventually married Emma when he was 61 in 1791, but he accepted with complacency her attachment to Nelson. In Palermo, and again in England, the three shared a home.

During the last years of his life, Nelson was totally dependent emotionally upon Emma. She bore him the only child he was to have, a daughter, Horatia. A second child died soon after birth. Nelson called her his 'wife', and after Sir William's death she most certainly was in every way but the legal formalities. Nelson's evident wish to remake her into the domestic anchor which he had lost in Fanny,

however, showed the limitations of his perceptiveness.

She was no less devoted to him. When the Franco-Spanish fleet was assembling in the late summer of 1805, however, she understood that he could not be happy unless he took command of the forces arrayed against them. According to Southey, she said:

> Nelson, however we may lament your absence, and your so speedily leaving us, offer your services immediately, to go off Cadiz; they will be accepted, and you will gain a quiet heart by it.

Nelson, it was reported,

> looked at her ladyship for some moments; and, with tears in his eyes, exclaimed – 'Brave Emma! Good Emma! if there were more Emmas, there would be more Nelsons; You have penetrated my thoughts.'[27]

Probably this recollection, which must have originated with Emma herself, was a pastiche. Nevertheless, it is consistent with her regard for Nelson as a hero who must be faithful to his duty. In his will, witnessed in the cabin of the *Victory* just before she came within range of the enemy guns, Nelson left Emma and Horatia to the care of his 'King and Country'. Sadly to relate, both failed in their obligation to him.[28]

Nelson's fatherly interest in his midshipmen continued all his life, and took the place of the son he never had. He tried to promote the naval career of Fanny's son Josiah, and was exasperated by the latter's drunkeness, but Josiah may perhaps be excused his failures which came to a head at the time of Nelson's triumph at the Nile and betrayal of his mother. He later did well in business. Nelson had more success with his protégés such as William Holst, Edward Parker who died of wounds after the abortive raid on Boulogne in 1801, and John Quilliam who was first lieutenant of *Victory* at Trafalgar.

26. M Eyre Matcham, *The Nelsons of Burnham Thorpe*, London: John Lane, 1911, pp182–83.

27. Southey, pp 330; DLN VII pp26–7.

28. Codicil to Lord Nelson's Will, 21 October 1805, DLN VII pp140–41.

29. Nicholas Tracy, 'The Falkland Islands Crisis of 1770 – Use of Naval Force', *The English Historical Review*, Vol XC, January 1975, No CCCLIV, pp40–75.

Top left:
The Reverend Edmund Nelson (1722-1802), Horatio's father, by Sir William Beechey (1753-1839). He was a kindly father who made a success of raising a large family after his wife's early death. (National Maritime Museum, London: BHC 2881)

Top right:
Catherine Nelson (1725-1767), Horatio's mother. Horatio's chief memory of his mother was that she hated the French. (National Maritime Museum, London: BHC 2879)

Nelson's Early Career

It is only necessary to sketch in the chronicle of Nelson's life before he came to assume the responsibility of commanding British battle-fleets. From the contemporary biography by Robert Southey, whose brother saw service at Copenhagen, to those by Tom Pocock and Christopher Hibbert, Nelson's life has been the subject of numerous books.

He was born in Burnham Thorpe in Norfolk in 1758, the son of the rector. His mother died when he was young, leaving him with the chief recollection that she 'hated the French', and a great sense of loss he was never able to resolve. Horatio first joined the navy in 1770 when the fleet was mobilised during the Falkland Islands crisis.[29] His mother's brother, Captain Maurice Suckling, introduced him to the service. When the danger of war passed, Nelson made a voyage on a commercial vessel to the West Indies, and then on the *Carcass*, a survey vessel, which penetrated the ice fields north of Spitzbergen where Nelson had to be rescued from a youthful effort to kill a polar bear. He then made the voyage in a frigate to the East Indies. His promotions came fast, helped by Suckling's

appointment as Comptroller of the Navy Board in 1775 which gave him a patron with influence enough to take the exam for lieutenant at the early age of 18. Suckling had also given him a good grounding in seamanship, and in human relations.

In 1779 Nelson was 'made' Post Captain at the very early age of 20 by an appointment to

Captain Maurice Suckling (1725-1778), by an unknown artist. Captain Suckling, Horatio's maternal uncle, introduced him into the navy and helped him begin his career. (National Maritime Museum, London: BHC 0345)

Nelson and the Bear, by Richard Westall (1765-1836). Clearly if Nelson had got this close to the bear he would not have been able to make such an impression on the French later in life. (National Maritime Museum, London: BHC 2907)

A View of the City of Quebec, the capital of Canada, published by Carington Bowles about the time that Nelson visited Quebec. At Quebec he very nearly married a local girl but was dissuaded by his friends. (National Maritime Museum, London: PAD 2013)

command the frigate *Hinchinbrook*. In 1780 he saw his first active service in a land operation against San Juan de Nicaragua, and nearly died there of fever. He recovered when he was invalided home, and an appointment to command the frigate *Albemarle* which took him to the healthier climate of Canada completed the cure. After the conclusion of the American Revolutionary War, Nelson was fortunate enough to obtain the appointment to the frigate *Boreas* in which he sailed to the

West Indies with Lady Hughes as a passenger.

It was during his service in the West Indies that he made enemies amongst the merchants and senior officers by his insistence on enforcing the Navigation Acts against the King's former American citizens who were attempting to continue their trade with the Islands. Despite the reputation this gave him in the planter community, his offer of marriage was accepted by Frances Nisbet. He had, however, to cool his heels for five years, perhaps because

his officious probity had made him enemies at the Admiralty, or perhaps because his friendship with Prince William Henry was not regarded with favour by King George III. He was not employed during the crisis of 1790 occasioned by the Spanish attack on British interests at Nootka Sound on Vancouver Island. He was too capable an officer, however, to be overlooked in the greater crisis of war with revolutionary France.

The execution of Louis XVI in January 1793 was quickly followed on 1 February by the declaration of war by France on England, Spain, Austria and the Netherlands. The day before, Nelson had been appointed to command a 64-gun ship of the line, the *Agamemnon*, with orders to place himself under Admiral Lord Hood who was to be Commander-in-Chief in the Mediterranean. The reputation he had already acquired in Norfolk by his concern for the sufferings of the poor, and for his readiness to greet warmly old friends from all stations in life, enabled him to fill his needs for ships company with Norfolk men without extensive reliance on the press. When later Hood offered him a 74-gun ship he declined to leave those who had been loyal to him.

The Spanish participation of the First Coalition against the French Revolution was a result not only of the hostility of deeply monarchist Spanish sentiment, but also of resentment of French betrayal at the time of the crisis over Nootka Sound. It gave Nelson an opportunity to observe Spanish army and navy commands as an ally, and he was not impressed. In Cadiz, which he visited on his way to the Mediterranean, he was shocked by the inefficiency with which the Spanish navy manned their otherwise excellent ships.

A royalist insurrection in southern France, supported by a badly directed Spanish force, opened the port of Toulon to the British Navy in August 1793. Nelson was involved in the operation, most notably by his effective diplomacy at the Court of Naples which led to Neapolitan soldiers being rushed to Toulon. It was on this mission that Nelson met Sir William Hamilton and Emma. It proved im-

Left: This profile of Horatio Nelson was made by Cuthbert Collingwood, who was to be his second-in-command at Trafalgar, when they both were lieutenants in the West Indies. (National Maritime Museum, London: PAD 3164)

Below: John Adams, alias John Wilkinson, Boatswain's Mate on the Agamemnon; *painted in June 1840 by F Cruickshank when Adams was a pensioner at Greenwich naval hospital. (National Maritime Museum, London: PAH 3992)*

possible to defend Toulon against the army of the French Republic, however, and the irresolute behaviour of the Spanish army holding part of the perimeter was a major contributing cause. Artillery, commanded by the young General Napoleon Bonaparte, forced the Royal Navy to leave the harbour before the task of burning the Toulon fleet was complete. The failure of Spanish incendiary parties to carry out their task properly no doubt added to Nelson's conviction that the forces of Spain were not to be rated highly. This was not blind prejudice, but it was an over-reaction which cost him dearly at Tenerife in 1797, and influenced his tactics at Trafalgar.

Nelson later played an active part in an operation intended to liberate Corsica, and he was the driving force behind the siege and capture of Bastia, although this was never acknowledged in dispatches. And it was at the

The Port and Harbour of Toulon, engraved by P Starckman. (National Maritime Museum, London: PAD 1628)

works before Calvi, which later fell, that he lost the sight in one eye from gravel thrown up by a mortar bomb.

His resourcefulness and determination ashore was more than matched afloat. The disgust Nelson had expressed to Fanny when Hotham broke off an indecisive action against the French off Toulon in March 1795 is the more understandable because it was in that action that Nelson had so brilliantly distinguished himself in the fight with the 84-gun *Ça Ira*. The general action was no more than a skirmish, but over a thousand men were killed or wounded on each side. When two French ships, the *Ça Ira* and *Jean Bart*, collided, and the former lost speed, Nelson hauled the 64-gun *Agamemnon* out of the line and headed for her. Nelson's journal gives a stirring account:

March 13th–At daylight the Enemy's Fleet

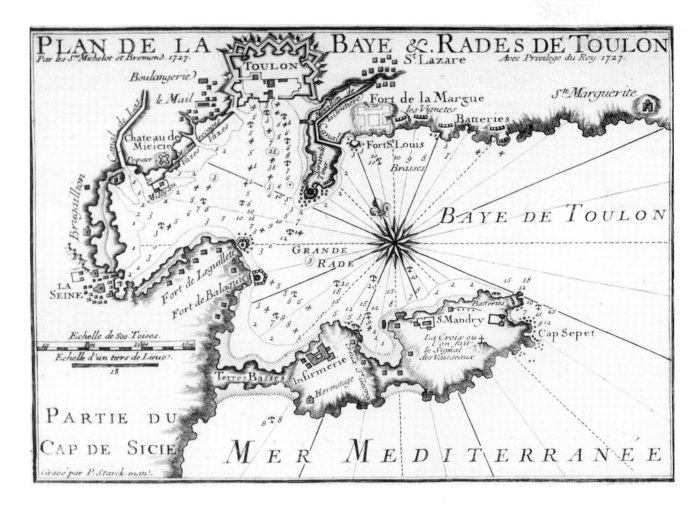

This painting, by Nicholas Pocock, purports to be a representation of the Agamemnon *'engaging with the* Ça Ira *within gunshot of a tremendous force'.* (National Maritime Museum, London: Neg 8308)

in the S.W. about three or four leagues with fresh breezes. Signal for a General chase. At eight A.M. a French Ship of the Line carried away her main and fore topmasts. At a quarter-past nine, the *Inconstant* frigate fired at the disabled Ship, but receiving many shot, was obliged to leave her. At ten A.M., tacked and stood towards the disabled Ship, and two other Ships of the Line. The disabled Ship proved to be the *Ça Ira* of 84 guns . . . [supported by the] *Sans Culotte*, one hundred and twenty guns; and the *Jean Bart*, seventy-four guns. We could have fetched the *Sans Culotte* by passing the *Ça Ira* to windward, but on looking round I saw no Ship of the Line within several miles to support me: the *Captain* was the nearest on our lee quarter. At twenty minutes past ten the *Ça Ira* began firing her stern-chasers. At half-past ten the *Inconstant* passed us to leeward, standing for the Fleet. As we drew up with the Enemy, so true did she fire her stern-guns, that not a shot missed some part of the Ship, and latterly the masts were struck every

shot, which obliged me to open our fire a few minutes sooner than I intended, for it was my intention to have touched his stern before a shot was fired. But seeing plainly from the situation of the two Fleets, the impossibility of being supported, and in case any accident happened to our masts,

Nelson's attack 13 May 1795 on the Ça Ira *which was damaged by an accident and was being towed by a frigate.*

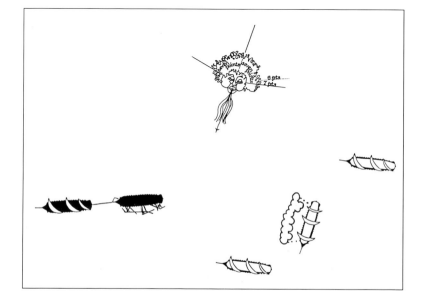

the certainty of being severely cut up, I resolved to fire so soon as I thought we had a certainty of hitting. At a quarter before eleven A.M., being within one hundred yards of the *Ça Ira's* stern, I ordered the helm to be put a-starboard, and the driver and after-sails to be braced up and shivered, and as the Ship fell off, gave her our whole broadside, each gun double-shotted. Scarcely a shot appeared to miss. The instant all were fired, braced up our after-yards, put the helm a-port, and stood after her again. This manoeuvre we practiced till one P.M., never allowing the *Ça Ira* to get a single gun from either side to fire on us. They attempted some of their after-guns, but all went far ahead of us. At this time the *Ça Ira* was a perfect wreck, her sails hanging in tatters, mizen topmast, mizen topsail, and cross jack yards shot away. At one P.M., the Frigate hove in stays, and got the *Ça Ira* round. As the Frigate first, and then the *Ça Ira*, got their guns to bear, each opened her fire, and we passed within half pistol-shot. As soon as our after-guns ceased to bear, the Ship was hove in stays, keeping, as she came round, a constant fire, and the Ship was worked with as much exactness, as if she had been turning into Spithead. On getting round, I saw the *Sans Culotte*, who had before wore with many of the Enemy's Ships, under our lee bow, and standing to pass to leeward of us, under top-gallant sails. At half-past one P.M., the Admiral made the signal for the Van-ships to join

him. I instantly bore away, and prepared to set all our sails, but the Enemy having saved their Ship, hauled close to the wind, and opened their fire, but so distant as to do us no harm; not a shot, I believe, hitting. Our sails and rigging were very much cut, and many shot in our hull and between wind and water, but, wonderful, only seven men were wounded.[30]

The next day the fleets fought a passing action at long range, with the British to leeward, and doubled by the *Ça Ira* which was to leeward under the tow of *Le Censeur*. Eventually, these isolated ships were beaten into surrender, and Nelson was on hand to send a lieutenant to hoist British colours. At this point, however, the fleets fell apart, and Hotham, to Nelson's disgust, made no effort to regain contact. After this action, he was rewarded with the courtesy rank of Colonel of Marines which added to his pay without adding to his duties.

Poor Fanny Nelson completely failed to fall in with Nelson's mood. She was so worried for his safety that she fretted herself into ill-health. It was in vain for him to write to reassure her that a heroic death was to be envied. His inability to understand how distressing to her must be his accounts of his personal heroism, it must be said, was a failing many of his brother officers shared. In Leghorn at this time Nelson was keeping company with Adelaide Correglia, an opera singer, with whom his friends thought he was making himself ridiculous. It was common for officers who had been away from home for years to make such friendships, but Nelson had no capacity to do so discretely. How significant was Fanny's failure to flatter his ego is a matter for conjecture, but it is significant that Emma was more than happy to oblige in this respect.

In December 1795 Admiral Sir John Jervis succeeded to the Command in Chief of the Mediterranean station. He was a commander to Nelson's exacting standards, and in Nelson he recognised a subordinate of the highest capacity. On their first meeting in January 1796 Jervis offered Nelson promotion to Rear

Sir William Hotham's engagement 14 March 1795. Nelson, in Agamemnon, *was directly ahead of the flagship and took the opportunity to urge decisive action, but Hotham was content with the capture of the isolated* Ça Ira *and the* Censeur.

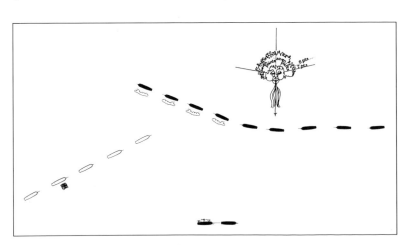

Admiral, if approved by the Admiralty, and an immediate promotion to the post of Commodore which was then a temporary rank.

Nelson's service with the Mediterranean fleet was important to his later triumphs because he experienced Jervis's methods of discipline, and of fleet management. Jervis was a very strict disciplinarian, but his severity was all directed to the goal of conditioning officers and men for combat, and training the fleet for action in all weathers. Conditions of service at the end of the eighteenth century had grown increasingly hard, and the French Revolution stood as an awful warning of the consequences of the breakdown of authority. Irish nationalism added to the discontent in a fleet manned with pressed men of whom many were Irish. In the summer of 1797 the discontent was to turn to mutiny at the fleet anchorages at Spithead off Portsmouth, and the Nore in the Thames estuary. The Spithead mutineers, who would certainly now be thought of as taking highly responsible collective action and who were careful to leave no one exposed to reprisal, succeeded in their demands for improved conditions, and received a royal pardon. Those at the Nore were more isolated, the mutiny was crushed, and a man who had allowed himself to appear as a leader was hanged. There was to be no mass mutiny in Admiral Jervis's command, however, because he resolutely stamped out any sign of disaffection, and because he took good care to look after his men's health.

Courts martial became a regular occurrence on the ships which were sent out to join his command in the months after the mutiny, and when the death sentence was passed it was always carried out. Jervis once ordered four mutineers hanged on a Sunday to demonstrate his determination, and sent home Vice Admiral Charles Thompson when he protested at the profanation of the Sabbath. He always obliged the condemned man's messmates to carry out the execution, and ordered that two armed marines from each ship be sent to ensure that it was carried out. This fierce control was matched by a no less fierce insistence that the ships and supplies sent to him

Parker the Delegate, published by W Holland in June 1797 and purporting to have been sketched by 'a naval officer'. Richard Parker allowed himself to be identified as a leader of the mutiny at the Nore and was hanged. (National Maritime Museum, London: PAD 3033)

should be in a condition fit for service, and for consumption. It is significant that the soups and citrus fruits needed to prevent scurvy were first issued to Jervis's command. It was Jervis's training which made the officers who were to be Nelson's band of brothers at the battle of the Nile.

The general action under Hotham was the first in which Nelson had held command. From that date, however, his career was to be meteoric. *Agamemnon* was worn out with service, many of her original crew had been dispersed, and Nelson was persuaded to hoist his new flag on the 74-gun *Captain*. As her captain, and commodore, he was to establish his reputation so strongly at the battle of Cape St Vincent that a year later he was appointed over the heads of more senior officers to command the detached force with which he annihilated the French Mediterranean fleet at the battle of the Nile.

30. Transactions on Board His Majesty's Ship *Agamemnon,* and of the Fleet, as seen and known by Captain Nelson, DLN II pp10–15.

Sea Power

Nelson is remembered for the battles he fought, for the tactics he used which made the best use of the high morale he inspired in the officers and men of his ships. To a considerable extent because of Nelson's successes, great battles came to be regarded as so self-evidently the means of winning wars that they virtually became an end in themselves. When

in 1902 the Admiralty prepared a 'Memorandum on Sea-Power and the Principles Involved' for the Imperial Conference, they advised the Dominion leaders that

To any naval Power the destruction of the fleet of the enemy must always be the great object aimed at. . . . In the foregoing

Sketches of capstans and anchors, by William Payne, Dover 1815. (National Maritime Museum, London: PAD 8591, 8592)

remarks the word defence does not appear. It is omitted advisedly, because the primary object of the British Navy is not to defend anything, but to attack the fleets of the enemy, and, by defeating them, to afford protection to British Dominions, supplies and commerce. This is the ultimate aim.[31]

Great victories can be sterile, however, or even counter-productive–the Pyrrhic victory of classical times. The task of the fleets Nelson commanded was fundamentally that of supporting the foreign policy of the British government in peace and war. If war could not be avoided it had to be won, but battles were only a means to that end. As battle-fleet commander on detached service, Nelson was well aware, as the Prussian General Von Clausewitz was to write a few years after Nelson's death, that 'war is simply a continuation of political intercourse, with the addition of other means'.[32]

During the eighteenth century the French navy had gradually developed a strategic *modus operandi* which largely sought to avoid battle. The task of French fleets was to mount enough of a threat that invasion of France became a difficult operation, and to maintain contact with French garrisons in America and Asia. Generally, these purposes could be undertaken while avoiding battle. Besides those defensive necessities, the French navy had a tradition of supporting the efforts of privateers who sought to make a profit out of naval war. This objective could be served by the maintenance of forces 'in being', safe in defended harbours. Because they might sortie at any time, Britain was obliged to keep her fleets in tactical formations ready for battle. Offensive use of the French navy to escort troop carriers, for invasion of the British Isles or other states, posed a greater risk of battle. There was always the hope, however, that clever deployments might enable the navy to evade British defences. This was Napoleon's intention when he took an army to invade Egypt in 1798, and during the following years when he sought to concentrate Franco-Spanish naval forces for the invasion of England. His commanders were under in-

struction to avoid battle unless the odds were very much in their favour.

The incentive to avoid battle was great because France, although a richer country than Britain, had to devote resources to the defence of her borders with continental neighbours. The French navy never had the same claim on the treasury as did the British navy. Furthermore, the fact that pre-revolutionary France did not give political power to the bourgeoisie ensured that they were unwilling to pay the taxes needed to support a fleet capable of seeking a quick decision in battle. Navies are capital-intensive institutions, and depended more on a money economy than did unmechanised armies. The revolution changed the political structure of France, but a partnership between commerce and government could not be created instantly. When Napoleon came to power he employed the French navy in a traditional strategy of manoeuvre while avoiding battle unless circumstances were ideal.

The naval potential of Britain was greater than was that of France for several reasons. Perhaps most important was the respected position commercial interests held in British society, unlike the situation in absolutist France. The partnership between businessmen, the aristocracy and government meant that there was more money in circulation in Britain even though its total economy was smaller than was that of France. The important role of the House of Commons in British government, and the presence of trading interests in the House, meant that it was easier for British administrations to raise tax revenue to pay for the navy which benefited all, but especially the monied interests. In the middle of the eighteenth century Parliament was even willing to permit the administration to run a debt for the maintenance of the navy, which periodically Parliament was asked to pay off. In effect, Parliament was willing to trust the administration with a blank cheque for the support of the navy.

The trading community in Britain supported the largest mercantile marine in the world, with the largest number of sailors. This made

31. Papers relating to a Conference between the Secretary of State for the Colonies and the Prime Ministers of Self-Governing Colonies, June 30–August 11 1902. Great Britain, House of Commons, 1902 vol LXVI p451. Sessional Paper Cd 1299.

32. Carl Marie von Clausewitz, *On War*, Peter Paret and Michael Howard, editors, Princeton: Princeton University Press, 1976, p 605.

THE PRESS GANG

William Robinson, who was a sailor on board the *Revenge*, published his memoirs in 1836, *Nautical Economy or Forecastle Recollections*, under the pseudonym of 'Jack Nasty-Face' which was the 'polite' name he was given by the officers. Jack was a volunteer, but nonetheless his experiences with the press were degrading.

> On being sent on board the receiving ship, it was for the first time I began to repent of the rash step I had taken, but it was of no avail, submission to the events of fate was my only alternative, murmuring or remonstration, I soon found, would be folly. After having been examined by the doctor, and reported *sea-worthy*, I was ordered down to the hold, where I remained all night [9 May 1805] with my companions in wretchedness, and the rats running over us in numbers. . . . Upon getting on board [the Admiral's tender] we were ordered down to the hold, and the gratings put over us; as well as a guard of marines placed round the hatchway, with their muskets loaded and fixed bayonets, as though we had been culprits of the first degree, or capital convicts.

Later, after fighting in the battle of Trafalgar, he experienced at first hand the activity of the press-gangs when he went to London for six days' leave. Being dressed in a seaman's short coat, he was chased by bounty hunters and questioned by army patrols. Jack Nasty-Face, *Nautical Economy*, pp1–2 and 38–40.

it possible for Britain to maintain in wartime the largest fleet. The availability of sailors was the true test of the capacity of a nation to keep a fleet at sea. In the Seven Years War Britain had been able to raise 84,770 sailors to man about 129 ships of the line, and in the following decades those numbers were used as benchmarks of the total naval effort of which Britain was capable.[33] In 1795 the British battlefleet listed 123 ships of the line, and in 1805 that number had been pushed up to 135, but to do so conditions of service were made so hard

that it led to the 1797 general mutiny at the fleet anchorages of Spithead and the Nore.[34]

The principal restraint on Britain's capacity to man her fleet was the means of recruitment. Britons cherished the personal liberties which had been established over the centuries. As a consequence, they were not willing to see the development of a methodical system of conscription. The result, perversely, was that wartime recruitment was left on the basis of medieval concepts of compulsory service, which by the eighteenth century was only enforced on professional sailors. These were still held to have an obligation to provide their services to the Crown in time of war. The Crown enforced this obligation by the rugged means of the impressment service. Popular commanders like Nelson were often able to fill their ships' crew lists with volunteers from their own districts, but, where dependence had to be placed on the press, recruitment was grossly inefficient. The benchmark provided by the Seven Years War indicated that the British were unlikely to be able to man more than thirty-nine ships of the line at the end of the first year of mobilisation. At the outbreak of war there was a danger that the French, who did have a system of conscription established by Colbert at the end of the seventeenth century, would be able to get their fleet to sea sooner.

Ultimately, if they could avoid defeat in the first months, the British could always keep a significantly larger fleet at sea than could the French. But when France was allied with Spain, as she was for much of the eighteenth century, or when France controlled the fleets of the Netherlands and Italy as she did under Napoleon, the pressure on British naval resources became more demanding. In 1795 there were 512,000 tons of ships in the Royal Navy, 284,000 in the French Marine, and 264,000 in the Spanish navy. The smaller navies totalled 565,000 tons, of which the largest was the Russian navy with 140,000 in the Baltic and 42,000 in the Black Sea. At the time of Trafalgar, the Royal Navy had 569,000 tons of shipping, the French Marine 182,000, the Spanish navy 139,000, and the smaller navies totalled 465,000 tons.

Britain had a greater need for cruisers, which in the eighteenth century was a term used to identify older and smaller warships stationed at focal points in the sea lanes to protect merchant shipping, and to deny the sea to enemy ships and for convoy of trade. Accordingly, the figures for total tonnage are not an adequate measure of the ability of the Royal Navy to contain the Franco-Spanish battlefleet. In 1760 Britain had had a battle fleet 3 per cent larger than that of France and Spain combined,

but in the American Revolutionary War France and Spain were able to build up a battle fleet strength nominally 44 per cent larger than that of the British navy, and for a while even dominated the English Channel. In 1790 they still had a 34 per cent combined superiority. Spain was unable to build any more ships of the line after 1797, however, and French construction did not keep up with that in Britain. At the time of Trafalgar the French could put to sea only forty-four ships of the line, and Spain only thirty, provided they could be manned. The 135 ships of the line Britain was then able to put to sea outnumbered the combined battle fleet to such an extent that the chance that the Franco-Spanish commanders would be able to defeat an isolated British squadron was small. For that matter, Nelson expressed his belief that the British must inevitably win such an encounter strategically, even if they lost it tactically, because they could afford to take much heavier losses.

The surprise declaration of war the British Government made in 1803, putting an end to the brief and hostile Peace of Amiens, was important to the relative naval strength Britain was able to command in the following years because British cruisers were able to sweep up the French merchant marine. An important part of the pool of French seamen was denied to the French navy. Because the relative weakness of the French navy made it necessary to avoid encounters with the British except under ideal conditions, it could not give the inexperienced replacement men enough sea time to develop their skills. In comparison with the French, however, Spanish ships were far worse off for skilled seamen. The Spanish mercantile marine employed less that 6,000 seamen on seagoing vessels, but the navy needed in the order of 90,000 men.[35] The ships of which the complements ranged from 606 to 1,113 men were only able to put to sea with crews of landsmen and soldiers stiffened by sixty or at most eighty experienced seamen.

The French and Spanish navies had different loyalties and different strategic objectives. The extent of the Spanish empire meant that her alliance was nearly as much a liability as it was

33. PRO 30/8/79 f 279. See: Nicholas Tracy, *Navies, Deterrence, and American Independence*, University of British Columbia Press, 1988, p29.

34. Jan Glete, *Navies and Nations, Warships, Navies and State Building in Europe and America, 1500-1860*, Stockholm: Almqvist & Wiksell, 1993, I p276 table 23:16; II pp376 and 396, tables 23:35, 23:43.

35. Report of Mazarredo to the King, 10 May 1801, *Duro*, VIII pp230–237

an asset for France, apart from the money that Spain was able to contribute to the common cause, and the diversion of British energies which occurred when campaigns were launched to seize Spanish resources.[36] It was the Spanish strategic objective of keeping the scene of naval conflict well away from their empire that led to the 1779 Franco-Spanish deployment to the Channel, where they heavily outnumbered the British but were so poorly co-ordinated that they were more a danger to themselves than to Britain. The people of Devon and Cornwall stopped eating fish because of the number of dead bodies which were thrown overboard from the combined fleet. In 1803, on the other hand, Admiral Don Frederico Gravina, who was then ambassador to Paris, made it clear to Napoleon that the Spanish navy did not want to become locked up in Brest as it had between 1799 and the Peace of Amiens. His secret instructions were based on the need to have forces available to protect the Spanish coast, and on the cold fact that it was not in the interest of Spain that England should be invaded.[37] Napoleon did not allow his plans to be affect-

ed by Gravina's representations, but two years later Gravina commanded the Spanish forces in the campaign leading to Trafalgar. His influence over the French commander, Admiral Villeneuve, may have been important in ensuring that, in fact, the combined fleet did not sail for Brest.

The principal incentive for the British to seek decisive battles with the French and Spanish fleets was that, ultimately, they did have to be able to defeat at sea any invasion attempt escorted by a battlefleet. The British army was too small to defeat an invasion in force once it was ashore. That which might have to be faced in the end might as well be faced at the onset.

The other strategic motive for seeking battle was that Britain's capacity to influence events on the continent depended largely upon the effectiveness of their fleet, both in the defence of trade and in the capacity to provide support for allies. If British forces were contained by Franco-Spanish squadrons maintaining fleets-in-being in defended harbours, few resources would be available for more offensive pursuit of British foreign policy.

Plymouth Dockyard, 1798, by Nicholas Pocock. Pocock had a long and productive life as a marine painter. This bird's-eye view of Plymouth was executed in 1798. (National Maritime Museum, London: BHC 1914)

Britain's Naval Strategy

The most important reason for Britain maintaining a navy was to prevent invasion from the continent. The Trafalgar campaign, which ended in Nelson's last and greatest battle, had started as a classic effort at power projection. Napoleon was frustrated in his conquest of Europe by the continued resistance of Britain and determined to take it off the map by invasion. To do so, he concentrated soldiers in the northern departments of France, built landing craft, and attempted to deploy French, Spanish and Dutch naval forces so that they could support a crossing of the short sea route to southern England. The British Government constructed coastal defences, notably the famous Martello Towers, to make it difficult for the soldiers to get ashore, but the principal defence against invasion was recognised to be the effective counteraction of the Royal Navy.

Next in importance to the defence of British shores, was the defence of Britain's allies. The inability of the small British economy to support an army on the scale of that of France,

Spain or Austria meant that alliances with one or more continental military powers was an essential defensive requirement. It was necessary to ensure that the French could not concentrate their efforts upon building naval forces. The classic expression of this concern, that 'France will outdo us at sea, when they have nothing to fear by land', had been made by the Duke of Newcastle in 1749.[38] The armies of her allies were important to Britain's naval defences.

Over the course of the century it had been learnt that the best way for London to acquire influence in central and eastern Europe, in order to construct alliances which could preoccupy French military planners, was by acquiring a dominant position in the naval affairs of the Mediterranean. In the Mediterranean area, where roads were long and difficult, or non-existant, naval forces possessed the greatest influence through their capacity to convoy troop ships. The acquisition of Gibraltar in 1704 gave the fleet a forward base

'East Indiaman taking a Pilot, off Dover.' This lively picture by Robert Dodd (1748-1816) shows a British East India Company ship homeward-bound with a cargo most likely loaded in Canton. She has hove to with foresails backed. (British Museum: PS 300389)

36. Nicholas Tracy, *Manila Ransomed*, Exeter: Exeter University Press, 1995.

37. Julian de Zulueta, 'Trafalgar–The Spanish View', *The Mariner's Mirror*, vol 66 1980 pp293-318

38. Newcastle to Hardwick, 10 September 1749, Add MS 35,410, ff 153–4.

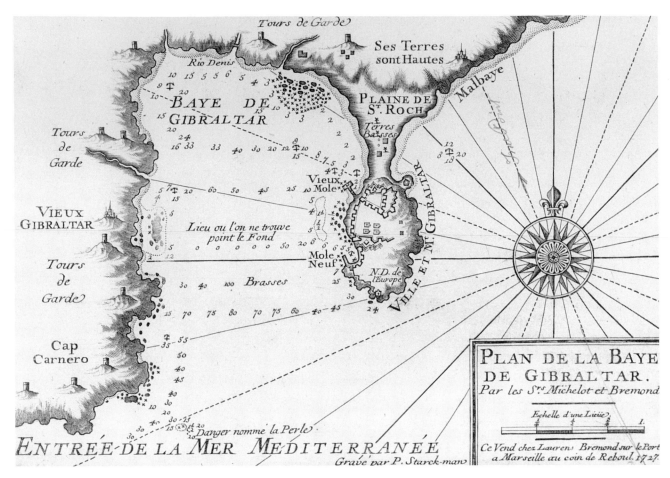

Tours de Garde

Ses Terres
sont Hautes

Rio Denis

BAYE   DE
GIBRALTAR

Tours
de
Garde

PLAINE DE
St ROCH

Malbaye

Terres
Basses

Vieux
Mole

Lieu ou l'on ne trouve
point le Fond

VIEUX
GIBRALTAR

Mole
Neuf

N.D. de
l'Europe

VILLE ET Mt GIBRALTAR

Tours
de
Garde

Brasses

Cap
Carnero

Danger nommé la Perle

ENTRÉE DE LA MER MEDITERRANÉE

Gravé par P. Starck-man

PLAN DE LA BAYE
DE GIBRALTAR.
Par les Srs Michelot et Bremond

Echelle d'une Lieüe.

Ce Vend chez Laurens Bremond sur le Port
à Marseille au coin de Reboul 1727

*Plan of the Bay of
Gibraltar, published by
Lauren, Marseille, 1727.
(National Maritime
Museum, London:
PAD 1651)*

which made possible year-round deployment
into the Mediterranean. The mobility this provided for the small British army, and for the
armies of the smaller Mediterranean states
with which Britain might be allied, put a significant political lever into British hands.
French, Spanish and Austrian interests con-
verged in the area. In the wars at the beginning
of the eighteenth century London, by deploying a fleet to the Mediterranean coast of
France, had tied down large French armies far
away from the decisive theatres in Germany
and Flanders. The capacity of the British
Mediterranean fleet to provide protection for
allies threatened by seaborne attack was even
more important.

British governments were aware of the need
to support the prestige of the Royal Navy by
reacting to any use of naval power by other
states which might undermine Britain's role of
naval arbiter. The mobilisation of 1770 in

response to a Spanish attack on British interests in the Falkland Islands, which was the
occasion for Nelson's first joining the navy,
was primarily motivated by the need to protect
the reputation of Britain's naval power.[39] The
circumstances of that crisis were as much concerned with the affairs of the Mediterranean as
they were with those of the South Atlantic. In
1790 Spain was warned off interference in
British interests in Vancouver Island, and for
the same reason.

When in 1796, after the defeat of the
Royalist uprising in Toulon, the decision was
taken to withdraw the British fleet from the
Mediterranean, the effect on British affairs in
the region was most unfortunate. The defec-
tion of Austria from the first coalition against
France followed. The damage done to British
interests began to be repaired in 1798 when the
deployment of a squadron under Nelson defeated the French at the Nile putting an end to

Napoleon's ability to determine events by moving a French army about the Mediterranean. The consequence was that Turkey concluded an understanding with Britain. Turkish and British armies were transported to Egypt, and eventually the army that Napoleon had abandoned there to its fate was defeated. The Kingdom of Naples threw off its restraint, and openly returned to hostilities with France. In December Russia concluded an alliance with Britain, and extended her protection to Naples. In 1799 a joint Turkish and Russian army expelled the French from Corfu and a Russian army of 6,000 was left as a garrison. Austria adhered to this second coalition against France. The ambition of the Russians to acquire their own naval footing in the Mediterranean, however, complicated Anglo-Russian relations in the 1800s, as indeed it had in the 1760s under Catherine the Great.

Gibraltar was an inadequate base for the Royal Navy because of its distance from Toulon, because of the prevailing northerly winds and the current through the Straits into the Mediterranean, and because the harbour was open to attack by Spanish gunboats. A British squadron based on Port Mahon in Minorca had commanded the western Mediterranean in the mid-eighteenth century, but Minorca was lost in the American War, and was not again available for British use until it was captured by Captain Duckworth in late 1798. It was returned again to Spain at the peace of Amiens in 1802. Naples provided supplies for the Royal Navy from time to time, but was vulnerable to the French army in northern Italy. The only really secure base which could provide distant support for the ships watching Toulon, and also block French ambitions in the eastern Mediterranean, was Malta. This island with its superbly fortified harbour had been captured by Napoleon on his way to Egypt in 1798, and was subsequently taken from its French garrison after a prolonged siege. The desire of the mad Tsar Paul to obtain Malta was a contributing factor to the Baltic crisis in 1801. The Addington Ministry agreed as part of the 1802 peace treaty with France that Malta should be

returned to the Order of St John which Napoleon had driven out, but backed out of the commitment when it became apparent that Napoleon did not intend to honour the spirit of the treaty. Britain declared war on France, and Pitt, who was returned to power, refused to cede Malta to Russia even when Tsar Alexander I made that a condition for accession to the third coalition against Napoleon. Alexander only changed his mind in July 1805 because he was insulted by Napoleon's proclaiming himself an Emperor, and alarmed by his seizure of Genoa.

The British refusal of the Russian demand was based on a concern that the Russian navy would not be able to contain the French Mediterranean fleet, and was consistent with the long-standing reluctance to share naval power with Russia. Russia and Britain were so far able to cooperate, however, that a joint military force was deployed to Naples at the time of Trafalgar to provide security against a French army which had occupied Taranto.

Naval control of the Baltic was no less important than was a commanding naval position in the Mediterranean, because of the continuing need for naval building materials from the north. Long before the end of the eighteenth century, the domestic British supply of timber had become inadequate. The need to import the great trees which were used to make masts and yards was older still. The best foreign source of supply for timber, masts, and for tar, hemp, canvas, and iron for fastenings, anchors and guns, was from the states around the Baltic. Efforts had been made periodically to develop North American sources of supply, but only in the case of masts had this been successful. France and Spain were very nearly as dependent on Baltic sources for naval stores as was Britain.

The objectives of British naval control of the Baltic trade were to deny to their enemies access to naval building material, and to ensure that British dockyards would be well supplied at a reasonable price. Before the development in the nineteenth century of the idea that neutrals had an obligation to act impartially, and to avoid destabilising the balance of power,

39. Tracy, *Navies*, pp69–99 *et passim.*

these objectives were practically speaking the two sides of the same coin. The same naval operation could deny the enemy access to supply, and ensure British supply. At the same time, the work of the British cruisers also helped to ensure that British trade was profitable enough to pay for the supply. This last, the purely mercantilist objective of using force to dominate trade, was as important as was the blockade of French dockyards.

In the eighteenth century blockade operations were rarely able to deny an enemy access to strategically important cargoes, and instead concentrated on making a profit by seizing enemy ships and cargoes for their monetary value. The profit made from the sale of prizes, and from carrying on the trade which the enemy lost through late delivery and increased costs, was strategically important because the wealth gained could be extracted in taxes and used to support the war effort. The chances of enemy shipping being able to run a blockade were good enough, on the other hand, that there was little strategic value in attempting to block supplies of most of the materials used for military purposes, let along block consumer goods. Only when efforts were narrowly focused on a few harbours, and on heavy cargoes which could not be transported by land, was there much prospect of preventing supplies getting through. In this respect, geography gave Britain an important advantage over the French. Naval stores were so bulky and so heavy that they could only reach their destinations by sea. When the Royal Navy was strong enough, as it had been following the battle of Quiberon Bay in the Seven Years War, it was able to impede the repair of the French fleet by cruises along the Normandy and Brittany coasts. Victuals for the fleet at Brest also had to be shipped by sea, because Breton farms could not supply the needs. Napoleon solved the problem of bringing supplies from central France by building canals, but naval stores from the Baltic continued to be sent by sea close by British naval harbours.

In the seventeenth century the British had had to fight to prevent the Dutch intercepting supplies to British dockyards, but the French did not enjoy a similarly powerful geographic position. Arrangements to convoy the cargoes of naval stores to England were well established, and there was little prospect of French privateers being able to intercept more than a small proportion of them.[40] It was a usual practice for French privateers to ransom their captives while they were still at sea so that they could continue their voyage. Furthermore, traditional French interpretation of international law protected neutral vessels carrying enemy-owned cargo. What London had to worry about was not the strangulation of supply so much as the prospect that the neutral Balts would drive up the price of naval stores to a degree which threatened Britain's ability to pay, and at the same time facilitate the armament of the French and Spanish fleets.

Apart from the blockade of naval stores, maritime control of the Baltic had important offensive as well as defensive implications. At the turn of the nineteenth century, Britain was not able to use her commanding position at sea to threaten the French Republic and Empire, except to support with limited success the independence of the smaller nations of Europe. It was only because of the economic pressure which a naval power could exert that the British Government was able to avoid a strategic stalemate. Napoleon was scathing about British subsidies which were paid to continental states to support their belligerence against France, but armaments cost vast amounts of money. Without the wealth Britain earned from overseas trade, it is doubtful whether Austria, Russia or Prussia would have been able to support the expense of resisting French power, or been induced to make the attempt. In 1804 the annual revenue of the British treasury was £40 million from which a subsidy was agreed with Austria and Russia of £1 million for every 100,000 soldiers put in the field against Napoleon.

Wealth earned in trade, and paid as customs dues and income taxes, was also vital to the capacity of the British Government to keep its own fleet at sea. Timber merchants, victuallers, and all the commercial concerns which were needed to sustain the navy were willing

40. A N Ryan, 'The Defence of British Trade with the Baltic, 1808-1813', *English Historical Review*, 74 (1959) p443; and 'Trade with the Enemy in the Scandinavian and Baltic Ports during the Napoleonic War: for and against', *Transactions of the Royal Historical Society*, series V 12 (1962) p123.

41. Nicholas Tracy, *Attack on Maritime Trade*, London and Toronto: Macmillan and University of Toronto Press, 1991, pp30–40, and *passim*; Minutes of a conversation between Count Bernstorff and Messrs. Drummond and Vansittart, Saturday March 14, 1801, Add MS 38537.

to supply their goods on the credit of Navy Board bills, but their faith in eventual repayment was based on the responsibility of government, and on their belief that the navy would hold its own.

Despite the growth of the idea in the last half of the eighteenth century that free trade was in the general interest, 'mercantilism', the use of tariffs and other controls to restrict the profitability of rivals' access to international markets, was still a prevailing economic doctrine. Mercantilism had an obvious strategic role in wartime when the relative wealth of nations, not their absolute wealth, was all important. Britain, because of her commanding leadership in the industrial revolution, had products that could hold their own in any market. In effect, a successful campaign against enemy trade by Royal Navy cruisers and by British privateers served to funnel money into the pockets of the British merchants and British insurers. The English were all the more successful at this game because the London insurance market had learnt how to make a good profit out of insuring ships and cargoes in wartime, even extending their services to enemy merchants who paid the large premiums made necessary by the activity of British privateers and the Royal Navy. British interpretation of the laws of war permitted the arrest of neutral merchantships if they were carrying enemy-owned cargoes, or cargoes which in peacetime the enemy would only permit their own nationals to carry.

The ability to intercept the flow of naval stores from the Baltic, was dependent upon the balance of power. Generally the masts, timber, hemp and tar were freighted in neutral merchantmen. Although British interpretation of international law asserted the right of a belligerent to seize enemy-owned cargo carried in neutral bottoms, the Baltic neutrals did not acknowledge that right, and resisted when they could.[41]

The Baltic states might have had little reason to wish French arms to triumph, but neither did they wish Britain to have the ability to determine to whom and at what price they could sell their commodities. British mercan-

tilism was in conflict with that of the Baltic states, which had very deep roots. British merchants had established strong connections with the primary producers, which tended to foil any attempts by the suppliers to push prices up to a level which could affect the ability of the British navy to keep the sea in sufficient numbers. However, there was a long history of Baltic states exploiting their geography and naval forces to profit from wars fought by their neighbours. For nearly three centuries Denmark had collected a toll on

Two views of a mast hulk, by J T Serres. (British Museum BM 1872.8.10.759)

trade passing the fortress of Elsinore to or from the North Sea.

To be able to profit from the wars of their neighbours, the Balts needed to be able to confront force with force. In the American Revolutionary War, under the leadership of Tsarina Catherine the Great, a League of Armed Neutrality was brought together to resist British naval and mercantile control. The objectives of the League were those of self interest. The new idea of free trade was used as justification for a strictly mercantilist purpose.

So great had been the threat, that the British Government declared war on the Netherlands in 1780 to pre-empt their intended joining of the League. The Netherlands suffered severely in consequence, but Britain was at such a disadvantage during the American War that the Royal Navy had not possessed the power to make effective the strategy of sea control in the face of Baltic resistance. Prussia had also joined the neutral League, Austria and Russia had concluded an alliance, and Britain had had to accept on face value the 'naturalization' of Dutch ships under Prussian and Austrian flags. In 1780, only 671 Prussian ships passed the Sound, but in 1781 the number rose to 1,507. The measure of Britain's failure is that between 1778 and September 1782 Riga exported 996 masts to Britain, 868 to France (with an additional twenty-nine sent via Genoa), 405 to Spain, and 1,855 to the Netherlands, only 600 of which were on the account of the Dutch navy.[42] The rest were probably reshipped to French ports.

In the war against the French Revolution and Bonapartism, London was determined not to let the Baltic situation again get out of hand. Britain could not afford to let France have free access to naval stores, and had to ensure that her own supply was safe, and that her trade was profitable. Royal Navy enforcement of the blockade of supplies to the French dockyards led to a clash with a Swedish convoy in January 1798, and when in December 1799 a Danish frigate tried to prevent the search of a Danish convoy, shots were fired. This was followed by a more serious action in July 1800 when a Danish frigate and her convoy were captured after a violent exchange.[43] The Danish Government, dominated by Count Bernstorff, demanded satisfaction, and the British Government sent a fleet to the Sound to underline its determination to enforce its sea control. The Danish court appealed to the mad Tsar Paul for support. It was to crush this threat that a British fleet was sent to Copenhagen, in 1801. Nelson commanded the detachment that destroyed the navy of Denmark.

Tsar Alexander I tried to stipulate in 1803 that the British give up their concept of maritime law before Russia would join the coalition against Napoleon, but Pitt refused to concede the point. In 1812 American resentment at British arrest of neutral shipping to manipulate trade was to lead to the United States declaring war on Britain. The strategic reality, however, was that it was only because of Britain's successful pursuit of mercantilism that Napoleon's conquest of Europe was eventually reversed. Free trade was the growing economic policy of peace, but mercantilism was the necessary strategy for naval war.

Britain's naval strategy could not concentrate entirely on European waters. The French empire at the end of the eighteenth century was a small remnant of what it had been when Nelson was born during the Seven Years War. Accordingly, the wars of the French Revolution and Empire were largely fought in European waters. The importance of overseas trade to Britain's war effort remained considerable, however. Sugar from the West Indies, furs from Canada, tea, spices, silk and porcelain from Asia all provided British merchants with stock in trade which ultimately provided the taxes that supported the war effort. Accordingly, the British navy, as well as guarding Britain's shores against invasion, and dominating the naval affairs of the Mediterranean and Baltic, had to ensure the safe passage of trade convoys from across the Atlantic, and from Asia. Fortunately, however, the same deployments which contained French and Spanish naval threats to home waters also served to minimise the scale of threat overseas.

42. Isabela de Madariaga, *Britain, Russia and the Armed Neutrality of 1780.* London, 1962; pp377–86; Alice Clare Carter, *Neutrality or Commitment: The Evaluation of Dutch Foreign Policy, 1667-1795.* London, 1975, pp97–103; and Bernard Semmel, *Liberalism and Naval Strategy, Ideology, Interest, and Sea Power During the Pax Britanica.* Boston, 1986, pp14–20.

43. See ADM 1/4186.

Operational Strategy

The operational strategy of the Royal Navy to guard against invasion, to protect her allies from invasion, and to control trade, had been developed over the century. The hinge of the entire strategy was the Channel Fleet, sometimes known as the Western Squadron: unless the French could meet the Western Squadron in battle, and defeat it, they could not invade England. Unless the French were able to concentrate a decisively superior force, no French admiral could take the risk of entering the Channel before the prevailing southwesterly winds and with an undefeated Western Squadron behind them. It was the usual practice for the Channel Fleet to lie at anchor in a safe harbour where it would not be subjected to damage from weather, and its crews would be less subject to ill health brought on by poor food and water. The danger of the French sailing had to be accepted, and in any case no close blockade could prevent them getting out of Brest in the immediate aftermath of a westerly or southwesterly gale during which a blockading force would have to seek searoom.

Two views of the British fleet off Ushant, 1 June 1794, by Nicholas Pocock, watercolour and wash. (National Maritime Museum, London: PAD 8701, 8703)

The admirals who commanded the Channel Fleet during the early years of the Revolutionary War, Howe and Bridport, favoured keeping the fleet as far east as Spithead where it could be supplied easily.

The disadvantage of Spithead, however, was that it could be very difficult to take the squadron down Channel should the Brest fleet move to the westward, as it did in 1796 to support a landing in Ireland, or to the southward to co-operate with the Spaniards, to cross the Atlantic, or to enter the Mediterranean. This difficulty was especially significant as, resources being limited, the Channel Fleet had to be treated as a strategic reserve from which detachments could be made to counter detachments from the French Atlantic Fleet at Brest, or from the other French dockyards in the Bay of Biscay and the Mediterranean. The Western Squadron was also, as Admiral Lord Barham, First Lord of the Admiralty at the time of Trafalgar, put it, 'the mainspring from which all offensive operations must proceed.'[44] During the American Revolutionary War, it had been very difficult to react in a timely manner. The strategic problems in the war against revolutionary and imperial France were less intractable, but still sufficiently demanding. In consequence, when Admiral the Earl St Vincent was made First Lord of the Admiralty in 1800 he applied the experience he had gained keeping the Mediterranean Squadron on station off the Spanish dockyard at Cadiz to the problem in the Channel, and established a close blockade of Brest. The Channel Fleet was stationed off Ushant with frigates and support units close to the entrances of the Rade. Admiral William Cornwallis commanded the Western Squadron, or Channel Fleet, during the Trafalgar campaign of 1805, operating from Torbay and Plymouth with Portsmouth to leeward for a main supply and repair base.

The French navy was dispersed to four dockyards in metropolitan France, at Brest, Lorient, Rochefort and Toulon, with ships deployed to protect French interests in the West Indies and the Indian Ocean. These squadrons had considerable value in the containment of British resources, and for supporting privateer action against trade, but separately they could not risk action unless the British forces offshore should be reduced by storm or accident. The Spanish navy in European waters depended on Cartagena in the Mediterranean, Cadiz at the southwest corner of Spain, and Ferrol at the northwest, and always had a sizeable detachment in the West Indies and South America. By stationing blockading forces close to these ports, and dominating the maritime communications between, the Royal Navy was able to keep on top of the aggressive use of French and Spanish naval forces.

The Royal Navy's most important overseas command was the Mediterranean Squadron. The acquisition of Gibraltar had made it possible for British ships to remain in the Mediterranean for extended periods, but Gibraltar was not well placed for supporting a blockade of Toulon because of the prevailing northeasterly and northwesterly winds. Minorca was preferable, and several times during the century Britain held Port Mahon as a forward base. Nelson, however, did not have the use of Port Mahon which had been returned to Spain as part of the peace settlement after the American Revolutionary War. Instead he had to use the undeveloped Magdalena anchorage in northern Sardinia. From this station he maintained a distant watch on Toulon, hoping to entice the French fleet out to sea where he expected to be able to defeat it.

When the Toulon fleet did come out, it was a problem to discover where it had gone. In 1798 it went to Egypt; in 1805 it went to the West Indies. It was standing orders for squadrons deployed outside home waters that, if the forces they were watching managed to escape, they were to concentrate on the Western Squadron. In 1798, however, Nelson decided that the French must have gone to Egypt, and took the risk of going there himself. In 1805 he concluded that they had gone to the West Indies and again took the risk of following them. He then had to follow them back, consumed with anxiety that they might get to Ushant ahead of him, join with the Brest squadron, and defeat Admiral Cornwallis

44. Cornwallis, 15 August 1805, HMC VI p411.

commanding the Western or Channel Fleet. In making his judgements, Nelson was able to depend on over a century of collective service experience about the effect of terrestrial geography, meteorological and hydrographic conditions on the potential movement of fleets.

To guard against the threat of invasion during the campaigns of 1804 and 1805, the Royal Navy deployed flotillas along the Channel coast. These ensured that no sudden assault could be attempted without heavy support. They were given close cover by a squadron of frigates and a few ships of the line based on the Downs, the roads to seaward of the white cliffs of Dover, the Nore command in the mouth of the Thames, and Great Yarmouth in Norfolk. Another cruiser squadron was based on the Channel Islands where it was to windward of the embarkation ports during the prevailing southwesterlies. The Western Squadron off Ushant provided the ultimate muscle.

Nelson – the Diplomat Sailor

British foreign policy in the late eighteenth century was controlled by the Secretary of State for Foreign Affairs, and to the extent that foreign policy could be said to be 'made' in London, it was made collectively by the Ministry acting in the King's name, and with King George III exercising some influence. Throughout Europe were stationed British envoys who were the agents of the Secretary of State. For practical reasons, however, naval commanders often had to take great responsibility for developing and supporting British policy. Communications were so poor that in peacetime it would take up to a month for letters to pass between London and the Mediterranean, and in wartime when the French mail service could not be used and letters had to be diverted over the Alps and through Germany, or take their chances of a fair wind for a passage by sea around Spain, they could take much longer. A detached naval commander at a foreign court, such as was Nelson at the Court of Naples after the battle of the Nile, had to undertake the task of coordinating naval and diplomatic action, and work to develop the policies of Britain's allies along safe and useful lines. After the battle of Copenhagen Nelson played a vital role in putting an end to the hostile policies of Russia, Sweden, and Denmark. It was his victories at the Nile and Copenhagen which made his diplomacy influencial.

⁂

Nelson died of his wounds during the battle of Trafalgar. It was others who profited from that victory, and had to exploit it. Nelson's last great battle reduced the naval forces available to Napoleon to such an extent that he was unable to dictate the course of European history by continuing to threaten invasion of Britain. Neither could he extend his control of the Mediterranean although he was able to overrun Naples from the land. Operationally, it freed the Royal Navy for other tasks, the most fundamental of which was the defence of trade. Strategically, this operational freedom at sea ensured that British trade would be able to pay for the subsidised armies that ultimately defeated Napoleon.

Part II

GUNS, SHIPS AND BATTLE TACTICS

NELSON'S THREE great battles, the Nile, Copenhagen, and Trafalgar, were almost the last acts of an era of naval warfare which had begun 250 years before when sailing vessels equipped with heavy cannon took the place of oar-propelled galley fleets as the dominant tactical force at sea. In 1571 the fate of the western Mediterranean had been decided when a coalition of galley fleets organised by the Papacy defeated a similar fleet of the Ottoman Porte at the battle of Lepanto. Seventeen years later, in 1588, Philip II of Spain's attempt to invade England with an Armada of great sailing ships armed with cannon was defeated by an English fleet of sailing ships. Not only did this signal the triumph of one weapon system over another at sea; the marriage of sail propulsion and massed artillery made possible the ascendancy of the Atlantic seaboard states of Europe, first over the Mediterranean, and then over much of the rest of the world.

The fleets that Nelson commanded, and the tactics he employed, had developed gradually since the sixteenth century. Fleet tactics of the sailing era were necessarily complicated because sailing warships were more limited in their tactical mobility than had been the galley fleets of earlier years, or the steam navies which eventually replaced them. The powerful combination of sail and cannon was the only weapon system ever developed which could only deploy its weapons at right-angles to its line of advance. It was their strategic qualities, their capacity to sail half way around the world without touching shore for supplies for their relatively small crews, and their ability to mount a great battery of guns, that caused them largely to take the place of galleys as the primary instrument of sea power. The traumatic social consequences of the French Revolution at the end of that period inspired Nelson with a determination to push his force to the limit so as to totally annihilate the enemy, and made it possible for him to employ tactics which were themselves revolutionary.

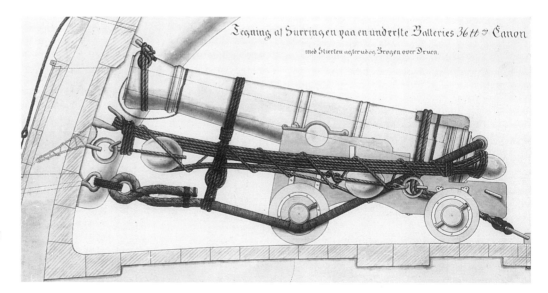

This beautiful drawing of a Danish 36-pounder gun shows the precautions which had to be taken to secure the gun carriage so that it would not break free in a seaway. (Rigsarkivet, Copenhagen)

The Ship of the Line

The basis of naval tactics must always be the principal weapon available to the admiral. The capabilities and limitations of the smoothbore cannon had a powerful direct effect on the way he had to go about his business, and also an indirect effect because it was a major determinant in the design of warships, the abilities of which also profoundly effected the admiral's art. Nelson's genius most particularly lay in his leadership of men, but he was also a master of ship-handling and gunnery.

The heaviest guns in general ship-board use in the late eighteenth century were smoothbore muzzle-loading cannon capable of firing a 32pdr shot. The gun itself weighed over 6,000lbs and was mounted on a truck carriage with four wheels (or trucks) so that it could recoil when fired. A heavy rope fastened to ringbolts at each end and passed round the breech of the gun, where it was secured by passing through an eye, or breech ring, above the cascabel, was used to limit the recoil, and a pair of tackles were used by the 13-man crew to run the gun up to the gunport for firing. The gun was elevated by a wedge, or quoin, placed under the breech, which needed to be hove into position by men employing handspikes. Handspikes were also used to lift the gun carriage across the deck to aim it to the right or left through the port.

The gun was loaded by ramming a flannel bag of black gunpowder down the barrel, followed by a spherical iron ball and a wad to keep it in place. For close action, it was the practice to load two, or even three, balls for the first discharge. Once engaged, however, the confusion of action made it necessary to stick to the simplest possible routine to reduce the risk of accidents. In order to fire, an awl was driven down through the touch hole breaking a hole in the charge bag, and a goose quill filled with fine gunpowder was inserted. By the end of the century the actual firing would be done by a flint-lock which was triggered by a long cord. The gun having been run out by its crew, it would be fired by the gun captain. The spark from the flint would flash down the firing quill and ignite the propellant, which would drive the shot out the barrel. The gun would then be sponged out to ensure there was no lingering scrap of the powder bag which might prematurely ignite the next change, and then it would be reloaded.

Because of limitations to the milling of the barrel and the imprecision of casting shot a ¼in 'windage' was necessary between the diameter of the ball and that of the barrel. As a consequence, anything up to half the force of the charge was wasted by blowing past the shot, and the shot was likely to fly off at a slight angle to the direction the gun was pointing.

Lighter 24pdr guns were used on the middle and 12pdr on the upper gundecks, but they had considerably less penetrating ability. Even lighter guns like 9pdrs were used as chase guns, and on smaller warships.

In the 1770s lightweight short-barrelled carronades were introduced into the fleet. Using a smaller charge, these guns could fire the same weight of shot but to a shorter range. Their milling was more accurate, so that the windage allowed was about half of that of the long guns. They were usually provided with a slide mounting, instead of a truck carriage, and recoiled along a bed on the mount. Because their weight was only 2,000lbs it was possible for a crew to run them forward without wheels. The mounting itself had wheels, but these were arranged to make it easier to train the gun. Elevation was usually controlled by a screw rather than by quoins.

Initially, the guns had been of most importance in providing merchantmen with an adequate defence. Only gradually during the sixteenth and seventeenth centuries did their value as offensive weapons become clear. They did so only when it was learnt how to use the massed firepower of hundreds of guns together, by concentrating the guns in powerful batteries along the sides of increasingly long ships, and by learning how to manage the firepower of fleets of such ships.

Other navies took considerable interest in the carronade, initially a uniquely British weapon. This Scandinavian drawing shows a 24-pounder carronade, dated to 1795.

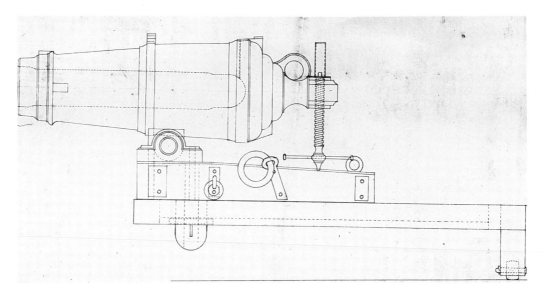

When cannon were first mounted on sailing vessels, the heaviest guns, like those of the galleys, were the chase guns firing over the bow. This arrangement enabled galleys to sweep an enemy deck before boarding, but the guns themselves could rarely be decisive. The rate of fire of great guns was slow because of the difficulty reloading in a seaway, and there was too little space in the bow to make it practicable to use a battery of smaller guns which could be reloaded more easily to develop decisive firepower along the axis of the ship. For this reason, boarding remained the decisive weapon of the galley.

Sixteenth-century sailing vessels disposed their smaller guns so as to ensure that at least one weapon could be brought to bear on any relative bearing. A ship lying-to could defend itself against galleys attacking from any direction. This arrangement served the needs of the armed traders who first made use of great sailing ships, but it was less useful for a ship of war pressing home an attack under sail. To employ its full gun power it was necessary to turn in a circle so as to present each gun in turn. The turning movement made close cooperation with a squadron difficult. It was impossible to concentrate enough weight of shot at any point to achieve decisive results, and naval battles continued to be decided by boarding.

The problem of concentrating fire was solved in the mid-seventeenth century by the development of the line of battle, and of ships suitable for fighting in it. If relatively lightly-manned sailing vessels were to hold their own, they had to make good use of their capacity to carry large numbers of guns. Few of these could be carried in the bow, but unlike galleys, sailing vessels were built heavily enough, and with enough beam, to permit firing guns at right angles to their keel. The concept of the ship of the line grew out of the twin impulses to build ships capable of carrying a very large numbers of guns, enough of which could be fired on the same relative bearing so as to produce decisive firepower, and ships capable of fast sailing. These design objectives called for increasing the length of ships, the penalty for which was a reduction in tactical manoeuvreability.

By the time that Nelson first went to sea in 1770, ships of the line had evolved into several distinct classes distinguished by their number of guns. The largest, with 100 guns or more on three gundecks, were considered First Rate ships. The most famous of all was HMS *Victory*, which had been launched in 1765 to a design by Thomas Slade and was to be Nelson's flagship at Trafalgar. She was 186ft long on the gundeck, and displaced 2,142 tons. Her armament was originally thirty smooth-bore cannon capable of firing a 42pdr solid shot, twenty-eight 24pdrs, thirty 12pdrs, and eight

French corvette, careened and having her bottom cleaned by burning. Drawn and engraved by Baugean, 1826, published by Jean. (National Maritime Museum, London: PAD 7400)

6pdrs. The difficulty of handling 42pdrs was such, however, that they were replaced in 1778 by 32pdrs which were capable of a greater rate of fire. Her broadside was thus 1,020lbs of shot. She was small compared to the ships which were being built at the end of the century. The First Rate *Hibernia* which was launched in 1804 displaced 2,530 tons and threw a broadside weight of 1,476lbs of shot.

Second Rates were three-decked ships with less than 100 guns. By the end of the century they were nearly all armed with 98 guns, the heaviest of which were 32pdrs. The *Prince of Wales*, which was launched in 1794, displaced 2,010 tons, and threw a broadside of 958lbs of shot. Third Rates were all two-decked ships, armed with 64, 74 or 80 guns. The 80s were a recent revival, but a considerably larger ship than the 80s of the early eighteenth century which had been small, over-gunned, three-deckers. At the end of the century the 74s were the most numerous two-deckers. The

Drawing of the Third Rate Culloden, *grey pen and ink with wash, possibly by John Christian Schetky. (National Maritime Museum, London: PAF 5783)*

Centaur, launched in 1797, had a tonnage of 1,842, and an armament of twenty-eight 32pdrs, thirty 24pdrs and sixteen 9pdrs, throwing a broadside of 880lbs. By the end of the century these numbers tended to understate the weight of fire because of the increasing use of short, heavy carronades to augment and replace long guns firing lighter shot.

The batteries, on two or three or even four decks, occupied all the length of the ship. For normal cruising, the after end of each gundeck was partitioned off to provide cabins for officers, with an elegant row of windows and a gallery closing the after end of the middle and upper decks. In preparation for battle, however, these partitions were either swung up on hinges under the deckhead, or struck down into the hold, so that the gundeck was uninterrupted. This would clear access for the powder monkeys, and give the gun crews room to work their weapons. It also minimised the amount of light timbering which could be reduced to lethal splinters by enemy shot.

Above: Port quarter of the model of the Royal George, *by John Christian Schetky.* (National Maritime Museum, London: PAF 6101)

Right: British two-decker, unrigged, by Nicholas Pocock c1800. (National Maritime Museum, London: PAD 8792)

Interior of the stern gallery in a ship of the line, c1819. (National Maritime Museum, London: PAF 5857)

British 32pdr long guns were capable of a range of about 2,900 yards, but battles were not fought at that range because the kinetic energy of the shot would be so diminished that its capacity to penetrate heavy timbering would be greatly reduced. Furthermore, too much of the shot would be wasted by falling into the sea. The cast iron, smooth-bore gun was optimised for rapid fire by a relatively un-skilled crew. Its windage was too great for it to be accurate, and its elevation system for long-range fire did not permit continuous laying, the continuous elevation and depression of the guns to compensate for the rolling of the ship. It was necessary for gunners to judge the pre-cise point in the role to fire, and the difficulty was increased if the gun were elevated. Point-blank range of 350 yards, when no elevation was required, was considered maximum battle range, and the effectiveness of fire could be in-creased by using double shot at a range of only 100 yards. Carronades were optimised for ac-tion at that range, and had half the maximum range of long guns. It was risky to arm ships exclusively with short guns because they be-came very vulnerable to an enemy which had the speed to keep just out of their range.[1] At the battle of Copenhagen, however, one of the ships, *Glatton*, was an experimental conver-sion which was entirely armed with 68pdr and 42pdr carronades on the gundecks. As part of

a mixed fleet which contained ships armed with long guns able to provide protection against longer–range fire, such a ship could be a very powerful force multiplier.

Before sailing on the Copenhagen campaign in 1801 Nelson agreed to his friend Sir Edward Berry's request that he meet an inventor who was working to improve the aiming of guns. However, he wrote,

> I hope we shall be able, as usual, to get so close to our enemies, that our shot cannot miss their object; and that we shall again give our northern enemies that hailstorm of bullets, which is so emphatically de-scribed in the *Naval Chronicle*, and gain our dear country the domination of the seas...[2]

It was possible for a fully worked-up British ship of the line at the end of the eighteenth century to sustain a rate of independent fire of one round every minute. In 1805 Colling-wood's *Dreadnought* was able to deliver three full broadsides every three and a half minutes. French and Spanish ships rarely met these standards. When in 1793 Admiral Gravina, briefly an ally of the British, visited Ports-mouth Dockyard he concluded that British superiority in gunnery was a result of the su-periority of the British gun carriage, and the

1. Robert Gardiner, *The Line of Battle, The Sailing Warship 1650-1840,* Conway's History of the Ship, London: Conway Maritime Press, 1992, pp146-163.

2. Nelson to Berry, 9 March 1801, Clarke and M'Arthur (1840) II p385.

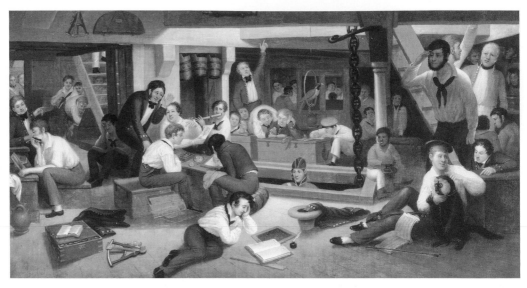

Life on the Ocean:
Midshipman's berth in a
British Frigate at sea, by
Augustus Earle.
(National Maritime
Museum, London:
BHC 1118)

use of the flint-lock for firing. Forty years ear-lier, during the Duc de Choiseul's effort to re-construct the French navy, the French had sought to induce British gun founders to move to France. Gravina, however, did not find any-thing remarkable in 1793 about British guns, despite Britain's leadership in the industrial revolution. British propellant was better due to the East India Company's control of sources of saltpetre. British gun crews may also have been drilled to a higher degree of performance.

Before the battle of the Saintes in 1782 Sir

Cook's Mate, by
Thomas Rowlandson.
(National Maritime
Museum, London:
PAF 5940)

Charles Douglas had experimented with alter-ations to the design of gundecks to improve the effectiveness of British gunnery in a pass-ing action. The three ships which he took in hand were converted by the addition of ring-bolts in the gundecks between the gun car-riages, so that their crews could heave them around, and by the reduction of the support-ing timbers called standards which were in-tended to stiffen the gun decks, but also re-stricted the degree to which guns could be trained fore and aft of the beam. These modifi-cations made it possible to train the broadside guns through 90 degrees fore and aft, which enabled those ships to simultaneously engage two ships of the enemy deployed in line ahead at two cables interval, at a distance of a quarter of a mile. 'Lieutenant Butler', Douglas wrote, 'says that from the middle deck of the *Formidable* he never fired less than two, some-times three broadsides at each passing French-man before such Frenchman could bring a gun to bear on him.'[3]

Captain Mansfield of the *Minotaur*, on the eve of the battle of Trafalgar, ended his address to the hands with a reminder of the need for gunnery discipline: 'I have only to recommend silence and a strict attention to the orders of your officers. Be careful to take good aim, for it is to no purpose to throw shot away'.[4] Almost everything depended on good gun drill. Victory depended on sustaining an effective rate of fire until the enemy gunners were killed or their weapons disabled. Shot from a 32pdr could penetrate the heaviest ship timbers at close range, destroy guns, and produce showers of splinters which killed or maimed the men. It required a high degree of training to ensure that a gun-crew could continue to work their weapon when subjected to such attack, and to do so safely. The recoil of the guns could kill their own crews if they were not well drilled, and if the rammer failed to sponge out the gun, or lost count and rammed in two charges, premature discharge, or the bursting of the guns was a real danger.

Explosive shells were rarely used in naval actions, except against shore targets, because of the very high trajectory used by the mortars which fired them. Any error in range, due to misjudgment of distance or time of firing on the roll, would result in a miss. Furthermore, the weapons were too dangerous to have onboard a major warship because of the chance that a mistake in fusing could lead to a shell exploding before firing, though the French experimented with firing shells from carronades. At the battle of the Nile, shells were fired from a shore position at the British fleet, but they had no success against moving targets. At Copenhagen the British fleet used mortar-armed bomb ketches against moored Danish warships, but their primary purpose was their potential against the Danish dockyard after the Danish battle line had been defeated.

Similar considerations prevented the use of red-hot shot onboard ships. It was too dangerous to keep furnaces lit during action. Shore batteries, however, did often have furnaces for heating shot. Besides solid round shot, shipboard gunnery included the use of grape and canister at short range against men assembled for boarding, and the use of chain shot or bar shot to cut the rigging and sails of the enemy ship. The newest weapons in the British arsenal were Congreve's rockets, which were fired from boats against fixed targets. A plan was being considered for their use against the Franco-Spanish fleet in Cadiz, to force it to sea, when Napoleon's orders produced the same result and precipitated the battle of Trafalgar.

The Ships

The French marine had perfected the 74-gun ship, a long two-decker, because it needed ships which could sail fast and carry a reason-

3. Douglas to Middleton, 4 May 1782. *Barham* I p284.

4. William Thorpe.

A 74-gun ship of the line in the Solent, c1780, by Serres. (National Maritime Museum, London: PAG 9682)

able armament. The British navy admired them, and built many of their own which tended to be shorter than the French 74s, but their strategic needs were different. British security depended ultimately upon the battle-fleet being able to meet the worst the enemy could put to sea, and defeat it. There was no way that battle could be avoided if the enemy were determined. The tendency, in consequence, was to cram as much armament into a ship as was possible, and to build the ship with as heavy timbering as was possible. The strategic bottom line also gave the British navy a strong incentive to keep the sea off the enemy's ports so that their fleets could be defeated in detail. Three-deckers could survive such treatment for longer periods than could two-deckers. Their greater girder strength meant that they were less apt to be strained by prolonged use at sea.

The French, on the other hand, had the population and economic base to enable them to defend themselves ashore. Their navy was for offensive purposes if the chance offered, and to maintain communications with imperial holdings. On the whole it could do its job if it could present a creditable threat while avoiding battle. Fast, weatherly ships were of great value to them. The Spanish navy had a strategic purpose similar to that of France, except for the consideration that the Spanish empire

was much larger than that of France and of much more economic importance. This ambivalence of purpose was reflected in the fleet, which had a long tradition of building ships of the largest classes, timbered to take the maximum punishment.

The reconstruction of the Spanish fleet by Charles III had led to that navy obtaining some of the best ships in the world. At first Spain tried to copy English designs, and employed English shipwrights, but came to prefer French models, and French shipwrights. Nelson, when he visited Cadiz in 1793, was most impressed by Spanish ships of the line, and Vice Admiral Collingwood referred to the *Santa Ana* which he engaged at Trafalgar as 'Spanish perfection'. The *Santisima Trinidad* was the world's largest warship, being the only four-decker afloat. She was much admired by the British. She narrowly avoided capture at the battle of Cape St Vincent, and was wrecked after being captured at Trafalgar. She was less admired in the Spanish service, however, where she was known to be a crank sailer.

Following the American War, the French, encouraged by their success even if they had lost the last battle at the Saintes, had begun to build new, very large, three-deckers. The British Admiralty under Admirals Keppel and Lord Howe ordered an increase in the number of three-deckers to match developments in France. When the Royalists seized control of Toulon in 1793 the British took possession of fifteen French ships of the line, including the 120-gun *Commerce de Marseilles* which amazed them with its superb sailing qualities. On the other hand, she proved to be structurally too weak to survive under British operational conditions.

French 74s proved to be faster than those in the British navy, and their greater beam helped to ensure that they could stay upright enough to use their lower deck guns in a hard blow. In response, the Admiralty ordered new 74s more than 10ft longer on the gun deck. The British introduction of two-decked 80s during this period, because they were faster and also cheaper than the Second Rate 98s, also fol-

Heaving the Lead, by John Augustus Atkinson. (National Maritime Museum, London: PAD 7765)

5. Brian Lavery, *The Ship of the Line,* London: Conway Maritime Press, 1983, pp119-129.

Drawing by John Cantiloe of 'A two-decker furling sails.' Executed in 1835, this drawing shows the reinforced rounded bow which was given to ships after the battle of Trafalgar to strengthen them for bows-on attacks. (National Maritime Museum, London: PAF 6084)

lowed French example. Admiral Lord Howe had decided not to impose a close blockade on Brest, as had been the usual British practice, so British strategic requirements came closer to those of France than they had in earlier years.[5]

The trend to really large ships of the line, however, did not become definite until after the defeat of Napoleon. The cost of the new, larger, 74s was in the order of £46,000, compared to £37,000 for the more traditional

Watercolour of HMS St Vincent *with topmasts struck and yards lowered at Portsmouth, 1835.* (National Maritime Museum, London: PAD 8972)

A 38-gun frigate of the 1790s. The standard heavy cruising ship of the period, she would have been armed with a 18pdr main battery and 32pdr carronades. (National Maritime Museum, London: PAF 5984)

British 74. A big three-decker like the *Caledonia* cost £80,000. This was a serious consideration for a navy which needed to be able to fight coalitions of continental navies. Nelson's victories using a fleet predominantly made up of the older, smaller, 74s put a hold on further copying of French ship design.

Later, however, Nelson's tactics at Trafalgar – head-on assault on the enemy line – were to bring about the last structural change in the design of ships of the line. The last First Rates of the mid-nineteenth century were built with much heavier timbering at the bow, replacing the old open head. At the same time, the great weakness of the traditional ship of the line, the highly vulnerable stern so exposed to the

broadside of a ship lying across it, was addressed by replacing the open and elegant stern galleries of the eighteenth century with a heavy rounded stern capable of taking much greater punishment. The development of new constructional techniques employing diagonal bracing between the timbers and diagonally laid deck planking made it possible to build very much larger ships, which were able to accommodate heavier guns. Ultimately, this process led to the introduction of cast-iron knees to support the deck timbers, and then to the use of iron diagonal bracing.

Battle tactics were based on the capabilities of ships of the line, but the strategic employment of fleets also required other types of ships. The need to keep battle squadrons united for tactical action meant that they had a very limited visual range. Frigates, lighter and faster than ships of the line, were required as scouts. They were also used as minor warships to escort convoys, and at the battle of Copenhagen frigates and smaller sloops were used in the firing line against Danish batteries and hulks. Their light scantlings made them more vulnerable to Danish shot, but their shallow draft made them useful in confined waters. The bomb ketches employed at Copenhagen were small vessels mounting two mortars.

The strategic mobility of fleets of ships of the line exceeded anything in the later steam navies, until the development of nuclear power. Ships could, and did, undertake voyages around the world lasting years, often even refitting on undeveloped beaches; and part of the admiral's art was that of managing the health of his seamen. Many a fleet lost so many men to disease that they ceased to be operational. The achievements of great naval leaders, such as John Hawkins in the sixteenth century, St Vincent and Nelson in the late eighteenth, were products as much of their care for the supply of healthy victuals and drink, the discipline they imposed, and their routine, as they were of their tactical dispositions. Leadership requires a gift for human relations, but is also a very practical management problem.

Signals and Instructions

The tactics employed by admirals in the age of sail were logical consequences of the technology available to them, and of the ageless factors of human endurance and morale. Nelson's tactical plans were based on the experience of a naval service with over 300 years of a tactical tradition which was the collective memory of the more or less successful efforts of admirals to make effective use of their fleets. These had been drawn up as sailing and fighting instructions by successive admirals.

Until the development of Admiral Home Popham's system of naval telegraphic signals in 1800, and its unofficial adoption in the navy, there was no way of signalling an idea which had not been established as a formal instruction prior to the engagement, unless a boat were sent through the fleet so that an officer could pass on the instruction by a shouted message to each captain. The result was that admirals had little means to undertake tactical manoeuvres in response to unexpected developments in the course of battle. Battle fleet control depended essentially on an admiral bringing his captains to a thorough understanding of his intentions before engaging the enemy, and of convincing them of the practicability of his plans. The subordinate captains did not have a full set of flags issued to them, so that they had little capacity to convey tactical intelligence to the admiral. Signals were used to indicate one or more of the fighting instructions which had been issued to the fleet prior to the battle, or even prior to the beginning of the cruise. These would usually be similar to those issued by earlier admirals, with whatever additional instructions experience had shown to be useful. From 1691 the Admiralty provided printed copies of the Fighting and Sailing Instructions, but they were still issued in the name of the fleet commander who had considerable latitude to change them, provided he could persuade his captains to change their way of going about their business.

Until late in the eighteenth century the signalling system employed in every navy consisted of flags of different colours flown from particular locations in the rigging. Each location and flag specifically referred to one of the articles of the Sailing or Fighting Instructions. If that particular signal were made, subordinate admirals and captains knew to conform to the instructions in that article. Lantern signals employing the same principle were devised for night manoeuvres, and fog signals employed guns, drums and bugles. Because of the dangers inherent in such conditions, however, the signals were never as comprehensive as those devised for use in clear daylight.

Captain's undress coat, painted at Malta c1795-1812 by Anton. (National Maritime Museum, London: PAD 3111)

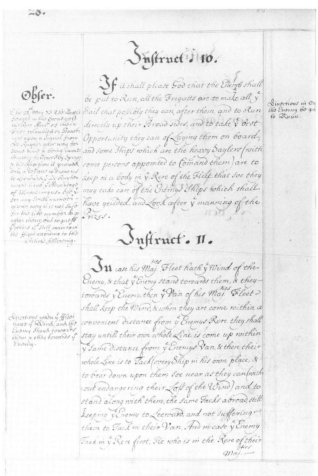

Pages from William and Mary Sailing and Fighting Instructions. (© Crown Copyright/MOD)

Sir Walter Raleigh and his cousin Sir William Gorges who commanded squadrons in the defence against the Spanish Armada of 1588 appear to have been the first English naval commanders to formally issue their captains with written instructions about their tactical intentions.[6] In 1625 Sir Edward Cecil, Viscount Wimbledon, issued instructions which divided his fleet into three squadrons, and placed the admiral, vice admiral and rear admiral respectively at the head of each.[7] His captains, however, expressed concern whether they would in fact be able to keep station in a seaway. As it was not until the end of the seventeenth century that ships began to be equipped with fore-and-aft sails on their stays, their difficulties were no doubt real. Somewhat more comprehensive instructions were issued by admirals during the Anglo-Dutch wars, and those of 29 March 1653 which were

issued to the whole fleet contained both Sailing and Fighting Instructions. Eight of the articles were provided with a flag signal so that the admirals could indicate at sea that their captains were to carry them out.[8] None of them referred to tactical manoeuvre of the fleet, but it appears that at the battle of the Gabbard the English fleet may have employed something like a line of battle for the first time.

During the eighteenth century the system of signalling was gradually improved, largely by the efforts of individual officers and even private publishers. The oldest existing privately-produced English signal book is dated 1711.[9] It began a process by which the deficiencies of the Admiralty publication were supplemented by individual effort. They were primarily of use for reading signals, and intended for junior officers, because they were organised by the location from which a flag might be flown,

6. *Fighting Instructions*, p42.

7. *Fighting Instructions*, pp52-64.

8. 'Laws of War and Ordinances of the Sea ordained and established by the Commonwealth of England', S R Gardiner and C T Atkinson, eds., *Papers relating to the First Dutch War*, Navy Records Society vol 30, London 1906; III pp293-301.

9. SIG/B/1.

starting with the mainmast head and working down, then the fore and mizzen masts. Sensibly enough, care was taken that different tactical instructions were signalled by flags flown from widely different locations so as to reduce the chance of confusion.

The introduction of signal tables into the French navy after the Seven Years War, of numerical signals into the British fleet in the last quarter of the century, and finally the issue of Popham's telegraphic signals to the fleet in September 1805 in time for Nelson to employ them at Trafalgar, improved the ability of commanders to communicate at sea and to receive intelligence from subordinates. Nevertheless, tactical signalling, however good, could never be an adequate substitute for the creative professional relationship between admiral and captains which so distinguished Nelson's leadership.

IN PORT

the seamen had their wives, sweethearts, and temporary friends onboard. Jack Nasty-Face wrote that

> After having moored our ship, swarms of boats came round us; some were what are generally termed bomb-boats, but are really nothing but floating chandler's shops; and a great many of them were freighted with cargoes of ladies, a sight that was truly gratifying, and a great treat; for our crew, consisting of six hundred and upwards, nearly all young men, had seen but one woman on board for eighteen months . . .

> So soon as these boats were allowed to come alongside, the seamen flocked down pretty quickly, one after the other, and brought their choice up, so that in the course of the afternoon, we had about four hundred and fifty on board.

> Of all the human race, these poor young creatures are the most pitiable, the ill-usage and the degradation they are driven to submit to, are indescribable; but from habit they become callous, indifferent as to delicacy of speech and behaviour, and so totally lost to all sense of shame, that they seem to retain no quality which properly belongs to a woman, but the shape and name. When we reflect that these unfortunate deluded victims to our passions, might at one time have been destined to be the valuable companions and comforts of man, but now so fallen; in these cooler moments of meditation, what a charge is raised against ourselves; we cannot reproach them for their abject condition, lest this startling question should be asked of us, who made us so?

(National Maritime Museum, London: PAD 5794)

The Line of Battle

Before the development of line tactics in the mid-seventeenth century, tactical organisation had consisted largely of mutual support. An admiral in his great ship surrounded by his fleet fought his battle like an armoured knight surrounded by his men-at-arms. When he steered into contact with the enemy his subordinate officers kept in station, and provided support. Their loyalty to him, and to their service, was central to tactical control. The earliest fighting instructions were more concerned with fleet discipline than tactical finesse. Captains had to be restrained from abandoning tactical formations in order to take prizes. They had to be instructed to hold their fire until they were within effective range. And at their peril they were never to fire on the enemy over, or through, a friendly ship. The development of line tactics changed things only to the extent that the admiral would instruct his squadron to take place in line ahead and astern of his flag. Instruction 18 of the

1799 Admiralty book of Signals and Instructions provided for immediate suspension 'if there should be found a captain, so lost to all sense of honour, and the great duty he owes his country, as not to exert himself to the utmost to get into action with the enemy.'[10]

From the time of the Second Dutch War, the standard tactical formation for the fleets of sailing warships became a close-order line of battle ahead because it ensured that ships which were designed to carry a heavy armament along their broadsides, and were thus long and slow-turning, would be able to minimise their vulnerability to raking fire against their bows and sterns. Each ship, except for those at the head and tail of the line, had their most vulnerable parts protected by their next in line. Linear tactics also ensured that each ship would be able to make good use of its firepower. In the Admiralty's signal book of 1799, the advantages of linear tactics were stated to be

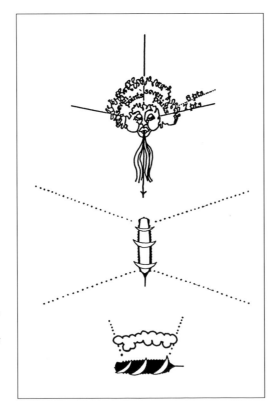

Typical arcs of fire from the broadside batteries of ships of the line. The line ahead tactical formation developed in the mid-seventeenth century was intended to ensure that the vulnerable bows and sterns of individual ships were protected by those ahead or astern in the formation.

that the ships may be able to assist and support each other in action; that they may not be exposed to the fire of the enemy's ships greater in number than themselves; and that every ship may be able to fire on the enemy without risk of firing into the ships of her own fleet.[11]

The line of battle, however, had more advantages for the defence than it had for offence. A fleet of ships mounting heavy batteries on their sides, drawn up in close-order line ahead, presented a tremendous weight of fire against the lead ship or ships in an approaching fleet, and could direct their fire at the structurally weak and lightly armed bows of the leading ships. The attacking fleet could only return fire if ships swung away from the line of advance to present their broadsides. If the attack was being made with line ahead formation there was a danger that the lead ship would be disabled, and block the advance of the remainder of the line. If the attackers adopted a line abreast formation and steered directly for the enemy they would cover the distance more rapidly, but all their ships would be highly vulnerable during the approach. In consequence, the central tactical problem in every battle of the sailing ship era was that of manoeuvering the ships of the line into firing range of the enemy.

The problem was further complicated by the need for an admiral who was determined to press home an attack to bring his fleet onto the same heading as the enemy fleet. If the lines of battle passed each other in opposite directions there was little chance of decisive results. Only by prolonged firing at very close range, no more than a few hundred yards and ultimately at ranges so close that there was a danger of muzzle blast setting both ships on fire, could the heavy sides of a First or Second Rate ship of the line be subjected to a truly destructive force.

Even when so engaged, decisive victory depended upon concentration of the fire on a part of the enemy line. With the longer-range guns which came into service in the late nineteenth century, concentration could be achieved by directing the fire of widely separated ships onto a single target. That was not possible with the short-range weapons available to Nelson. In *An Essay on Naval Tactics*, John Clerk of Eldin demonstrated in 1782 that ships moving in line ahead and a cable from each other, unless one of them swung out of line, could only fire on the same target if the enemy were over 720 yards away. At that range the kinetic energy of the broadside would be dissipated. Consequently, admirals sought to bring the enemy line between two fires, to 'double' the enemy line in the van or rear by detaching ships to pass around the van or rear of the enemy, or to cut through the line. To do so, without compromising the defensive strength of his own line, it would be necessary for an admiral confronting an enemy of equal strength to space out his own line so as to release forces for the enveloping movement. The thinned line might be able to contain the enemy because of the difficulty the latter would experience in employing its unen-

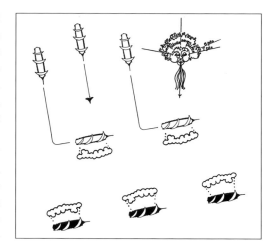

The line of battle was so strong defensively that it was difficult to develop tactics for the offensive. A head-on approach in line abreast from the windward was unsatisfactory because all the ships would be exposed to hostile fire without being able to reply until they bore up. Station keeping was always more difficult in line abreast than it was for a fleet in line ahead, especially when running downwind when it would be impossible for captains to back topsails to wait for slower ships. The result could be that when the leading ships turned to form line of battle they would block the slower ships from taking an active part in the action.

Because of the limited arc of fire of ships of the line, an admiral commanding a fleet with a smaller number of ships could reduce the danger by increasing the intervals between them. Some of the enemy ships would be left without a target. If they bore up to direct their battery at a ship forward of their station in the line they would slow down and cause bunching. If the enemy were sailing close hauled, the 'spare' ship could be taken aback, opening a wide gap in the line which the enemy might exploit by tacking through it to double the rear.

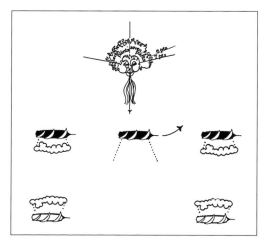

10. *Fighting Instructions*, pp274-275.

11. TUN/18 and 19; SIG/B/16, 74, 75 smf 78; HOL/51; DUN/32.

gaged ships without disrupting his tactical movement.

The development of systems of tactical manoeuvre to enable fleets of ships of the line to force decisive battle on their enemies was a result of experience, and theoretical analysis, over the century and a half leading to the wars of the French Revolution and Empire. This

For the attacking fleet to windward, a decisive concentration of fire could be brought upon the enemy rear by cutting through the enemy line, raking the bow and stern of the ships ahead and astern of the break, or by the rear of the line bearing down to 'Double' the enemy rear, and bring it between two fires.

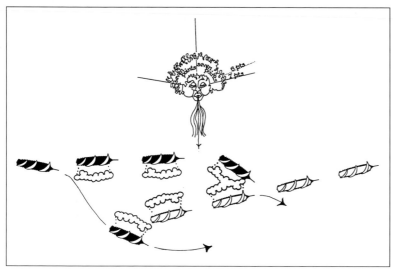

Decisive results could not be obtained by firing while passing the enemy on a reciprocal course. It was standard British practice, if the race for the windward position was won, to sail the length of the enemy line and then to tack in succession, starting with the rear. This would bring the fleets onto the same course, and in close firing range.

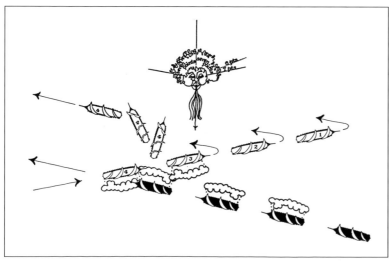

experience, and tactical conception, was drawn up by successive admirals in the Sailing and Fighting Instructions which they issued to their subordinates. Admirals could learn from their mistakes and issue additional instructions which might be useful in a subsequent battle, and their ideas were frequently adopted by subsequent commanders so that they became part of the tactical culture.

Providing the admiral was able to deploy his fleet from order of sailing to order of battle, it was then open to him to manoeuvre to engage the enemy to good advantage. From the Second Dutch War, admirals began to issue additional instructions setting out their intended method of making the dangerous approach, and of responding to moves of the enemy. These were consolidated in 1672 or 1673 when was published under the name of James Duke of York a volume containing all the standard signals and instructions.[12] Article 4 instructed commanders to place their ships in a close hauled line to windward. This was to become very much the standard practice, because an admiral who kept his fleet in line ahead to windward was more likely to be able to control the subsequent encounter with the enemy. It was only possible to keep formation seven points (79 degrees) off the wind, or at best for a well-drilled French fleet of the mid-eighteenth century, six points (67 degrees). Since this limitation was common to all fleets, commanders could seek to exploit each other's mistakes.

Article 7 instructed the fleet to endeavour to keep to windward of the enemy. A windward position had several advantages, not the least of which was that when the admiral judged it time to close with the enemy the dangerous approach could be made more quickly. Article 8 instructed the leading squadron to steer for the leading ships of the enemy fleet. Should it be necessary to reverse the fleet to bring the enemy to action on the same tack, Article 1 established the principle that the rear ships of the line should be the first to begin the deployment. In the 1690 Sailing and Fighting Instructions, this instruction was renumbered as Article 17.

Two pictures of Mary Anne Talbot, otherwise known as John Taylor (1778-1808). There were women on board some of the ships in the navy, some of whom were the wives of sailors. Most of the stories, however, are about women who adopted men's clothing as a disguise.

Right: by James Green, artist, and G Scott, engraver. (National Maritime Museum, London: PAD 3120)

Left: by John Chapman, engraver. (National Maritime Museum, London: PAD3119)

Above: A coloured wood-cut of another female sailor, Anne Jane Thornton, c1800-1802. (National Maritime Museum, London: PAD 3045).

Right: 'The Sailors Will and Power'. (National Maritime Museum, London: PAF 5809)

Tacking into battle from leeward could expose the lead ships to protracted punishment. If a fleet were forced into the leeward position, however, Article 3 instructed it to attempt to cut the enemy line and so pass through to the windward side. This cutting manoeuvre was by no means universally approved, and as late as the mid-eighteenth century there was no signal in the Fighting Instructions which called for it. At the end of the century, however, the analytic work of John Clerk of Eldin, experience, and the innovative dedication of Admiral Lord Howe increased its popularity. Nelson was known to have taken an interest in Clerk of Eldin's work, and much admired Lord Howe. At Trafalgar he deployed his fleet into two columns, and used them to punch through the enemy line in two places from windward.

12. SIG/A/1, and NM/104.

Growth of the Tactical Tradition

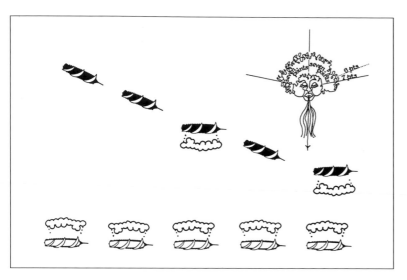

An oblique approach reduced the danger, but required skillful shiphandling if the forward motion of the fleet was not to be impeded.

The problem of engaging from windward in an orderly manner was addressed by Lord Dartmouth when he issued instructions to the fleet which was assembled in 1688 to prevent a landing by William of Orange. His idea was that a long approach should be made at an oblique angle to the enemy wake which would not expose his ships heads to a fire they could not return. Progress was to be controlled by the captains conforming to the movements of the flagship. From time to time, as appeared necessary, the ships were to swing round so that they could open fire on the enemy ships ahead of them. Then the admiral would bear down again with his ships taking their cue from his movements. When nearly within gunshot of the enemy, the ships were to 'lask away', taking the wind on their quarters and steering courses to intercept their opposite number. At no point were they to head directly for the enemy when they would be exposed head-on to a raking fire.[13]

Given the disparate nature of the English fleet at the time, this tactical plan may have been somewhat fanciful. It was to be attempted by Admiral Byng in 1756 at the battle of Minorca, but he failed because his leading captain did not understand what was expected of him.

In another version of the Duke of York's

Sailing and Fighting Instructions, a manuscript version probably dating from after the Glorious Revolution of 1688, the question of how to bring preponderate force against part of the enemy line was developed. Cutting the enemy line from leeward was not favoured, except in desperation if being driven on a lee shore. The limited capacity of seventeenth-century ships to work to windward, while firing on the enemy, and the danger of the ships which made their way to windward being themselves cut off by the enemy, argued against that tactic. The preference was for an attack from the windward, with a concentration of force against the head of the enemy line, or the windward-most part of the line if the head had fallen off to leeward. It was felt that those ships which were most to windward would be those with the best sailing qualities, and that it would be difficult for those left to leeward to work up under fire to provide relief.[14] In 1691 Admiral Russell put his name to a reissue of the Fighting Instructions, with a few additions, and his name continued to be attached to what became in fact, but not in law, an official Admiralty publication.[15]

Tourville and Hoste

At the end of the seventeenth century the French navy rapidly developed a science of naval tactics which more than caught up with the empirical growth in Britain. Louis XIV's Admiral, the Comte de Tourville, drilled the French fleet to unprecedented skill in manoeuvre, and established for it a prowess which was to survive until the French Revolution decimated the professional officer corps. For the campaign designed to put James II back on the British throne, Tourville published General and Sailing Instructions, and a Signal Book, which were revised each year from their first appearance in 1689. By 1693 the signal book contained 229 items, providing comprehensive tactical control of his fleet.[16]

Tourville had a protégé by the name of Père

13. Sloane MS 3560, printed in *Fighting Instructions,* pp168-72.

14. Ec/48 and *Fighting Instructions* pp139-40, 152-63.

15. SIG/A/2.

16. HOL/6.

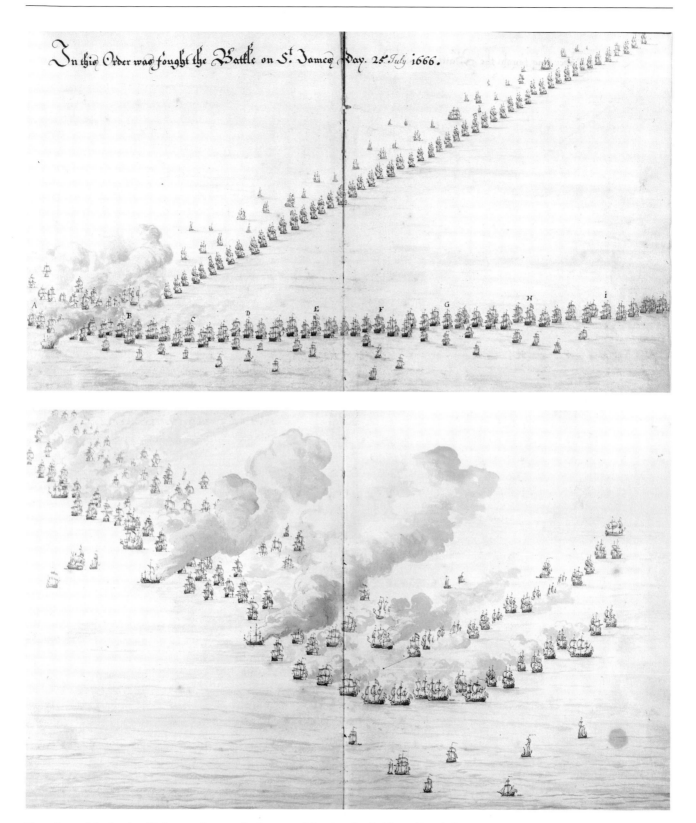

In this Order was fought the Battle on St. James Day. 25 July 1666.

Two views of the battle of Sole Bay showing the first use of the close-hauled line of battle formation, from James Duke of York's Sailing and Fighting Instructions *c1688.* (© Crown Copyright/MOD)

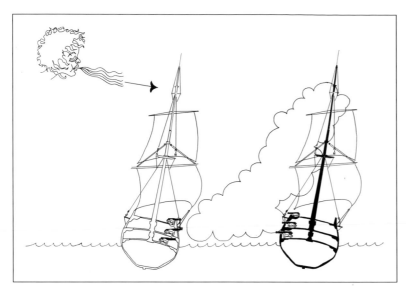

The advantage of fighting from the leeward position in a strong wind was that the fleet could engage the enemy with all the guns on the windward side, which would be heeled up above the harbour water line, but its opponent might not be able to open its lower-deck gun ports which would be low to, or even below, the water line. On the other hand, the leeward ship would find it harder to aim its guns because of the smoke blown back into the faces of the crew.

Paul Hoste who published in 1697 one of the great books of naval tactics, *L'Art des Armées Navales ou Traité des Evolutions Navales.* He developed a system of tactics based on five *ordres de marche* which were adopted by the French navy, and remained its standard throughout the entire era of sail-driven warships. Hoste believed strongly in the necessity for admirals to adopt a line-of-battle close-hauled to windward when engaging the

The leeward position was defensively stronger because damaged ships would drift behind their own line, to a position of safety. Captains of ships in the windward fleet, however, recognising their vulnerability, could be expected to fight with all the more determination.

enemy, as being most likely to put their fleets in the windward position. His five orders of sailing were designed to permit rapid deployment into that battle order.

He wrote that the windward position not only gave the initiative to the fleet possessing it, but also facilitated doubling the enemy rear. It facilitated attack by fire-ships on disabled enemy ships, attack on enemy ships trying to escape, and cutting the enemy line. The smoke of battle would be carried down onto the leeward fleet making it harder for them to retain cohesion. On the other hand, the heel of ships to a strong wind could make it impossible for those on the windward side to open their lower gun ports which would be close to sea level. More than one warship was sunk when water flooded in through open gun ports. The leeward fleet also had the advantage that ships which became disabled aloft tended to drift into safety behind their own line, although the fact that captains in the windward fleet knew that they had no easy line of retreat may have stiffened their resolve. The admiral commanding the leeward fleet could more easily take advantage of the onset of night, or a shift of wind, to break off action. An admiral of Nelson's stamp, who could develop and depend on his fleet's morale, would find a windward position to his advantage.

Hoste's sailing formations were adopted or adapted by all fleets because of their tactical utility. His First Order of Sailing was a close-hauled line of bearing on either tack. The ships could be sailing in any direction the wind permitted, but would be in a line formation the axis of which was 6 points off the wind. At any time the admiral could order his ships to bear up, and they would then be immediately in a close-hauled line of battle. Later in the eighteenth century this formation was developed into a line of bearing on any compass point, which permitted the rapid deployment of a line of battle on any possible course. When this devolution took place Hoste's Second Order of Sailing, a line of bearing at right angles to the direction the wind was blowing, was subsumed. The British navy came to call Hoste's first order a 'bow and quarter line', but were content with keeping 7 points off the wind so as to make it easier for captains to keep in station.

Hoste's Third Order of Sailing was for a squadron or fleet to be divided into two divisions, in a 'V' formation with the flag at its leeward apex. Each arm of the 'V' was 6 points off the wind respectively on the port and starboard tacks. Again, the fleet could be sailing in any direction the wind permitted, but on a signal from the admiral it could form a line ahead close-hauled to windward. The advantage of this formation was that the fleet could deploy on either tack, with the division at the end of the line coming down on the wind to form a continuous line.

Hoste's Fourth Order of Sailing was for the fleet to form its three squadrons into columns deployed to port and starboard of the admiral's squadron, and to divide each squadron into two divisions each. The squadron flags would take up position leading and between the divisions, and the centre squadron would be somewhat advanced over the van and rear. The axis of the formation would be down wind, but the ships' headings could be anything for which the wind served.

The Fifth Order divided the fleet into three squadrons deployed to port and starboard of the admiral, in close-hauled lines of battle 6 points off the wind. Although it would take longer to deploy into a single line of battle from this formation than it would from the first order, the fifth order was of practical utility because it kept the fleet closer together, and more under the admiral's eye.

Hoste's preferred means of bringing preponderate force against a part of the enemy line was to double on the enemy rear. The general preference was for doubling the van, because it was thought that the forward movement of the enemy line would be disrupted by the engagement of the van. This, however, Hoste discounted, especially in the case of an attack on a fleet to leeward. The damaged ships could drift to leeward and be sheltered by the undamaged ships moving up into position. There was a danger that the attacking ships would themselves be overwhelmed.

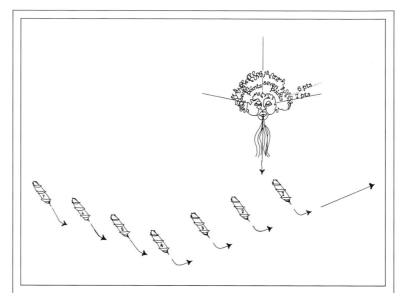

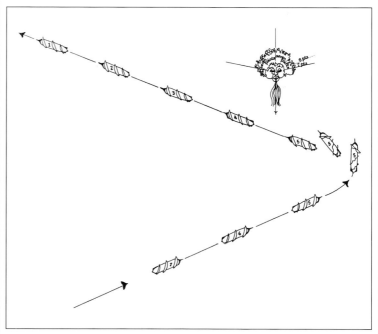

HOSTE'S THIRD ORDER OF SAILING, AND TACKING

The fleet is sailing with the wind on the port quarter in Hoste's Third Order of Sailing, in a 'V'-formation able to deploy on a close-hauled line of battle 6 points off the wind on either tack. On a signal, all ships turn together, the leaders on the larboard line of battle bracing hard up, and the rear following round when they reach the apex of the old formation. Finally the fleet tacks in succession onto a close-hauled line of battle to starboard, 6 points off the wind. Tacking a fleet risked confusion because of the danger that one or more ships would miss stays, and force those following them to bear away. For that reason, admirals preferred to wear fleets in the presence of the enemy. French fleets were drilled to form line 6 points off the wind, but British practice was to work 7 points off the wind so as to make it easier for ships forced to bear away to avoid collision to regain their stations.

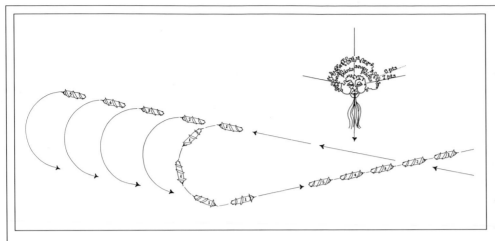

BOW AND QUARTER LINE, WEARING

The fleet is sailing in a 'bow and quarter line' with the wind on the starboard quarter, and ready on the signal being given to brace up into a close-hauled line of battle on the starboard tack, 7 points off the wind. What the British called a 'bow and quarter line', because the admiral ordered both the fleet's heading and the relative bearing each ship should keep from the flagship, was the same as Hoste's 'First-Order of Sailing', except that a French fleet could manage to deploy into line of battle 6 points off the wind. In order to deploy on a close-hauled line of battle on the port, or 'larboard', tack, the fleet then wears in succession starting from the last ship. This is a more reliable manoeuvre than would be tacking the fleet in succession starting with the leading ship, but it reverses the order of battle, putting a more junior commander, and possible weaker ships, in the lead.

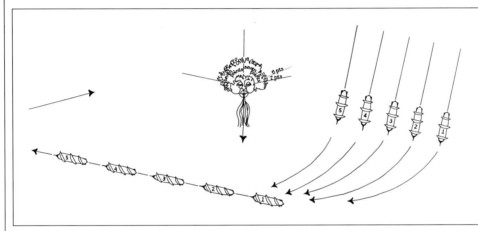

Doubling on the rear, on the other hand, could rapidly isolate those attacked from their line which would be drawing away all the time. Ships damaged in making an attack on the rear had a good chance of getting clear without pursuit.

Hoste suggested five methods by which admirals in danger of being doubled, because of their inferior number of ships, could protect their fleets. If in the windward position, they could deploy against the enemy centre and rear only. The enemy van would then be useless, because it could not put about to engage without risking being cut off. An admiral commanding an inferior force to leeward could not risk leaving the enemy van unengaged, because it could easily come about to double his own van. Instead he would have to space out his squadrons, or the ships within the squadrons. The latter was less satisfactory because in light airs each would be in danger of engagement by more than one of the enemy. Spacing out the squadrons would leave some of the enemy ships without anything to engage. This could be done by leaving a large gap in the centre, which might have to be covered with fireships, or by ordering the squadron admirals to engage their opposite numbers. A more sophisticated solution would be for the squadron commanders to engage ships to the rear of their opposite number so that the head of each of the enemy squadrons would be unengaged.

Hoste did not reckon that cutting the enemy line had great potential for disabling it. If it were to be done, however, he believed that the way to go about it from the leeward was for the line to tack in succession, and then again once the van had successfully passed through the enemy. This would bring the enemy between fires immediately ahead and astern of the point of cutting. For the windward fleet to counter the cutting motion, its admiral should order it to tack together. This could be done before the enemy actually made the cut, or after, in which case the van of the leeward fleet risked being cut off itself.

Although Hoste's work was a tremendous advance for the art of tactics, it did little to alter the fact that the line of battle was a stronger defensive than offensive formation. He devoted much more time to discussing its defensive qualities than he did to the methods of pressing home an attack with success.

The English did not approach Hoste's methodology. Instead, Admiral Russell's Sailing and Fighting Instructions were re-issued in Queen Anne's reign, with some further detail, but without Russell's indices which had been deleted by Admiral Rooke in 1702.[17] Although the 'Permanent' instructions were never more than printed by the Admiralty, and acquired their authority only when an admiral issued them to his subordinates, they nonetheless acquired a status which made it virtually impossible for admirals to deviate from accepted practice. Article 17 was amplified to make it absolutely clear that a fleet engaging the enemy from the windward on converging courses must be tacked, starting with the rearward ships, to bring it on a parallel course. Article 19 made it equally clear that once on a parallel course, the van was to attack the enemy van. The apparent rigidity of the tactical system was further emphasised by the fact that there were so few manoeuvering signals provided for the admiral that he would have difficulty undertaking any tactical variant. All the same, the tactical concept was not so rigid that admirals were prohibited from continuing to add additional instructions, some of which became accepted general practice. For seventy years some of England's most successful admirals were able to work within the limitations of the Sailing and Fighting Instructions without apparent difficulty.

The Order of Battle

The instructions issued at the beginning of the Second Dutch War, in 1664, were an advance on earlier practice because they indicate that it had been decided to give each ship a pre-assigned position in each squadron's battleline.[18] This was necessary because fleets were made up of ships with differing weight of timber and gun, and commanded by officers with different degrees of capacity. In the mid-seventeenth century fleets were more disparate than they were to become by Nelson's time, but the fleets of the late eighteenth century were by no means homogeneous. No navy could afford to build all its ships of the largest rate, because they had to be constructed from the largest trees, which were relatively scarce. This made them disproportionately expensive. In any case, admirals needed battle lines with roughly the same number of ships as those of their enemy so as to limit the danger of being overwhelmed by concentrations of force. These numbers could only be achieved by compromising on ship size. It was also important for an admiral to have smaller ships for detached duties, which could sail faster in light winds and manoeuvre easily. All the great sea powers had overseas empires which needed naval defence, which was best provided for by the maintenance of large fleets of Third Rates.

Joining such disparate ships into a battle line was part of the admiral's art. Experience eventually led to admirals generally placing their flag in the centre of the line where it was easiest to keep in touch with developments and exercise control. Admirals would fly their flag in one of the largest ships, which would provide the best accommodation, and provide maximum force where the fight would be heaviest. The tradition whereby capturing the enemy admiral was tantamount to victory en-

17. 'Instructions for directing & governing Her Majesties Fleet in sailing & fighting by the Right Honourable Sir George Rooke . . .' Add MS 28126; and the Permanent Sailing and Fighting Instructions, NM/80.

18. WYN/12/1, 5, 8 and WYN/13/1.

sured that the flagship would be subjected to the heaviest attack, and would set the pace for offensive action. Heavy ships commanded by senior captains typically would be stationed either side of the flag to ensure good support, and at the head and tail of his squadron because their captains would have considerable responsibility in carrying out the tactical plan, and because they might have to endure a considerable weight of fire unsupported during the approach phase. Some admirals placed their subordinate flag officers near the ends of their divisions to ensure that the lead ship carried out tactical orders effectively, but this practice died out in the eighteenth century in favour of consolidating the maximum power in the centre of each division and squadron.

Towards the end of the eighteenth century the formal order of the line began to appear less important than before, and Admiral Lord Howe issued a signal in 1794 which specifically instructed captains to take whatever place in the line that they found most immediately convenient. This helped to reduce the time it took for a fleet to get into battle formation, but probably was only possible because by then the majority of the fleet was made up of ships of similar force. Howe's instruction called for flag officers to assume their appointed places notwithstanding, and as they flew their flags from three-deckers the need to have a concentration of force at the centre of each squadron was ensured despite the relaxation of order.

Nelson placed himself, and the majority of his three-deckers, at the head of the columns attacking the Franco-Spanish fleet at Trafalgar. This he did partly because the plan of his attack exposed the head of the line to heavy fire, which a First Rate could better withstand. At the head of his column, Nelson was also in the best position to direct the attack. Most important of all, however, was the psychological necessity that he place himself in the position of most danger.

The difficulty of manoeuvering a squadron to take station in the line of battle in time could be considerable. Sailing vessels of different sizes and rigs responded differently to different sailing conditions, and could also be affected to different degrees by the fouling of their bottoms, which would effect the leeway they would make. Where there were so many variables, there was scope for ships' captains to deviate from the plan consciously or unconsciously. The success of an admiral's efforts to get his ships into the line could depend on the order in which they had been sailing. However, the order of sailing was based on different considerations than was the order of battle. The older tradition of sailing in line abeam, derived from the battle formation of galley fleets, survived until late in the eighteenth century. When in order of sailing, seniority rather than tactical utility determined stations. Traditionally, the Vice Admiral's station was to starboard of the Admiral, and the Rear Admiral's to port, and the captains of each division took station to starboard and port of their divisional commanders in order of seniority. Where the whole fleet was assembled, the White and Blue squadrons would take station respectively to starboard and port of the Commander-in-Chief in the Red squadron.

After the second battle of Schoonveldt in 1673 Admiral Spragge recommended that when there was sea room enough, fleets should always sail in the order of battle, in line abreast with the squadrons deployed ahead of each other.[19] Incredibly, however, the sailing order of the English fleet by seniority survived at least another hundred years. In the 1830s the younger Admiral Knowles was to write that in his early years it was still the practice for the second in command to sail immediately to starboard of the admiral, and the third in command on his port hand. They would have to make their way through the fleet to take their respective battle positions at the head of the line on starboard and port tack. During the blockade of Cadiz before the battle of Trafalgar, Nelson deployed his fleet in order of battle so that there would be as little difficulty as possible in bringing them into action. The full spread of canvas he then carried, however, defeated all efforts at station keeping.

19. Spragge's Journal, *Third Dutch War*, p321.

Lessons of Battle–The early eighteenth century

Malaga

The battle of Malaga in 1704 established in both British and in French tactical thinking the absolute importance of maintaining the defensive strength of a well-ordered line of battle. If defeat could be avoided despite the worst efforts of the enemy then there was the possibility that effective gunnery, aided perhaps by a lucky shift of the wind, might yield victory. This attitude was reinforced by the fact that, although Malaga was at best a tactical draw, it was nonetheless an important strategic victory for the British because it ensured their continued occupation of Gibraltar at the mouth of the Mediterranean. At the same time, Malaga reinforced French belief in the defensive power of a well-ordered line.

The fact that several fireships were available on each side at the battle of Malaga, but that neither side used them, is significant. In the seventeenth century fireships were regularly used. Their station was on the disengaged side of the line, sheltering behind the heavy sides of the great ships. Should circumstances permit their use, they would be steered towards the enemy by a volunteer crew which would set fire to the combustibles onboard and abandon ship at the last moment. Each side would use small vessels either to support an attack, or attempt to counter it. They were always impressive spectacles with a great potential to disrupt tactical formation, but the circumstances of eighteenth-century battles in the open sea tended to reduce their utility. They fell out of use, though Admirals Howe and Kempenfelt in the 1770s supported their reintroduction. It is arguable that Nelson should have used them against the French defensive line chained across the entrance to Boulogne in 1801.

French Fireships attacking the English Fleet off Quebec, 28 June 1759, by Dominic Serres (1722-1793). By the end of the eighteenth century the British had all but given up the use of fireships, but they might have been useful in the abortive attack Nelson ordered against the invasion forces at Boulogne. Congreve's rockets, had they been available, would also have been useful. Plans were afoot to employ them against the Franco-Spanish fleet at Cadiz in 1805, but the battle of Trafalgar put an end to the need. (National Maritime Museum, London: BHC 0392)

Admiral Sir Edward
Vernon (1723-1794), in
the style of Francis
Hayman (1708-1776).
(National Maritime
Museum, London: BHC
3069)

Admiral Sir Edward Vernon (1723-1794), in the style of Francis Hayman (1708-1776). (National Maritime Museum, London: BHC 3069)

Vernon

In 1739 Admiral Vernon issued several additional instructions to the fleet he commanded in the West Indies which significantly improved his ability to exercise tactical control. He established a signal, a yellow and white striped flag at the main topmast head, to be used if he found his fleet engaging a weaker enemy force. At the same time he would fly pendants indicating particular ships. These were to fall out of the line and form a reserve, which was to hold itself ready to support ships in difficulty. He appreciated that in the smoke of battle he might not be able to give particular direction to this reserve, but he had a confidence in his officers which served him as well as later it did Nelson: 'I principally rely upon their prudence and resolution in observing where such service lie open for your execution, or require your relief.'[20]

Another of Vernon's innovations was to provide instructions which enabled him to overrule the tradition that the van squadron led the line on the starboard tack, and the rear on the port. He made it clear that, if he ordered the fleet to tack together, beginning with the last ship, his intention was to reverse the order of the fleet. If, however, he ordered the fleet to tack in succession starting with the first ship, he wished to preserve the order. In this way, regardless of the direction of the wind, he was able to ensure that his more experienced vice admiral would be in charge of bringing the fleet into action, and was also able to ensure that the heavy ships which he stationed at the head of the van would be in position to lead the attack. Had Admiral Mathews issued a similar instruction to the Mediterranean fleet in 1744, for 'same ships to lead on different tacks', he might well have gone into action at Toulon in better order. Following the battle, and Mathews' recall, Rear Admiral Rowley promulgated the instruction.[21]

Vernon introduced night signals for ships deployed ahead of the fleet, so that they could report ships encountered, their number and relative direction. And he established night recognition signals for his fleet. These last, especially, suggest that he was contemplating the possibility of night action, despite the risks always associated with its uncertainties. Admiral Hawke also issued night recognition signals, as part of a list of eighteen additional night signals before the battle of Quiberon Bay in 1759.[22]

Vernon's additional signals were important in the process of developing more effective tactics for the Royal Navy, but Vernon was rather an exceptional admiral. His education included the study of Hebrew. The navy as a whole was not convinced of the need to study tactics. As Vernon wrote:

Our sea officers despise theory . . ., and by trusting only to their genius at the instant they are to act, have neither time, nor foundation whereby to proceed.

But Vernon himself thought there was merit in the anti-intellectual approach. There is more to tactics than evolutions: morale, ship design and gunnery all play important parts.

Where officers are determined to fight in great fleets, 'tis much of the least of the matter what order they fight in. . . . All formality . . . only tends to keep the main point out of the question, and to give knaves and fools

20. *Vernon*, pp290-1, 295.

21. TUN/12.

22. TUN/36.

23. *An Enquiry into the Conduct of Captain Savage Mostyn,* London, 1754.

24. Tunstall/Tracy, pp6-7.

25. Tunstall/Tracy, p213.

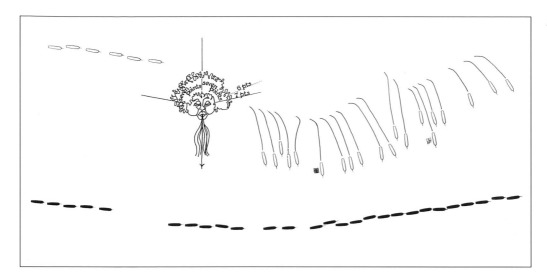

Battle of Toulon.

an opportunity to justify themselves on the credit of jargon and nonsense.[23]

This attitude continued throughout the age of sail in the Royal Navy. Manoeuvre well-conducted could certainly strengthen the capacity of a fleet to defend itself, but there was no certainty that it would ensure the ability of an admiral to force action upon an unwilling enemy. Admiral John Jervis, Lord St Vincent, was to observe that 'two fleets of equal strength can never produce decisive events, unless they are equally determined to fight it out or the Commander-in-chief of one of them so bitches it as to misconduct his line.'[24]

And he expostulated that 'Lord Hawke when he ran out of the line [at the Battle of Toulon] and took the *Poder* sickened me of tactics.'[25] Part of Nelson's genius lay in his ability to judge just how far he could depart from tactical conventions in order to get decisive, yet successful, action.

Toulon

The battle of Toulon was a national disgrace, but it led to a renewal of interest in tactical development. Admiral Mathews had attempted to bring on a general action by steering directly for the Franco-Spanish fleet, but the British

Contemporary plan of the battle of Toulon showing Admiral Mathews closely engaged, but Vice Admiral Lestock's squadron out of action. (National Maritime Museum, London: 8468)

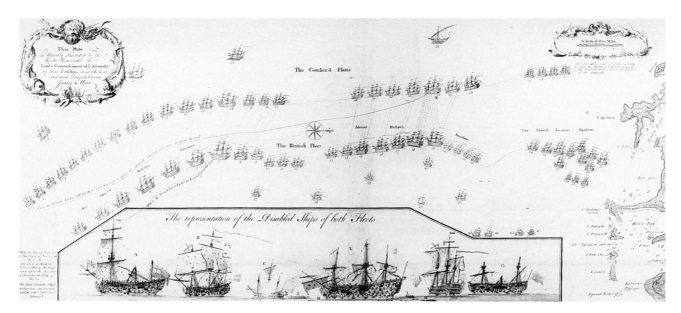

Admiral George, Lord Anson (1697-1762); print by J M Ardell after a painting by Sir Joshua Reynolds. (British Museum)

line was not well formed, and he confused his subordinates by leaving the signal for line of battle flying despite his approach nearly in line abreast. Once engaged with the Spanish flagship, the signal was understood by his Vice Admiral, Lestock, as requiring him to keep in formation even though the Spanish line had sagged far to leeward. Lestock was certainly working to rule, probably because of his personal dislike of Admiral Mathews. That the existing signals and instructions were defi-

Admiral Lord Edward Hawke (1709-1781), by Francis Cotes. (National Maritime Museum, London: BHC 2784)

cient, however, was indisputable. Following his assumption of command, Admiral Rowley not only introduced all of Vernon's additional instructions, he added others which usefully relaxed the discipline of the line of battle so as to make clear the overriding importance of mutual support.[26]

Anson and Hawke

Additional instructions did not necessarily become a permanent part of the tactical tradition, but the need for this flexibility was generally recognised. During his brief period in command of the Channel Fleet during the Seven Years War Admiral Anson issued an instruction that, if he found that not enough of his ships were able to engage the enemy while maintaining line discipline, he would haul down the signal for the line. Every ship was then to engage the ship opposite it in the enemy line.[27] The next year Rear Admiral Hawke amplified the same instruction when he took over command.[28]

In 1747 Hawke issued a set of additional instructions, which may have been devised by Anson, the Commander-in-Chief, and which were intended to increase the flexibility of line tactics by giving the admiral more control over manoeuvre, and also by trusting individual captains to make appropriate decisions.[29] Article 8 instructed the captains of the smaller ships, if the fleet was in action with a less numerous enemy force, to fall out of the line on their own initiative and manoeuvre to rake the enemy van or rear. Article 13 provided individual captains with a signal to other captains which they could use to help in station keeping. Articles 9 and 10 gave even more initiative to individual captains, in the particular circumstance of the pursuit of an enemy fleet which was unwilling to give battle. Anson had encountered this circumstance a few months earlier when he met a French convoy escort under De La Jonquière. Not only could deployment from order of sailing to order of battle take so long that the enemy would have time to retreat in good order, but the line of battle once formed could only advance at the

speed of the slowest of the ships from which it was composed. The signal ordering 'general chase', which permitted ships to leave the order of battle to pursue the enemy, was on its own only suitable if the enemy force were disorganised. Hawke, or Anson, introduced the idea of an emergency line of battle which would be formed by the captains of the faster ships as they came up with the enemy, the furthest advanced taking the lead without regard to seniority. This *ad hoc* line was to engage the rearward ships of the enemy, and try to pass on to the enemy van.

Anson also introduced into British tactics the Line of Bearing Formation, or the 'Bow and Quarter Line'. This was identical to Père Hoste's First Order of Sailing. As with the later versions of Hoste's order, the axis of the formation could be any bearing ordered by the admiral. The course set for the fleet could be anything the wind permitted. The term 'Starboard' or 'Larboard (Port) Line of Bearing' was used to indicate lines of bearing which could be made into a close-hauled line to windward on the starboard or port tack by ordering the ships to change course. If it was wanted to change the line of bearing, as opposed to the ships' heading, it was usually necessary to deploy into line ahead, and pay off

on the new bearing, before returning to the intended heading.

Minorca

The tactical lessons which had been learnt over the century, however, had not adequately addressed the problem of bringing a line ahead formation into action with a well-formed enemy line. When Admiral John Byng was

Lord Anson's victory off Cape Finisterre, 3 May 1747, by Samuel Scott (1701/2-1772). (National Maritime Museum, London: BHC 0369)

26. TUN/12.

27. *Barrington*, I, pp231-2 (30 August 1758).

28. *Barrington*, I, pp259-60.

29. CLE/2/19.

Admiral John Byng, by Thomas Hudson. (National Maritime Museum, London: BHC 2590)

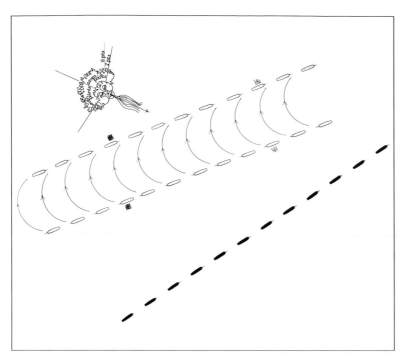

Battle of Minorca. Admiral Byng tacks his fleet in succession beginning from the rear in order to bring it on the same heading as the French fleet. This was required by Article 17 of the Fighting Instructions. Fleets passing on opposite directions did not have time to inflict decisive damage to each other.

Battle of Minorca. Once on converging courses, Byng ordered his fleet to lask down on the enemy, but the captain of the leading ship believed he had to conform to Article 19 of the Fighting Instructions directing him to steer to intercept the leading ship of the enemy.

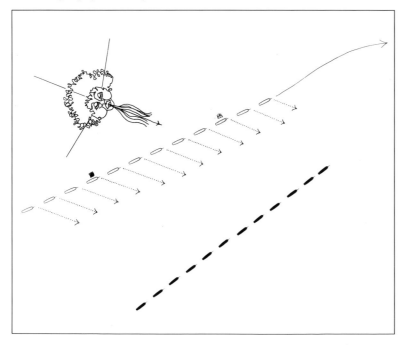

sent to the Mediterranean in 1756 to cover the British garrison on Minorca he was confronted by a French fleet fresh out of Toulon, covering the soldiers besieging the British at Port Mahon. A lucky shift of wind gave Byng the windward position, passing the French on an opposite course. This was the situation in which the virtually mandatory Article 17 of the official Sailing and Fighting Instructions required him to tack the fleet, beginning with the rearmost ship. This he did, although his timing would have been better had La Galissonière not ordered his ships to back their sails.

Once tacked, the two fleets were on slightly converging courses which would have permitted the British to ease down on the French line without exposing themselves to unacceptable damage. This is the tactic which Lord Dartmouth had recommended in 1688. Unfortunately, Article 19 required the leading ship, the *Defence*, to seek to engage the leading ship of the enemy. Her captain, Thomas Andrews, judged that he could not get up with the French leading ship if he continued on his course, so he bore up on one parallel to the French line of advance. This could not have helped much given the relatively clean hulls of the French ships, but repeated signals to bear down a point did not serve to correct the situation. Byng was too far back in the line to be able to see exactly what was required, Andrews was too unimaginative to understand the intent behind Byng's approach, and there was no way of communicating it to him because of the inadequacy of British signals.

Abandoning his effort at a subtle approach, Byng hoisted the signal to engage, and the entire fleet bore down on the French in a loose line of bearing. In doing so they were exposed to heavy fire without being able to reply, and suffered so much damage that they were unable to press home their attack. As Audibert Ramatuelle observed in *Cours Elémentaire de Tactique Navale* published in 1802, Byng's attack became a downwind run on which point of sailing it was impossible to ensure good station-keeping by backing the topsails of the faster ships.[30] As a result of the damage the fleet suffered Byng felt it necessary to retire to Gibraltar for repairs. The British garrison in Port Mahon had to surrender, which led to Byng being tried by Court Martial for failing to do his utmost to defeat the enemy. As Voltaire put it, Byng was shot, *pour encouragé les autres*.

Byng was at once the victim of an immature tactical system, and also of English politics. He was made a scapegoat for the Administration. All the same, he was guilty of two failures of command which stand in stark contrast to the qualities that Nelson was to show later in the century. In the first place, he evidently had not taken his captains adequately into his confidence in the weeks before the battle so that they thoroughly understood his tactical intentions, and he had not ensured that the fleet would be led by an officer who could be relied on to carry them out. Second, he had made a strategic mistake in not appreciating that the consequences of withdrawing to Gibraltar would be more serious than would be the consequences of fighting another battle despite the damage suffered by his ships. There was nothing in the Articles of War which referred to errors of strategic judgment, which is why he was charged quite unjustly with disaffection.

Lagos Bay

The night action of Lagos Bay in August 1759 was also affected by the need for more signals, the necessity for which Admiral Boscawen only recognised too late. He had not given consideration to the problem of the deployment of ships as they caught up with the rear of the French line. He had reissued Hawke's 1757 instruction that the leading ships should form an *ad hoc* line without regard to seniority, but what he recognised in retrospect was needed was an instruction to the effect that the leading ship should engage the enemy rear and that a line should be formed on it, in reverse order. The second ship to come up should pass by the fight on the disengaged side, and come into action with the next enemy ship. The third should pass the first two and engage the third from the enemy rear.[31] The Admiralty was eventually to establish a signal incorporating this idea in the 1770s.

Quiberon Bay

Hawke's triumph at Quiberon Bay three months later, on the other hand, demonstrates how much a commander could accomplish without sophisticated communications, pro-

30. Tunstall/Tracy, pp235-240.

31. Julian Corbett, *England in the Seven Years War*, London 1907, II pp37-8; and Tunstall/Tracy, p114.

Battle of Quiberon Bay, 20 November 1759, by Dominic Serres (1722-1793). (National Maritime Museum, London: BHC 2266)

vided his captains were thoroughly familiar with his intentions, experienced, and inspired by his example. The battle was fought in very dangerous conditions in a full gale on a lee shore choked with shoals and islands. Hawke used a minimum of tactical direction, merely signalling his fleet to form line abreast, and crowd on the sail. This served to bring his ships together, and propel them towards the French fleet which was seeking shelter in the Vilaine estuary. When Admiral Conflans deployed his fleet into order of sailing in line ahead, and led them into the bay, Hawke was permitted by the Admiralty instructions to order his ships to chase. He used his additional signal of 1747 to instruct the leading seven ships to form an *ad hoc* line as they came up on the French rear. It was not until 2.30pm on that short winter's day that firing started, when Hawke flew the signal to engage. The

fighting was confused, and did not last long. As the dark came on shortly after 5.00pm Hawke ordered the fleet to anchor where they were amongst the shoals. One French ship surrendered, two were sunk, and four were wrecked. One of the latter was Admiral Conflans' flagship which had anchored in the dark in the midst of the British fleet, and in the morning was lost when trying to get away. Those ships which escaped into the river only did so by jettisoning their guns and stores, effectively putting them out of the war. The threat of invasion of England was eliminated, at the cost of two British ships wrecked, and some fifty men killed. Hawke was justified in writing: 'When I consider the season of the year, the hard gales on the day of action, a flying enemy, the shortness of the day, and the coast they were on, I can boldly affirm that all that could possibly be done has been done.'[32]

Tactical Development During Nelson's Early Service

Nelson's victories at the end of the century and the beginning of the next, were won by fleets which were little different materially from those of the first half of the eighteenth century, although the ships were a little larger and their armament somewhat lighter and more effective. Their tactical capabilities, however, were developed significantly during the early years of Nelson's career in the navy, notably by Lord Howe, and they were opposed by a French fleet which had also acquired new tactics, although the process was cut short by the French Revolution. The new methods reflected a new flexibility of mind, which enabled Nelson to achieve annihilating victories such as had never previously been seen.

The Seven Years War was followed by a period of naval development on both sides of the English Channel. The Duc de Choiseul believed that it should be possible for France to neutralise her land frontiers, and concen-

trate on preparation for a naval war to recover her wartime losses to England. For this purpose he set in train an ambitious fleet construction programme, which in the end proved to be beyond the financial capability of the regime. He also persuaded Charles III of Spain to rebuild the Spanish fleet. The British were aware of Choiseul's efforts, and those of the Spanish navy, and tried to match them while at the same time paying off as much of the debt accumulated by the Navy Board as possible. During the years before the American Revolution there were repeated trials of strength between England and the 'Family Compact', the alliance between the Bourbon kings of France and Spain. The most dramatic was the crisis which was triggered when a Spanish force expelled a British post on the Falkland Islands. This was recognised to be a critical moment in Choiseul's manoeuvres to regain Bourbon ascendancy, and the British

32. Hawke to Cleveland, 24 November 1759, *Hawke*, p347.

33. Nicholas Tracy, *Navies, Deterrence, and American Independence, passim.*

34. *Tactique Navale au Traité des Evolutions et des Signaux*, Paris, 1763.

Government of Lord North acted decisively by mobilising a fleet and threatening war. With some compromise on Britain's part, her superior naval position was successfully asserted, and the fleets were demobilised without blows. It was this crisis which brought Nelson into the navy as a midshipman.[33]

Morogues

All this naval activity stimulated interest in tactics. His experience at Quiberon Bay inspired the Vicomte de Morogues, captain of the 74-gun ship *Magnifique*, to publish a book which drew together ideas on tactics and signalling which he had been circulating for several years amongst his fellow officers.[34] In some respects it was derivative of Père Hoste's work seventy years before, and defeat evidently reinforced the tendency of French tactics to emphasise defensive considerations.

Morogues' book, however, was written by a seaman for the use of other seamen. He suggested methods of doubling an enemy line from windward or leeward which were more practical than anything Hoste had developed from mathematical models.

Morogues recognised that tactics were more than just evolutions. From his perspective as captain of a 74-gun ship of the line at Quiberon Bay who had tried to work his guns in a gale, he was persuaded of the tactical value of three-decker ships, especially for an inferior fleet. The larger ships mounted heavier guns, were stiffer in a hard blow and in a really bad blow when lower deck ports could not be opened, a three-decker would be capable of twice the firepower of a two-decker. The larger ships were also more difficult to board. A small, well-handled fleet of heavy ships he believed would be able to hold their own against a larger fleet of smaller ships.

These two plates from Le Vicomte de Morogue's *Tactique Navale ou Traité des Evolutions et des Signaux, Paris, 1763, show ships signalling with skyrockets, and points of sailing.* (National Maritime Museum, London: P4577-1,-2)

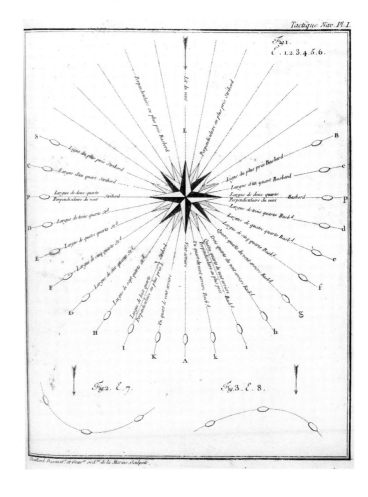

French signals

The most important contribution Morogues made to French tactics was his collection of signals, running to 200 pages and 300 signals. The value of his work lay in the structure of his book which included a 40-page index that simplified signal recognition, and thereby made tactical communications a more practical operation. Unfortunately, however, he made no major improvement in the method of signalling. This continued to depend on the use of a large number of wildly patterned flags flown from particular locations in the rigging, locations which in any given circumstance might not provide a good line of sight.

A much better system had already been devised by Mahé de Bourdonnais, an officer of the French East India Company. This was described by Bourdé de Villehuet in a book published in 1765.[35] It reduced signals to a digital equivalent. There were only ten pendants, and these could be hoisted together to indicate any number. If three sets of pendants were carried, 999 different signals could be sent. This was the ultimate answer to the problem of signalling at sea, although when the Royal Navy adopted it they devised a way of using only one set of number flags along with flags and pendants which were used to indicate repeats.

The French Navy, however, did not adopt Le Bourdonnais's system. Throughout the age of sail it continued to develop an inherently limited system devised by the Chevalier du Pavillon who published in 1776 a tabular system for encoding signals using two sets of ten flags flown where best seen. A flag signal was used to indicate when the admiral wished his fleet to go from one table to another. Each table had ten columns and ten rows, and a number flag was depicted at the top or end of each. By reading down and across the intersecting box could be located, and the number in it read off. Each number referred to an article in the signal book. Because du Pavillon began at the upper left hand corner with flag number one, however, instead of using a zero, the numbers in the box were always ten behind the apparent value given by the two flags,

except in the bottom row of the table where, for example, flags one and ten gave the value of ten. There were three tables using the same flags, and one of them replaced the use of numbers with letters. Du Pavillon's tabular signalling system was a very great improvement on the old system, and it was possible for officers to overcome the difficulty of using the table on deck by transcribing the signals into book form. However, it was more limited than was the true numerical system which with slight modification it could have been.

The content of du Pavillon's signals was certainly an improvement on older practice, although they were rather more complicated than necessary. For example, the system included the use of a two-flag hoist to command the fleet to change from any of the standard sailing or tactical formations to any other one. The need for such multiplication of signals is unclear. The fleet might be expected to be aware of the formation they were in at the beginning of the manoeuvre without reminder. However, du Pavillon was to be chief of staff to Admiral d'Orvilliers in 1778, and a version of his tabular signalling system was used to good effect during the battle of Ushant. Both sides experienced difficulties with communications, but they effected the tactical disposition of the British fleet under Admiral Keppel more significantly. Another version of the tabular system was also used for the combined Franco-Spanish fleet of 1779, and José de Mazarredo Salazar developed a tabular system for the use of the Spanish Navy.[36] Du Pavillon's tabular signalling system was firmly established in the French Navy until after the end of the War of the French Empire.[37]

Lord Howe's reforms

Meanwhile, in England the first text on naval tactics in the English language was published, in 1762, by Christopher O'Bryan.[38] About a quarter of the book was a poor translation of Père Hoste. The rest provides interesting insights into contemporary British tactical thinking. O'Bryan, for example, believed that admirals should be careful to respect the rela-

35. *Le Manoeuvrier, ou Essai sur la Théorie et la Pratique des Mouvements du Navire et des Evolutions Navales*, 1765.

36. REC/46; and *Rudimentos de Táctica Naval para Instruction de los Officiales Subalternos de Marina*, Madrid, 1776.

37. *Tactique Navale à l'usage de l'armées du Roi commandée par M. le Cte d'Orvilliers*, 1779.

38. *Naval Evolutions: or a System of Sea Discipline*, London, 1762.

39. *Naval Tactics; or a Treatise of Evolutions and Signals, with Cuts, Lately Published in France . . . Translated by a Sea-Officer*, Paris, 1767.

40. Tunstall/Tracy, p126.

41. Article 18, based on Hawke's article 9 of 1747.

42. HOL/21.

tive seniority of their commanders, keeping the most senior captains as seconds ahead or astern of the flag in the line, and as leaders of the squadrons. He believed that fleets should always be divided into three squadrons, even if a senior captain had to be designated as its commander, so that there would be a rear division to carry out a doubling action. He stressed the importance of reconnaissance, and recommended that action should be fought at point-blank range, that is 300 yards, so that the line could be kept better formed than would be the case if ships were allowed to conform more closely to the irregularities of the enemy line. In 1767 there appeared a poor English translation of Morogues's *Tactique Navale* which may also have been the work of Lucius O'Bryan, Christopher's brother.[39]

Although the O'Bryans' work was not itself of great importance, it was indicative of a growing interest in England in developing more scientific tactics for the navy. Of vastly greater importance was to be the work of Admiral Lord Howe. Howe was an inarticulate man, who may have become interested in signalling systems because he had such difficulty conveying his intentions in any way. During the Seven Years War he had issued additional instructions, and in the years of peace which followed he took up the problem of reform with great zeal. In 1770 he was appointed commander of the Mediterranean fleet which was intended for the Mediterranean in the event that the Falkland Islands crisis led to war, and that appears to have been the occasion for his publication of an undated book entitled *Signals & Instructions in Addition to the General Printed Sailing & Fighting Instructions by Day and Night.* As with Morogues's signal book, Howe's of 1770 was important chiefly for its organisation. Its indexing was a great development, and increased the ability of an admiral to deploy his fleet.

The Admiralty itself published in the 1770s *Signals & Instructions in Addition to the General Printed Sailing and Fighting Instructions.*[40] It was hardly progressive to provide officers with a multiplicity of badly organised books, but one of the additional in-

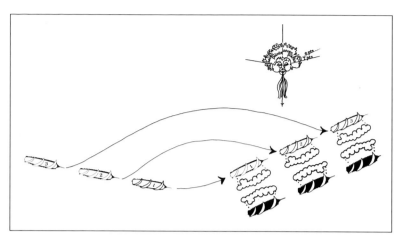

structions is important because it officially adopted Hawke's provision that in a chase the admiral could order his fleet to form an *ad hoc* line ahead on the rearmost ship of the enemy 'the headmost opposing their sternmost, the next passing on under cover of her fire, and engaging the second from the enemy's rear, and so on in succession as they may happen to get up, without respect to seniority or the prescribed order of battle'.[41]

The reform of British naval tactics did not get really under way until 1776 when Lord Howe arrived in New York to assume command of the North American Station. His fleet was engaged in operations against the American rebels, but he took the opportunity to organise it for battle, and provided it with a *Signal Book For Ships of War* which was such an important development on standard British practice that it eventually became the model for official publication.[42] The signals themselves were made in the traditional way with flags flown in particular places in the rigging, with the new feature that battle signals were to remain in force when hauled down, until they were annulled by signal. Howe issued a numerical code using ten flags and a substitute for repeated numbers, permitting ninety-nine signals, and a tabular code using two sets of ten flags was also provided, but it appears that these were only used for experimental purposes. In the case of the tabular code this was just as well.

The signal book itself was new and an important innovation. It organised signals into

The Admiralty's Additional Instruction of 1770 establishing the standard procedure for engaging a fleet which is endeavouring to avoid action.

useful groupings, and the references from it were not to the official fighting instructions, but to a companion book Howe published which expressed his tactical intentions in clearly worded standing orders.[43] A year later, in July 1777, Howe supplemented this book with *Additional Instructions Respecting the Conduct of the Fleet Preparative to and in Action with the Enemy*.[44] His tactical ideas were at once formal, and sophisticated, and called for a high degree of intelligent support from his captains.

Howe believed strongly in the importance of a well-ordered line of battle, and he renewed the ban on individual captains breaking the line to pursue individual ships of the enemy. His conservatism is revealed in his direction to his subordinate flag officers to engage their opposite numbers in the enemy line. But he also instructed the captains of ships which found that they could not keep up with the fleet to drop out of the line: 'The Captains of such ships will not be thereby left in a situation less at liberty to distinguish themselves; as they will have an opportunity to render essential service, by placing their ships to advantage when arrived up with the enemy, already engaged with the other part of the fleet'. The trust implicit in this instruction could not have been more revolutionary, and gives Howe a

strong claim to have sown the seeds which, under Jervis, and then Nelson, transformed the navy into 'the band of brothers' that won the battle of the Nile, and went on to win the battles of Copenhagen and Trafalgar.

Howe's appreciation of the need for flexibility, while retaining tactical purpose, continued to grow. The book of additional instructions opened with the statement that line tactics were necessary for defensive purposes, and to ensure that ships were provided with clear lines of fire, but that they also hampered captains from 'taking advantage of the favourable incidents which may occur in the progress of a general action'. Howe's purpose was to overcome the limitations of the line so that individual captains could seize opportunities 'by an authorised deviation from these restrictive appointments'. The requirements of defence continued to be given prominence. Captains were informed that it was Howe's general intention to engage the enemy line along its entire length, to prevent the enemy being able to double the British van or rear. If the enemy were a superior force, however, his captains were to take the initiative and pass by the weaker enemy ships so that the stronger could be engaged. Conversely, if the enemy were weaker the captains in the van or rear which found themselves unengaged were to leave the line on their own initiative and place their ships where they could most effectively support the fleet.[45]

Howe also developed a new tactic for engaging the enemy progressively from the rear. He instructed his van to open fire on the rearmost ship of the enemy, tack in succession, and then again so that the British van ships rejoined the line at the rear. This phase of the tactic resembled the long-outdated system used at the Armada battle, but was only intended to pick off the last ship in the enemy line, and possibly provoke an enemy reaction which could be useful. When it was judged right to extend the battle along the enemy line, Howe instructed his captains to deploy a line in inverted order. Superficially, this resembled the chasing order for the establishment of an *ad hoc* line, but when used in this way against

Howe's tactic for crippling the rear of a fleet attempting to avoid action. At the right moment, the last ship of the enemy rear would be closely engaged and the British line would deploy along the enemy, engaging it in inverted order as laid down in the Admiralty's 1770 Additional Instruction.

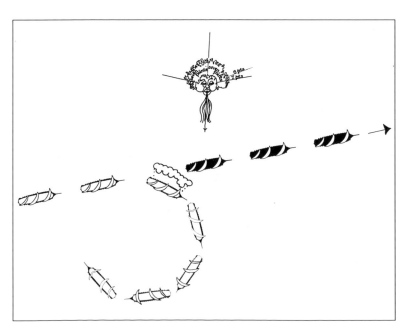

a well-ordered enemy the tactic retained the formal sequence in which the British line had been drawn up to ensure adequate mutual support. It was a sophisticated development calling for skill and judgment.

Howe made provision for the eventuality that irregularities in the enemy line might make it desirable to permit his captains greater latitude in their station-keeping. On the signal being made, individual captains were to continue to steer for those ships which in the sequence of the line ought to be their lot, making as little change of course as possible so that they would gradually work into position to engage without either exposing their own ship too greatly, or creating difficulties for the ships astern of them. They were free to engage from windward or leeward as they thought fit.

The trust Howe gave to his subordinates was important in developing the officer corps that Nelson commanded at the end of the century. He also provided the fleet with a system of night signals for frigates on reconnaissance which gave Nelson the means of maintaining a continuous observation of the enemy in Cadiz in the days before Trafalgar.[46] The frigates engaged in the service were to carry distinguishing lights so placed that they could be seen by the fleet off shore, but not by the enemy. They were to be especially careful to display their lights if the enemy were seen to be drawing towards or away from the fleet. This set of signals was reissued by Howe when he assumed command of the Channel Fleet in 1782, and became a permanent feature of all his future additional instructions.

Ushant

The French intervention in the American war, and the subsequent British declaration of war in 1778, led to the first test for Du Pavillon's system of tabular signals. The battle of Ushant was tactically a battle on the largest scale with both sides exhibiting their national characteristics. Admiral D'Estaing's fleet was marshalled into well-ordered lines and handled skillfully to ensure that no mistakes led to catastrophic losses. The first phase of the bat-

Admiral Augustus Keppel (1725-1786), watercolour by unknown artist. (National Maritime Museum, London: PAD 2931)

tle was a passing action on nearly opposite courses. It is indicative of the strengths as well as the weaknesses of the British fleet that Keppel ordered it to engage without forming line of battle because it would have taken too long to close up into formation. At his court martial it was easily accepted that it had been necessary to dispense with the standard form and, in fact, only Palliser's van division failed to interpret the order effectively. The French directed their fire into the rigging of the British, quite deliberately, though they were to windward where the heel of their ships would have tended to depress their guns' elevation. Disabled aloft, the British ships were unable to come again to close action. Both sides suffered from the limitations of their signalling systems, partly because flags were obscured by gun smoke. Keppel was reduced to sending a frigate to 'acquaint' Palliser that he was waiting upon him carrying out the order which had been hoisted to form line of battle. Palliser was accused by the opposition press of failing to provide effective support and demanded that Keppel be tried by court-martial. The court was heavily biased in Keppel's favour, and Palliser's career was ruined as a way of attacking the ministry.

43. *Instructions for the Conduct of the Ships of War, Explanatory of, and Relative to the Signals contained in the Signal-Book Herewith Delivered*, SIG/A/8 issued and signed 13 June 1776.

44. NM/88.

45. *Signals and Instructions*, pp108-9.

46. *Signals for the Frigates or other Ships of War appointed to observe the motions of a strange fleet discovered or enemy's fleet, during the night*, NM/34.

Rear Admiral Richard Kempenfelt (1718-1782), by Tilly Kettle (1735-1786). (National Maritime Museum, London: BHC 2818)

Kempenfelt

Admiral Richard Kempenfelt introduced Howe's signalling reforms into the Channel Fleet where he was Captain of the Fleet to three successive Commanders-in-Chief between 1779 and 1782, in which year he was drowned when the *Royal George* capsized and sank. He was an extraordinarily gifted staff officer, but a man in a hurry who experimented with tactics and signalling systems which the officers of the fleet had difficulty assimilating. It is unclear to what extent he was the follower of Howe, or the originator of some of the new publications and signaling projects which were issued to the fleet, or circulated for discussion.

Kempenfelt experimented with new orders of sailing which divided into more than the traditional three squadrons the large fleet concentrated to contain the Franco-Spanish fleet when it cruised in the Channel in 1779. He also introduced an order of retreat for a damaged or outnumbered fleet which resembled

Pére Hoste's Third Order, but with the apex of the formation to windward.[47] These ideas had no immediate practical application, but apparently when Admiral Lord Howe sailed in 1782 to escort a convoy to Gibraltar he was persuaded to adopt an order of sailing in six columns, dividing each squadron in half. Although deployment from this order of sailing into a line of battle could not be as rapid as when a fleet sailed in a starboard or larboard line of bearing, sailing a large fleet in six columns enabled its admiral to retain a closer control over his ships, and made it easier for individual captains to keep their stations. In the judgment of Admiral Sir Charles Knowles, writing in 1830, 'From the sailing in columns and the introduction and use of the signals by numbers may be dated the era of the improvement in the navy'.[48] Kempenfelt's order of retreat could have been deployed into line of battle by the leading ship paying off to leeward, but in doing so any hope of stealing the weather gage would have been lost.

Kempenfelt was aware of the numerical signal system, and issued it to the fleet, but his opinion of its value was not entirely clear. He was concerned that it would be difficult to distinguish the flags in a three-flag hoist flown where best seen. Under the old system it was possible to get an idea of the likely intent of the signal from the location in which it was flown, even when the distance was too great to be able to distinguish the colour. Nonetheless, he did issue in 1780 a numerical code for regular use in the Channel Fleet, as an alternative system.[49] On the other hand, he also introduced a version of the tabular system to the fleet. It evidently found greater acceptance amongst his fellow flag officers.[50]

In the matter of gunnery, Kempenfelt concluded from the experience of the battle of Ushant that the French practice of directing fire at the rigging could be tactically important, even for a superior fleet seeking to destroy the enemy. Admiral Keppel's disappointment at not being able to force a closer action upon the French at the battle of Ushant could have been avoided if the British too had sought to immobilise their enemy.

47. Tunstall/Tracy, p148.

48. *Observations on Naval Tactics*, p25.

49. NM/34 and Ec/50.

50. NM/53. See Kempenfelt to Middleton, 9 March 1781. *Barham* I pp430-41.

51. Rodney 15 and 19; NM/83. *Signals and Instructions* pp180-234.

Actions of the American Theatre of War

At the same time that Howe and Kempenfelt were groping their way towards a new system of signals and tactics for the Royal Navy, other British admirals were continuing to issue additional instructions. In 1780 Admiral Rodney issued Signals and Instructions in Addition which included a signal ordering 'all the three-decked and heavy ships [to] draw out of their places in the line of battle and form in the van [or rear] of the fleet'.[51] Rodney never employed this signal, perhaps because he never had under his command more than two ships of 90 guns or more which were not required as flagships. It may, however, have been the germ of the idea that led Nelson at the battle of Trafalgar to place his flag-officers, in their three-deckers, at the head of the columns where their heavier timbering could absorb the punishment that the leading ships must inevitably suffer.

Rodney also issued a new order of sailing which disposed his three squadrons into three arrowhead formations, each led by its flag-officer and deployed with the van and rear squadrons on the weather and lee quarters of the centre. The order of the ships in each squadron was the same as in the line of battle. It would have required considerable practice and seamanship to deploy from this cruising formation into a close-hauled line to windward. Perhaps his purpose in designing this formation, in fact, was to bring about a melée battle without forming a line at all. If so, this was a true anticipation of Nelson's tactics at Trafalgar.

Admiral Lord Rodney (1719-1792), by Sir Joshua Reynolds, painter, and Edward Scriven, engraver. Published by Charles Knight. (National Maritime Museum, London: PAD 3005)

The Moon Light Battle: the battle of Cape St Vincent, 16 January 1780, by Dominic Serres (1722-93). (National Maritime Museum, London: BHC 0430)

The Moon Light Battle

In January 1780 Admiral Rodney scored a notable success when he engaged a Spanish force of eleven ships on a lee shore in a gale. In the so-called 'Moon Light Battle', he used general chase to bring the enemy to action. By midnight seven Spanish ships had been captured, sunk or wrecked. His flag captain, Walter Young, who claimed to have directed the battle because Rodney was confined to his bed with gout, concluded that it would have been better to have used order of battle in line abreast rather than general chase as chasing strung out the fleet too much.

Grenada

Six months earlier, at the Battle of Grenada, a British fleet under Vice Admiral the Honourable John Byron had met a superior French force under the Comte d'Estaing, and demonstrated by example how important it was to get the right balance of tactical formality and initiative, and how important it was to have signals which could effectively convey the admiral's intention. The British were lucky to survive the heavy damage inflicted upon them. The circumstances of the battle were the French occupation of Grenada and Byron's escort of a troop convoy intended for its recapture. When he caught up with the French fleet it was just coming out of St George Roads, with orders to form an *ad hoc* line as they got clear of their moorings and came up.

Byron made his first mistake when he ordered general chase against what turned out to be a more numerous enemy; one rapidly scrambling into good order. He then signaled his seven leading ships to form an *ad hoc* line to attack the enemy rear, but the two fleets were converging at an acute angle, and this order obliged his ships to sail the length of the French fleet before coming to close action. His third mistake was to try and save the situation by ordering formation of the line of battle and close action. This obliged his ships to reorganise themselves into the formal line. The result of these tactical mistakes was that several

British ships were badly exposed to enemy fire and only avoided capture because of d'Estaing's preoccupation with the danger to his soldiers ashore. The latter was much criticised by Suffren, who was then captain of the van ship in the French fleet and was later to become one of France's most successful admirals, for not pressing home his advantage and destroying the British fleet. Perhaps d'Estaing's early career as a land-force commander made it psychologically impossible to take any chances with the men ashore.

A more positive view of Byron's tactics would call attention to the thought that if he had been able to surprise the French at their anchorage, his gamble of ordering general chase would have paid off. Equally creditable is the evident fact that his captains were fired with a fighting spirit, and determination to provide mutual support even at great cost. Their aggressive handling of their ships went a long way towards justifying Byron's pugnacious tactics. The letter of approval to Byron from the Admiralty Secretary remarked on his 'animated conduct', and the

> spirited example and gallant behaviour of Vice Admiral Barrington, and the Commanders of the ships who were principally engaged. The endeavour and strong desire of coming to a close engagement, which prevailed universally through the Squadron, and the bravery of the Officers and Men in general does great honour to them individually, as well as generally.[52]

His aggressive fleet tactics, and the rapport he had with his subordinates, give Byron something of the Nelsonic flair, without Nelson's good fortune. This action might have been as decisive as was to be the battle of the Nile.

The limitations of the existing fighting instructions is evident. Byron did not have a signal ordering his leading ships to form an *ad hoc* line attacking the enemy van, which was what would have been most useful. But he could have used signals directing his leading ships to chase to the southwest, or Howe's signal of 1762 which directed the chasing ships to

52. *Barrington,* II p319.

53. Tunstall/Tracy, pp162-4.

54. Young to Middleton, 28 June and 31 July 1780, *Barham,* I p72, II pp67-70.

55. *Barham,* I p1.

56. Tunstall/Tracy, op. cit. pp165-167.

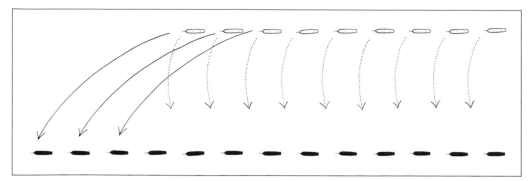

The battle of Martinique. Admiral Rodney's intention to concentrate on the enemy rear was frustrated by the vice admiral and the captains of the leading ships who conformed with the service tradition that their task was to contain the enemy van.

form line as they came up, which would have implied that the standing order to engage the enemy van should be complied with.[53] Clearly, however, he would have benefited by the possession of better two-way communications with his captains. Captain Young recommended that every ship be provided with a full set of signal colours so that they could repeat signals from the admiral, as was the French practice.[54]

Martinique

In April 1780 Rodney met the French fleet himself, now under Admiral de Guichen, off Martinique. In the battle that followed, Rodney's more skillful tactical direction was also frustrated by the limitations in the system of fighting instructions and signals. All might have been well had Rodney had the sort of relationship with his captains which Byron enjoyed, and which was to distinguish Nelson. However, Rodney was a martinet constitutionally incapable of confiding in his subordinates, whose failure to understand his intentions he attributed to disaffection.

Rodney had issued additional instructions which provided a signal indicating his intention to attack the enemy at the rear, centre or van, and he used it on this occasion. However, his signal which he made at the beginning of the action, that he intended to attack the rear, gave no executive direction as to how the attack was to be made. He apparently told his physician, Gilbert Blane, that he had verbally or in writing previously informed all his captains of his intentions. If so, they seem not to have understood him.[55] Consequently, when

he had successfully brought the fleet into position to carry out an attack on the rear, and then signaled for the fleet to bear down and engage, the vice admiral and several of the captains of the van understood from the wording of the instruction that they were supposed to stretch ahead to contain the enemy van. This was consistent with the traditions of the service, but it defeated Rodney's efforts to bring a decisive force against a part of the enemy line. The limitations of the system were also evident a month later when Rodney found himself in position to cut the French line from the leeward, but had he wished to make that tactical move he had no signal to order it.[56]

The Chesapeake

If Byron's failure was due to a reckless disregard to the need for tactical order, and Rodney's to his failure to take his officers into his confidence so that they really understood his intentions, the decisive defeat at the battle of the Chesapeake, which led to the defeat of the army at Yorktown, was a result of a failure of Rear Admiral Thomas Graves's cautious tactical plan because of the inherent confusion of the Fighting Instructions, signalling failure, and the unfamiliarity of the captains with their new admiral's intentions. His second-in-command, Rear Admiral Hood, later asserted that Graves missed an opportunity to defeat the French as they deployed out of their anchorage in an *ad hoc* line. He argued that an order to chase could have brought the whole weight of the British fleet onto the French van. Byron had failed to succeed in just that operation at Grenada, however, and maybe only a com-

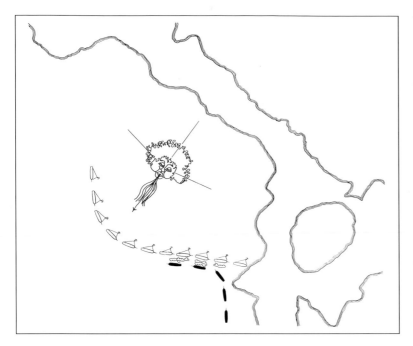

The battle of St Kitts. Rear Admiral Hood successfully anchored his fleet under fire along the line of a bank in good order. By swinging individual ships with the spring hawsers on their single anchors they could bring their guns to bear on the French under Admiral de Grasse during the subsequent action.

With consummate seamanship Hood was able to bring his ships while under fairly heavy fire to anchor in succession, inverting their line of battle in the process, along the edge of a shoal. Their formation at anchor was good enough that they were able to hold off a subsequent French attack. Once anchored, of course, Hood had no way of preventing the French concentrating on a part of his line. Everything then depended upon the ships being in close enough order, with springs on their warps, so that two or more ships could be swung around to engage individual attackers. Unlike Nelson at Aboukir Bay, de Grasse did not succeed in turning the British line to bring it between two fires.

The Saintes

In April 1782 Rodney and de Grasse fought the last great battle of the American Revolutionary War, near the islets known as the Saintes, north of Dominica. This was a remarkable encounter, yielding Rodney a tactical victory, but its strategic importance was limited because the outcome at Yorktown could not be reversed.

The battle was technically interesting because the British fleet, for the first time since the Dutch Wars in a major fleet action, cut the enemy line. The tactical movement which effected this, Rodney taking the centre through a gap in the French line, was probably unpremeditated, and led to captains ahead and astern of the flag taking similar action. Admiral John Jervis, Earl St Vincent, who more than anyone else was to be Nelson's mentor, and who trusted him with the detachment from the Mediterranean fleet which fought the battle of the Nile, was convinced that 'Lord Rodney passed through the enemy's line by accident.'[59] The danger of cutting the enemy line is that the ships passing through are vulnerable to raking fire from the enemy's previously unengaged side, and the tactical cohesion of the fleet making the cut is as disrupted as is that of the fleet which is cut. However, Rodney was presented with the opportunity to undertake the action because the

mander of Nelson's calibre could have appreciated in time the difficulties the French were experiencing in tacking out of the bay.[57] Instead, Graves deployed onto a line of bearing parallel to the French line, and then tried to bring it down obliquely and still in the same line of bearing onto the French. His captains, however, understood his signal for 'the leading ship to lead more to starboard' as calling for a turn in succession which put them in line ahead. This exposed the leading ships to heavy concentration of fire. Graves hauled down the signal for the line, and tried to bring about the deployment he wanted by steering directly for the French, but he was not supported by Hood commanding the rear who thought the order for the line was still in force. Graves's tactical purpose having been frustrated, the outcome was a tactical draw but a strategic defeat of the highest order.[58]

St Kitts

That the British fleet was capable of precise manoeuvre in difficult circumstances was demonstrated by Rear Admiral Hood in January 1782 when he was sent to St Kitts to relieve, if possible, the garrison besieged by a French force supported by Admiral de Grasse.

57. John Creswell, *British Admirals of the Eighteenth Century*, London, 1972, p162.

58. *Sandwich* IV p181-185; *Hood* p31; Tunstall/Tracy, pp172-174.

59. J S Tucker, (Jervis's secretary), *Memoirs of Admiral the Rt. Hon. the Earl of St. Vincent*, London, 1844, II pp281-3.

60. Tunstall/Tracy, pp179-182.

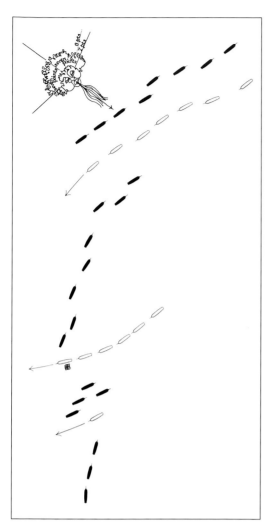

The battle of the Saintes. There is some dispute about Admiral Rodney's intentions, or whether in fact he was well enough to be said to have been in control at all, but the action of British ships in cutting through Admiral de Grasse's line of battle brought decisive force against the French centre and rear. The British victory, which came too late to prevent the defeat of Cornwallis' army at Yorktown and the independence of the United States, was to profoundly effect British naval tactics during the war against the French Revolution and Empire.

enemy fleet had become disorganised in the gun smoke, and he could take advantage of the accident without undue risk because he was conscious of the moral ascendence the British fleet had already gained. As they passed through the French, their gunners were ready to fire into the vulnerable bows and sterns of the ships on either side of the break, and then they were able to hold some of the French between two fires. Their success was a valuable lesson for the future.

The battle had been fought with the fleets passing on opposite tacks. This came about because when de Grasse tried to wear fleet to come onto the same tack, his captains refused to begin a manoeuvre which would expose their bows to raking fire at close range. The cutting movements took place in the context of this very close action, and it was significant that the British fleet was only able to carry it out as it did because it was fighting from the leeward position. British thinking about tactics was never the same again.[60]

The battle of the Saintes, 12 April 1782, by Thomas Luny (1759-1837). (National Maritime Museum, London: BHC 0438)

Clerk of Eldin

The idea that it could be easier to force a general action from the leeward position, and that the best way to do so was by cutting through the enemy line, was published by John Clerk of Eldin in 1782. The first important original study of naval tactics in the English language, the first part of his *An Essay on Naval Tactics* was printed as a limited edition, and when eventually reprinted it contained Rodney's approving marginal notes. Although some of his supporters claimed otherwise, there is no reason to believe that Clerk had been influential in Rodney's snap decision to cut the French line at the Saintes. Rodney, however, evidently thought that Clerk had got it right when he emphasised the importance of concentrating force against a part of the enemy line: 'during all the commands Lord Rodney has been intrusted with,' he noted in the margin, 'he made it a rule to bring his whole force against part of the enemy's and never was so absurd as to bring ship against ship, when the enemy gave him an opportunity of acting otherwise'. The proviso, of course, is important.[61] Furthermore, it is notable that the French ships isolat-

ed by Rodney's cutting movement, although badly battered, all escaped. The captures were made later by Rear Admiral Hood when he came upon ships including De Grasse's flagship *Ville de Paris*, which had been severely damaged in the battle, but had not been affected by the cutting action.[62]

Clerk noted with approval the tendency of French commanders to prefer a leeward position. Hoste had pointed out that attack from the windward was by no means easy, and Clerk of Eldin demonstrated why, using a geometrical model which he labeled the Curve of Pursuit. Ships bearing down from the windward and steering directly towards their designated opponent made good a course which inevitably became a curve as the enemy line moved forward. The speed advantage which the windward fleet might enjoy from sailing large would be dissipated by the longer distance they had to sail, making it necessary in the end for each ship to run the gauntlet of the enemy ships astern of their intended. The 'lasking' approach that Admiral Byng had tried to use at Minorca reduced the problem because the course sailed would be a chord of the curve, and therefore shorter. It was always possible for the leeward fleet meeting the assault, however, to back its topsails, and stop making way. The attackers would then have to come straight down on the wind, exposing their bows to fire they could not return. If they chose instead to continue their oblique approach their van would become extended beyond the enemy van, and their rear would be in danger of being doubled from leeward.

The difficulty of forcing a general action from leeward, however, were greater than Clerk acknowledged. As soon as the leeward fleet bore up to close the enemy line it was bound to lose speed. Its exposure to raking fire would be protracted, and it was quite possible that by the time it reached the position once occupied by the enemy fleet, it would find itself passing ineffectually across its rear. In a crossing movement such as had happened at

Clerk of Eldin demonstrated geometrically that a fleet making a down-wind run to engage an enemy inevitably will end up pursuing it, unless the enemy waits with topsails aback. The speed advantage enjoyed when coming from windward is not enough to overcome the greater distance which has to be sailed.

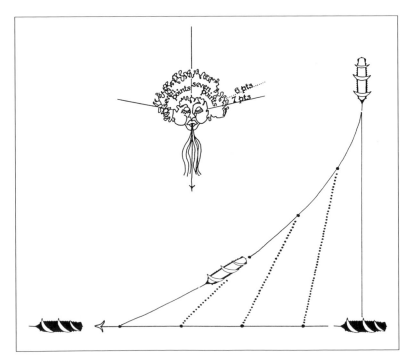

the Saintes close action could be less problematic, but in fact it had only occurred as a result of de Grasse's clumsy handling of his fleet. In any case, crossing actions rarely produced decisive results.

Clerk of Eldin continued to develop his work. Part was published in 1790 and it was finally published in finished form in 1797 four years after the beginning of the war against the French Republic. He was not interested in evolutions as such, and concentrated entirely on the problem of defeating the defensive strength of the enemy line of battle. Important as were his ideas, however, the impact of the work on British naval tactics came primarily from the clarity of his thought. An outsider with no financial stake in the acceptability of his ideas, Clerk served to stimulate discussion of innovative tactics during Nelson's years in higher command. Nelson is known to have been 'very fond' of hearing his chaplain, Mr Scott, read from it.[63]

Revolutionary Tactics

Howe's tactical instructions for the Nootka Sound crisis of 1790 were little changed from those he had issued to the American station early in the American War, and for the moment he continued to be issued as two separate books of *Fighting*, and *Additional* instructions.

He addressed the problem of bringing the French to close action, and holding them, by issuing a new signal, number 34, which was to be used 'If when having the Weather Gage of the Enemy the Admiral means to pass between the ships in their line for engaging them to leeward'. This manoeuvre would combine the advantages of the windward position for forcing action on the enemy, and the leeward for preventing them escaping once engaged. It is unclear whether Howe's intent was to make the approach in line of bearing, and so break the enemy line in more than one place. That was what he attempted to do at the battle of The Glorious First of June, but he tried then to convey his meaning by employing another signal, number 36, indicating that every ship was to steer for her opposite number and engage her. The result confused his fleet, and when the Admiralty reissued the signal in 1799 as its new number 27 it specifically directed captains to 'Break through the enemy's line in all parts where it is practicable, and engage on the other side'. Unfortunately, the Admiralty then contributed its own confusion by using the same signal, with the addition of a blue pendant, to order the fleet in close order line ahead to cut through the enemy in one place only, and presumably from the leeward.[64]

A new system of signals was adopted to implement the new tactics. In 1790 Howe, when in command of the Channel Fleet during the Nootka Sound crisis, issued a truly numerical signaling system.[65] It employed a hoist of two flags to signify digits and tens, with a pendant for the hundreds. Ten numerical flags were required, and substitute pendants for repeating numbers, as well as for the hundreds. The use of pendants overcame the problem of distinguishing a hoist of three flags. In this way most three-digit numbers could be signalled, using flags and pendants flown from whatever position in the rigging they could best be seen. Each paragraph in the sailing and fighting instructions was numbered. Even he could not break with tradition to the extent of issuing a full set of flags to every ship, and proposals for a partial return to the old signalling system continued to be put forward.

The great advantages of converting signals into numbers were the speed with which they could be read, and the ease with which new signals could be incorporated. It was also easier to change signals if there was a risk that the enemy had obtained a copy of the signal book. The adoption of a signalling system which enabled the flags and pendants to be flown

61. John Clerk of Eldin, *An Essay on Naval Tactics*, 3rd edition (1827), p18.

62. John Creswell, pp172-175.

63. C Ekins, *Naval Battles of Great Britain*, London, 1828, 2nd edition, p311.

64. John Creswell, pp187-188.

65. MKH/A/n/4. Tunstall/Tracy, p194.

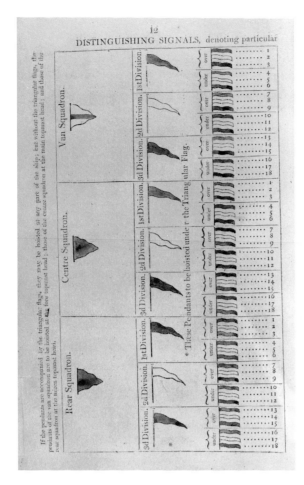

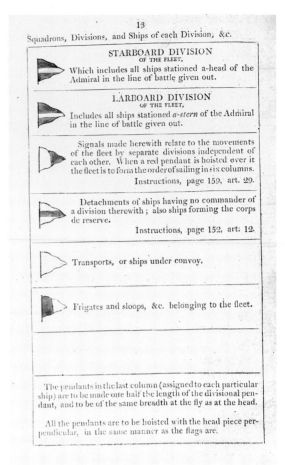

from the best position for them to be seen had obvious tactical advantages. The problem that the new numerical system depended on three-flag hoists which were relatively difficult to distinguish at a distance, and that no hint of their meaning could be ascertained from the location they were flown in as had been possible under the old system, had to be overcome by a supplementary system of 'distance signals'. These used a limited number of flags and shapes which were flown from the fore, main, and mizzen mastheads. They were slower to use, but could be read at ranges which made it difficult to distinguish colours. It was by this method that Nelson received the signal that the enemy were leaving Cadiz on the eve of Trafalgar.

In contrast, when the Royal Navy went to war in 1793 after the execution of Louis XIV and the French declaration of war against Britain, Spain, Austria and the Netherlands, it

was very different from that which had existed when Nelson was born, or even that which he had joined in 1770. The reforms in battle tactics initiated by Lord Howe, and developed by Kempenfelt, and the new atmosphere which encouraged the development of new methods, made a profound difference.

In 1793 Hood issued signals and instructions with the latter consolidated into a single volume, for the first time, and also issued *Night Signals & Instructions* which consolidated signals and instructions into a single volume.[66] The result of this work was that the Royal Navy began its struggle against the forces of Revolutionary France with a greatly improved system of tactical control. In 1799 the Admiralty, for the first time, was to issue its own consolidated signal and instruction book, using Howe's numerical system.

Victory in the American war had a less creative effect on French tactics, perhaps

Pages from the Admiralty Signal Book for the Ships of War of 1799. Someone has pencilled in different values for the flags, possibly at an order from a local commander wishing to enhance security. In the Explanatory Instructions at the beginning of the book the general system of signals is explained:

II The signals generally used to distinguish ships from each other will be single pendants shewn at different mast heads, or yard arms, as shall be appointed by the Admiral; but the distinguishing signals in the tables, pages 12 and 18 will be used to ships which, joining the fleet when no communication can be had with them, can have no particular pendant assigned them; or to ships which happen to be so placed as to render it impossible for them to see the part of the ship at which their single distinguishing pendant is hoisted. . . .

III The signals will generally be made without guns, except in cases where two or more guns are necessary to constitute a part of the signal.

IV All ships to which signals are addressed, are to hoist the answering pendant as soon as they see and understand them, which is to be kept flying until the Admiral's signal is taken in.

[In sections V to VII it was established that ships which could not read a signal were to signal to that effect, and stand towards the admiral. Other ships were to repeat the signal.]

VIII When the Admiral makes any movement, either with or without a signal for the purpose, the ships of the fleet are to regulate themselves thereby, in order to keep their appointed stations, unless the Admiral makes the signal that his motions are to be no longer an example to the fleet.

IX All signals are to continue in force until they are annulled, or countermanded by some subsequent signal, or completely obeyed. (© Crown Copyright/MOD)

inevitably. In 1787, however, a French flag officer, the Vicomte de Grenier, published a new tactical study *L'Art de la Guerre sur Mer* in which he attempted to refute the idea that ships armed with broadside batteries had to be deployed in a single line of battle. His observations during two wars, he believed, indicated that the English had already begun to abandon the idea. In every action, he wrote, they had tried to concentrate their force against a part of the enemy line, and they had not gone into action in careful order. He criticised the concept of the single line of battle as being inflexible, too long to control effectively, and easily thrown into confusion.

Certainly, the Royal Navy was moving away from the line concept, but they were far from abandoning it. Most of the effort in devising improved signals was intended to make the old tactical ideas more effective. The same can be said about the tactical latitude Howe had

given the junior captains. Nevertheless, the new confidence in the value of initiative and mutual support he exhibited was fundamentally important and almost revolutionary.

The French Marine did not take Grenier's ideas to heart, but in 1787 it did consolidate current practice into a single book, *Tactique et Signaux, de Jour, de Noit et de Brume, à l'Ancre et à la Voile.*[67] It was a major compendium of observations and analyses which provided officers with a tactical education as well as a set of signals and instructions. It was unquestionably too long-winded for easy use, but it was a major improvement on Morogues's book. The signal section was so comprehensive that it almost amounted to a barrier to decisive action, or at least an encouragement to the use of manoeuvre to avoid it.[68] In 1799 the book was reprinted in two volumes, to assist the deck officer by separating the treatises from the signals.[69]

66. SIG/B/36 and 64; KEI/S/10(c); TUN/109.

67. SIG/C/4 and 5.

68. Tunstall/Tracy, pp201-02.

69. SIG/C/6.

When the Revolution swept away the traditional officer corps, the Marine retained its pre-revolutionary tactical system. The junior officers and lower-deck seamen who were rapidly promoted to assume command under the Republic never managed to emulate the skill in manoeuvre of the old corps. Strategically, the French Republic had less incentive to avoid decisive combat because of the loss of most of the overseas empire during the Seven Years War, but the French Marine was all but paralysed by the break-down of central authority, and demoralised by failures of materiel, leadership and training. The strongly motivated revolutionary French army was able to develop new columnar tactics which accepted high casualty rates in thrusting through enemy lines of infantry, but the revolutionary Marine was not able to develop comparable tactics because navies needed such a high level of technical proficiency to carry out even the simplest manoeuvres. The fleet of the Revolution, and later of the Empire, went about its business in the old way but with somewhat less skill. Nelson became aware of this reality during his service life, and one of the great secrets of his success was his ability to exploit effectively this appreciation. In doing so, it was he who developed the revolutionary tactics which substituted shock for finesse.

After the end of the Nootka Sound mobilisation, and Howe's retirement, Admiral Hood continued to develop the sailing instructions. In particular, he experimented with sailing in three columns, and with the means of deploying them into a single line ahead.[70]

Three sketches by P J de Loutherbourg (1740-1812) of captured French ships after the battle of the Glorious First of June.
- Upper right are Le Juste *of 80 guns, and* L'América *of 70 guns, showing the jury masts fitted to bring them into harbour.*
– Middle is the stern of Le Sans-Pareil *of 80 guns.*
– Lower right: The sterns of the three ships in the view lower right, all floating high out of the water without the weight of their masts and yards, show the damage they received from cannon shot.
(British Museum: BM 1857.6.13.588, 600, 591)

The Glorious First of June

The British attack on 29 May. Rear Admiral de Villaret de Joyeuse fought a hard two-day action to protect a vital grain convoy. The British under Admiral Lord Howe broke through the French line of battle in line ahead on the 29th, and in line abreast on the 'Glorious First of June'.

The Glorious First of June 1794: Lord Howe on the deck of the Queen Charlotte, *by Mather Brown (1761-1831). (National Maritime Museum, London: BHC 2740)*

70. Tunstall/Tracy, p199; and *Signals and Instructions,* p68n.

Philip de Loutherbourg, self-portrait, engraved by Page and published 1 August 1814 by G Jones. Loutherbourgh had established his reputation in Paris, where he was elected to the Académie Royale in 1767. In 1771 he moved with his family to London where he worked on theatre set design for Garrick, exhibited at the Royal Academy, and became an academician in 1781. He invented a system of stage lighting, and was a faith healer under the influence of Mesmer, but is best known for his work as a war artist. (National Maritime Museum, London: PAD 3189)

FIRST OF JUNE

by P J de Loutherbourg. Having made careful sketches, Philip James Loutherbourgh proceeded to complete a full scale canvas of the battle of the Glorious First of June. It is a masterpiece, but he could not please all the sailors who wanted the picture to represent the tactical action accurately. In his *Naval History* first published in 1822, William James wrote that

> Soon after the battle of the 1st of June the justly celebrated marine painter, P J de Loutherbourg, was employed by some enterprising individual to represent the *Queen Charlotte* engaging the *Montagne*. . . . the grand mistake in it was, that the *Queen Charlotte* was placed where Lord Howe wanted to get, but never could get, a little before the lee beam of his antagonist. Amongst others, the officer, whose duty it was (and who would have succeeded, but for the hasty flight of the *Montagne* and the loss of the *Charlotte*'s fore topmast) to place the British ship in the desired position, went to see the picture. At the first glance the gallant seaman pronounced the picture a libel upon the *Queen Charlotte*; inasmuch as, had she been in the position represented, it would have been her fault for letting the *Montagne* escape. [William James, *Naval History* IV pp149-150].

(National Maritime Museum, London: BHC 0470)

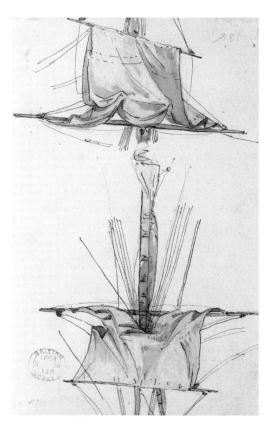

Queen Charlotte's Cathead

Four sketches by P J de Loutherbourg for his painting of the battle of the Glorious First of June.
Above and to the left: Sails brailed up,
Below: Howe's flagship, the Queen Charlotte
(British Museum)

At the opening battle of the war, Rear Admiral de Villaret de Joyeuse and his subordinate flag officers, all of whom were recent promotions from captain, lieutenant, or even from the lower deck, did a very creditable job of fighting an important grain convoy through to Brest against the worst that Admiral Lord Howe with an exceptional British fleet were able to do. Only by the strenuous efforts of a member of the Committee of Public Safety, Jeanbon Saint-Andre backed by the guillotine, had the Brest fleet been got to sea, and Villaret de Joyeuse had been threatened with death if the convoy were taken. The important features of the engagement on 29 May 1794, and on The Glorious First of June, were that Howe accepted battle from a leeward position, and that he ordered his fleet to cut through the enemy line, first in line ahead, and then in line of bearing. The former, however, only succeeded in bringing the English fleet into the windward position, and it was from the windward that on the 1st of June he succeeded in breaking up the French fleet's tactical organisation by cutting its line in five places and engaging it from the leeward.

Admiral the Earl of St Vincent succinctly described the action in a letter written in 1806

in which he diminished the influence of Clerk of Eldin's writing.

On the 29th May a manoeuvre, by which

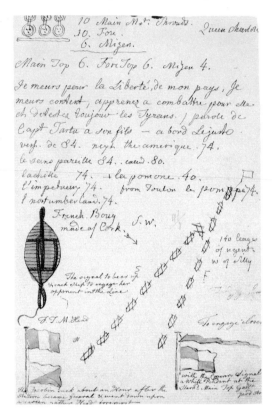

Two further sketches by P J de Loutherbourg for his painting of the battle of the Glorious First of June.
Above: Sketches of signals
Right: A plan of the battle.
(British Museum)

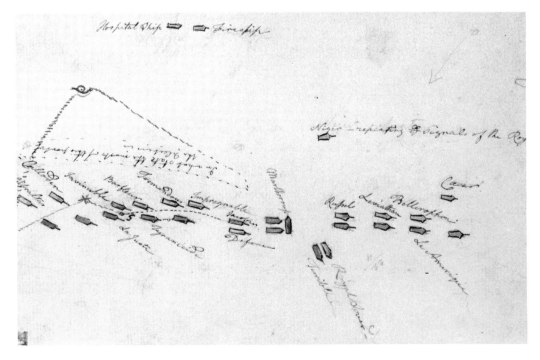

Lord Howe proposed to cut off the rear of the enemy, by passing through his line, failed in its effect, owing to the mistake or disobedience of signals; the only advantage gained was the weather gage, which he preserved to the first of June, when he ran down in a line abreast, nearly at right angles with the enemy's line, until he brought every ship of his fleet on a diagonal point of bearing to its opponent, then steering on an angle to preserve that bearing until he arrived on the weather quarter, and close to the centre ship of the enemy, when the *Queen Charlotte* altered her course, and steered at right angles through the enemy's line, raking their ships on both sides as she crossed, and then luffing up and engaging to Leeward.[71]

The fruits of victory were the sinking of one French ship of the line, and the capture of six more. Howe's tactical manoeuvres were successful because they made the best use of British superiority in gunnery, putting captains in a position where they could overwhelm individual French ships by their superior rate of fire.

Following the battle of The Glorious First of June Admiral Jervis issued a secret instruction to the Mediterranean fleet that, in the event that he was forced into action from a leeward position with the enemy on the opposite tack, he wished his ships to reduce sail so as to close up into a strong, cohesive force, which he intended should break through the enemy line.[72] Once through, they would be ordered to tack, and engage those ships which had been cut off in the van. Despite his assertion that he was 'sickened' by the study of tactics, it is evident that he gave considerable thought to his fleet's deployment. His flag captain, Sir Robert Calder, developed a number of hypothetical tactical plans which have survived.[73] When in 1799 the Admiralty republished his book virtually unchanged, Howe's tactical signals, and the numerical signaling system, was finally given official status.

Telegraphic Signals

The next year was also published the first version of Admiral Sir Home Popham's telegraphic signals which he developed during the 1800 deployment to Copenhagen, a year before the battle in which Nelson destroyed the Danish fleet. Alphabetical and numerical flags were used in three-digit numerical hoists to signal individual letters, and 972 words which Popham had drawn up in a dictionary. He soon added further lists of 972 words, and eventually adopted signals which mixed letters and numbers to increase the size of his vocabulary. Each 'word' included all the possible variants, such as visit, visited, visitation and visiting. Admirals for the first time were provided with the means of conveying ideas which had not been previously incorporated in an instruction, and at the same time they were provided with the means of getting detailed intelligence signalled from the ships in their fleet, or even from shore.

The version of *Telegraphic Signals or Marine Vocabulary* published in 1803 was the one used by Nelson at the battle of Trafalgar to keep in touch with his scouts, and to make his famous signal: England Expects that Every Man will do His Duty.[74]

At the same time as the numerical system of tactical signalling was perfected, the problem of strategic communication was taken in hand, first in France. Until the development of wireless telegraphy in the later nineteenth century, admirals were required to take great responsibility for deployment of their fleets, based on letters from the Admiralty which could take weeks or even months to reach them. In 1792 that responsibility was lessened somewhat when lines of shutter telegraph stations were constructed connecting French dockyards with Paris. In clear weather, it became possible

71. J S Tucker, pp281-3.

72. DUC/1/18, 31 January 1796. Tunstall/Tracy, pp213-16.

73. *Naval Miscellany* II, pp301-07; Tunstall/Tracy, pp214-15.

74. SIG/B/82, and NM/75.

to pass messages to fleet commanders while they were in port or close off-shore in a matter of hours. The British soon copied the French system, constructing in 1796 two chains which joined Dover with London, and London with Portsmouth and Plymouth.

Howe's innovative tactical ideas were important in providing Nelson with the tools he needed to achieve his annihilating victories. In that sense he was clearly the beneficiary of a service which had learned to reform itself. Howe, Kempenfelt, Byron, Hood, and even Rodney, and the civilian Clerk of Eldin, had all played their parts. The developments in the techniques of signalling were of great importance, but even more fundamental was the changed attitude of mind which was made evident by the recognition that effective two-way communication was necessary if battle tactics were to be appropriate and promptly carried out. All this said, however, it remains a fact that Nelson was a unique figure with a genius for leadership. It was his hand, his left as it were, which grasped the tools developed by others, and optimised them for his own use.

Page from Admiral Home Popham's Telegraphic Signals. This dictionary enabled the Navy, for the first time, to compose sentences and transmit them by flag signals. Nelson's famous signal at the Battle of Trafalgar, 'England Expects that Every Man Will do his Duty', could not have been sent before 1800 when Popham first tried his system during negotiations at Copenhagen.
(© Crown Copyright/MOD)

This engraving of the shutter telegraph was published in 1796, the year the chain of stations was opened between the Admiralty in London and the dockyard at Portsmouth. Chains also linked Dover with London, and the Portsmouth line was given a long spur to Plymouth dockyard. In clear weather, messages could be passed in minutes. This British system was inspired by those which were established between Paris and the French dockyards, and eventually connected to the Spanish dockyard at Ferrol. (National Maritime Museum, London: PAH 2206)

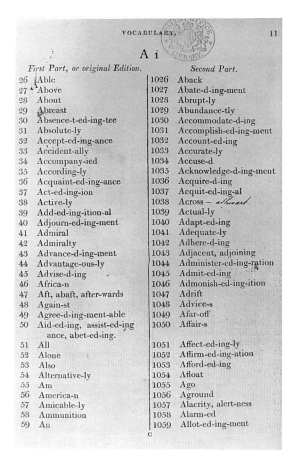

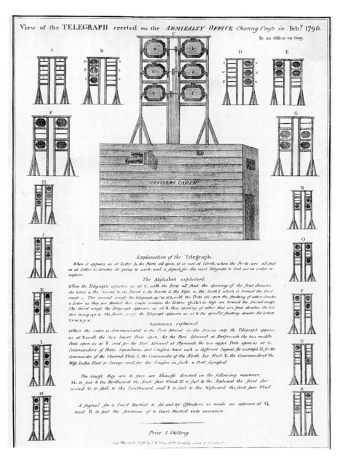

Part III

CAPE ST VINCENT AND THE NILE

THE GENERAL action off Cape St Vincent on St Valentine's Day, 14 February 1797, established Nelson's reputation. To those who had watched him on service ashore in Corsica, at the Court of Naples, and in the duel with the *Ça Ira*, Nelson was already recognised as being an officer of unusual ability. Admiral Jervis's appointment as commander-in-chief in the Mediterranean had ensured that Nelson's abilities would be exploited and developed to the full. It was his moral and physical courage at Cape St Vincent, and his calculated assessment of tactical requirements, which brought him to the attention of the world. His initiative at Cape St Vincent led directly to his being given command of the detachment which annihilated the French Mediterranean fleet at the Battle of the Nile, which in turn led to his victories at Copenhagen and Trafalgar.

The crisis which brought Nelson his first taste of glory was the decision in Paris to cut the Gordian knot by invading the British Isles. The British Mediterranean command, which extended west to the Atlantic coast of Spain, was involved because in 1795 Spain had been forced to conclude peace with France, and then in 1796 to sign the treaty of San Ildefonso by which the imbecile Charles IV was committed to war against Britain. The first invasion attempt was a strictly French effort. At Christmas in 1796 the Brest fleet had succeeded in carrying soldiers to Bantry Bay in the southwest of Ireland where they were to cooperate with Irish rebels led by Wolfe Tone. No British fleet was able to intervene. Ireland was always to be regarded as a weak point in British defences because of the relative ease with which the Brest fleet could sail there when the prevailing southwesterlies made it difficult for

the Royal Navy to get down channel. The need to guard the approaches to Ireland was one of the principal reasons why the cruising station for the Channel Fleet had to be close off Brest. As it happened, the French landing was prevented by a snow-storm, and when the wind turned to the east so that the Western Squadron could get out of the channel the French departed in haste. Paris, however, was not discouraged. Pressure was put on the Spaniards to undertake joint operations in the English Channel as they had in 1779.

London got advance warning of this development from the Queen of Naples, who gave Emma Hamilton a letter to copy, which she sent on to Nelson. The odds were thought to be too great for a battle fleet to be kept in the Mediterranean where it could not be used to reinforce the Channel Squadron, and the deci-

Rear Admiral John Jervis (1735-1823), by Sir William Beechey (1753-1839). (National Maritime Museum, London: BHC 3001)

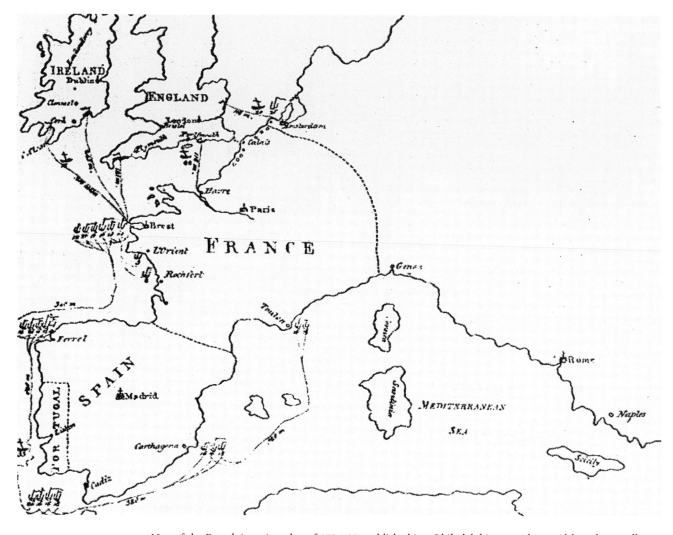

Map of the French invasion plan of 1796-97, published in a Philadelphia news sheet. Although a small force was landed in southern Ireland at Christmas 1796, and the mutiny of the fleet at Spithead and the Nore raised hopes in France, the battles of Cape St Vincent and Camperdown prevented the execution of the plan in its entirety.

sion was made to withdraw to a position off Cadiz. Naples was left to make the best peace it could with France, and the Austrians were given an excuse for doing so as well.

Nelson was left behind to cover the withdrawal, flying his flag in a captured French frigate, *La Minerve*. At the end of January 1797 he steered for the rendezvous with Jervis off Cape St Vincent in southwest Spain, sailing right through the Spanish fleet in the dark. The very fact that he was able to get away safely reinforced the impression that he had acquired at Cadiz in 1793 and later at Toulon that the Spaniards were not in good warlike order. He

was able to report to Jervis the next morning, and rehoist his flag on *Captain*.

During the following night, the signal guns of the Spanish fleet could be heard, and in the morning, one by one, ships loomed out of the fog, looking enormous to the British, 'like Beachy Head in a fog'. As Flag-Captain Sir Robert Calder counted them out, with the numbers eventually reaching twenty-seven to the British fifteen ships of the line, Jervis said sharply 'Enough, sir, no more of that. The die is cast and if there are fifty sail of the line, I will go through them'. In fact, the Spanish fleet numbered twenty-five ships, under Admiral

Cordoba, of which four were merchant *urcas* loaded with mercury under a strong local escort. The eight or nine ships of the convoy and its close escort were separated from the main body. To Jervis, however, it appeared as though the Spanish fleet was divided. He steered to keep the two parts of the fleet separate so that he could retain control of tactical developments.

Clerk of Eldin had demonstrated the value of cutting the enemy line by suggesting a scenario which proved to be a remarkable anticipation of the battle of Cape St Vincent. He had written that if a large fleet advancing in thick weather in an irregular line abreast with the wind abeam should run into a smaller fleet coming the other way in rough line ahead, the admiral of the latter could hardly do better than proceed on his course to split the larger fleet. Having passed through, raking the enemy to port and starboard, it could then tack so as to attack the windward half in the rear. The leeward half of the enemy fleet would probably be unable to get to windward to support those attacked.

Jervis ordered his captains to form a line of battle as convenient, and informed them of his intention to cut through the Spanish line. Captain Cuthbert Collingwood, who commanded the *Excellent*, wrote that

> The truth is, we did not proceed on any system of tacticks. In the beginning we were formed very close and pushed at them without knowing, through the thickness of the haze, with what part of the line we could fall in. When they were divided, & the lesser part driven to leeward, the Admiral wisely abandoned them, made the signal to tack, and afterwards stuck to the larger division of the fleet, which was to windward, and could not be joined by their lee division in a short time. After this we had neither order nor signals, for the Admiral was so satisfied with the impetuosity of the attack made by the ships ahead of him that he let us alone.[1]

Collingwood, however, was never to appear at his best as a tactician. Jervis's tactics were

P J de Loutherbourg's sketch portraits of
Top left: Thomas Ramsay, whom he has identified as one of the seamen who boarded the San Joseph;
Middle: Robert Williams, boatswain's mate of the Venerable
Bottom: The boatswain of the Venerable.
(British Museum)

1. To Carlyle, 3 June 1797, *Collingwood* #42 p83.

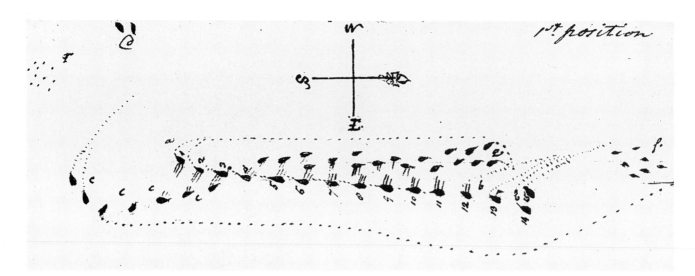

Naval officers could be as confused about the precise position of ships in a battle as were the wretched artists. These two sketch plans of the Battle of Cape St Vincent were preserved by Sir Samuel Hood in his papers now in the National Maritime Museum. The British fleet has been indicated by the numbers which have been placed beside each ship, but only five were identified in the accompanying list: 1 Culloden; *2* Blenheim; *3* Prince George; *12* Namur; *13* Captain. *The first drawing is inaccurate because it shows* Culloden *leading the British round the far side of the Spanish fleet, whereas Troubridge in fact tacked on Admiral Jervis's order and passed back along their engaged side. Nelson's action in taking* Captain *out of the rear of the British line and engaging the leading Spaniards is roughly shown. The second drawing is a better reflection of the battle, but has failed to show* Captain *where Nelson had put her, alongside the* San Nicolas. *(National Maritime Museum, London: MKH/102)*

2. Jervis to Nepean, 3 March 1797, DLN II p333.

3. J S Tucker, p262n.

intended to disorganise the Spaniards by the immediacy of the attack, and to make best use of his own fleet's seamanship and gunnery. As such they were a precursor of Nelson's, and in them a free and driving spirit like Nelson's could play an effective part.

Jervis, having passed through a gap between the main body of the Spanish fleet and the ships escorting the convoy, tacked the British Mediterranean fleet in succession to engage the rear of the loosely-formed Spanish fleet. Captain Thomas Troubridge, whom Nelson had met years before on his voyage to the East Indies, led the line in *Culloden*. So familiar was he with Jervis's intentions that he had his acknowledgment at the masthead, stopped and ready, before the signal was made to tack. He brought his ship around on the instant, and engaged the Spanish line with his port-side guns.[2]

The Spanish admiral, Cordova, responded by ordering his fleet to tack. They did not execute a coherent movement, but there was some danger that the Spanish van would be able to join the convoy escort passing across the British rear. To forestall this Nelson wore the *Captain* out of line, passed back through it, and attacked the Spanish van. This placed his ship in extreme danger, confronted by seven Spanish ships, three of which were of 100 guns, and a fourth the only four-decker in the world, the 140-gun *Santisima Trinidad*. Jervis immediately signalled Collingwood, last in the line, to leave his station and tack into Nelson's wake to provide support, and soon Nelson was also supported by the van coming down along the Spanish line. Calder later alluded to Nelson's breaking the line as unauthorised, and Jervis's responded: 'It certainly was so . . . and if ever you commit such a breach of your orders, I will forgive you also.'[3] Had the Spanish fleet been as well-trained and manned as was the British, Nelson's action would have been suicidal. But as it was, his prompt response to a tactical requirement was a nicely-judged stroke.

HMS Victory *raking the* Salvador del Mundo *at the battle of Cape St Vincent, 14 February 1797, by Thomas Luny (1759-1837).* (National Maritime Museum, London: BHC 0484)

Sir Thomas Troubridge, painted when a Rear Admiral, by Sir William Beechey. (National Maritime Museum, London: : BHC 3168)

Nelson receiving the surrender of the San Josef *at the battle of Cape St Vincent, 14 February 1797, by Daniel Orme (1767-post 1832) dated 1799.* (National Maritime Museum, London: BHC 0493)

The resulting meleé action led to the capture of four Spanish ships, two by Nelson in person. *Captain* took such a beating that she all but lost steerage way, and Nelson decided that the better part of valour would be to ram the

80-gun *San Nicolas* and board her. He insisted on commanding the boarding party himself, and when he found himself under fire from the *San Josef* of 112 guns which was close aboard the other side of the *San Nicolas*, he called for another boarding party and crossed over to her, sword in hand. This incident became known in the fleet as 'Nelson's Patent Bridge for Boarding First-Rates'.

Nelson's own account of the incident is breath-taking:

The soldiers of the 69th Regiment with an alacrity which will ever do them credit, and Lieutenant Pierson of the same Regiment, were among the foremost in this service. The first man who jumped into the enemy's mizzen chains was Captain Berry, late my First Lieutenant; (Captain Miller was in the very act of going also, but I directed him to

remain;) he was supported from our sprit-sail yard, which hooked into the mizzen rigging. A soldier of the 61st regiment having broke the upper quarter-gallery window, jumped in, followed by myself and others as fast as possible. I found the cabin door fastened, and some Spanish officers fired their pistols; but having broke open the doors, the soldiers fired, and the Spanish Brigadier (Commodore with a distinguishing pendant) fell, as retreating to the quarter deck, on the larboard side, near the wheel. Having pushed on to the quarter deck, I found Captain Berry in possession of the poop, and the Spanish ensign hauling down. I passed with my people and Lieutenant Pierson on to the larboard gangway to the forecastle, where I met two or three Spanish officer prisoners to my seamen, and they delivered me their swords.

At this moment a fire of pistols or muskets opened from the admiral's stern gallery of the *San Josef*; I directed the soldiers to fire into her stern; and, calling to Captain Miller, ordered him to send more men into the *San Nicolas*, and directed my people to board the First-rate, which was done in an instant, Captain Berry assisting me into the main chains. At this moment a Spanish officer looked over from the quarter-deck rail

Watercolour by Clarkson Stanfield entitled 'Jack Knocking the Frenchman Overboard' intended to illustrate Captain Marryat's novel 'Poor Jack'. (National Maritime Museum, London: : PAF 6064)

and said 'they surrendered'; from this most welcome intelligence it was not long before I was on the quarter-deck, when the Spanish Captain, with a bow, presented me his Sword, and said the Admiral was dying of his wounds below. I asked him, on his honour, if the ship were surrendered? he de-

The signatures of Horatio Nelson, Ralph Willet Miller, and Edward Berry on their account of the action off Cape St Vincent. This is one of the last documents Nelson was to sign with his right hand. (British Museum: Add MS 34,902)

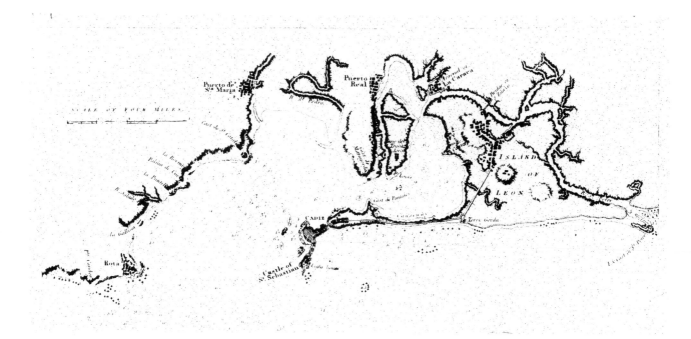

Plan of Cadiz, from a British chart of the south coast of Spain, dated 1804. (British Museum: BL Maps 18212(7))

4. 'A Few Remarks Relative to Myself in the *Captain*, in which my Pendant was Flying on the most Glorious Valentine's Day, 1797', signed by Nelson, Ralph Willett Miller, and E Barry; copy sent to HRH the Duke of Clarence, DLN II pp340-43.

5. 28 February 1797, Clarke and McArthur (1840) I p159 DLN II p358.

6. Lady Nelson to Nelson, 11 March 1797, DLN II p358; and Naish, p352.

7. 22 July 1797, *Wynne*, p277.

8. Nelson to his wife, 15 June 1797, DLN II p397.

9. Nelson to his wife, 11 July 1797, Naish, no 192 p330.

View of Cadiz, by Thomas Sutherland, engraver, published by S, A & H Oddy, 1 August 1808. (National Maritime Museum, London: PAD 1661)

clared she was; on which I gave him my hand, and desired him to call his Officers and Ship's company, and tell them of it– which he did; and on the quarter-deck of a Spanish First-rate, extravagant as the story may seem, did I receive the Swords of the vanquished Spaniards; which, as I received, I gave to William Fearney, one of my barge-men, who put them with the greatest sangfroid under his arm.[4]

This time, Nelson's got the credit he de-served, and was made a Knight of the Bath, which honour he preferred to being made a baronet because of the gaudy star he could wear on his uniform coat. His promotion to Rear Admiral had already been confirmed, but as a routine step rather than as a result of Jervis's request. Jervis himself was raised to the peerage as Earl St Vincent. To Fanny Nelson wrote that 'the Spanish War will give us a Cottage and a piece of ground, which is all I want. I shall come one day laughing back, when we will retire from the busy scenes of Life.'[5] Poor Fanny, however, could not share altogether in his happiness: 'What can I at-tempt to say to you about boarding? You have been most wonderfully protected. You have

Representation of the Advanced Squadron under the command of Rear Admiral Lord Nelson during the blockade of Cadiz. Published 1 July 1802 by Thomas Butterworth, artist, and T Williamson, publisher. (National Maritime Museum, London: PAG 7151)

done desperate actions enough. Now may I, indeed I do beg, that you never board again. *Leave it for captains.*[6]

Nelson was of quite a different mind. On 3 July he raided Cadiz with a bomb vessel guarded by the boats of the fleet. Against all precedent, he, a rear admiral, with Captain Fremantle, went in the boats. It was in the melée that followed that his coxswain saved his life three times, once interposing his own hand to stop a sword blow. Nelson knew that his willingness to share all the dangers with his men, to lead from the front, was the best possible means of dampening the undercurrents of discontent in the ships sent out from Spithead in the months after the mutiny. He had shifted his flag to the *Theseus* which Betsey Fremantle had found on her voyage out from England to be full of 'the most tiresome, noisy, mutinous people in the world'.[7] The impression he made on these men was such that a note was found dropped on his quarterdeck reading:

success attend Admiral Nelson! God Bless Captain Miller! We thank them for the Officers they have placed over us. We are happy and comfortable and will shed every drop of blood in our veins to support them, and the name of the *Theseus* shall be immortalised as high as the *Captain*'s.

It was signed: 'Ship's Company'.[8] On 11 July Nelson wrote home 'Our Mutinies are I hope

stopped here, the Admiral having made some severe examples, but they were absolutely necessary'.[9]

Nelson in Conflict with a Spanish Launch, July 1797, by Richard Westall (1765-1836). It was in this action that Nelson had his life saved three times by a sailor who even warded off a sword blow with his own hand. It was unusual for a rear admiral to expose himself in a boat action. (National Maritime Museum, London: BHC 2908)

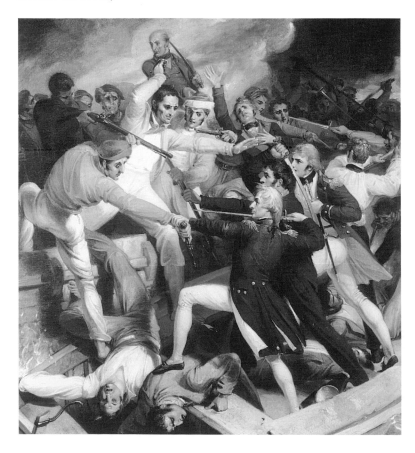

View of Santa Cruz de Tenerife, watercolour by J J Williams, 1830. (National Maritime Museum, London: PAF 5948)

Tenerife

Captain Thomas Fremantle, later Rear Admiral (1765-1819), by Domenico Pellegrini, artist, and Charles Picart, engraver. (National Maritime Museum, London: PAD 3287)

It would have been well for Nelson had he been more attentive to his wife's fears. A few weeks after the bombardment of Cadiz he was sent in command of a detachment to seize Santa Cruz de Tenerife and a valuable merchant ship sheltering in the harbour. This was not a successful operation, largely because surprise was lost due to an unexpected current along the shore. Nelson ordered a second assault immediately under the cover of fire from the ships, but at the end of the day the men had to be withdrawn because they were unable to carry the main defences by assault. However, a German deserter they brought back with them led Nelson to believe that the morale and numbers of the defenders were both low. Despite a gale that was blowing, he ordered another night assault on a much larger scale. He admitted later that his principal reason was his belief that Britain's honour was at stake. He determined to go in with the first wave, and Betsey Fremantle thought he was completely confident of success. He later wrote, however, that he 'never expected to return'.[10] He burnt all the letters from his wife before leaving *Theseus*, and bade farewell to Josiah. Fortunately for him, however, his step-son refused to leave him.

A fire of thirty or forty pieces of cannon, with musketry, from one end of the Town to the other, opened upon us, but nothing could stop the intrepidity of the Captains leading the divisions. Unfortunately, the greatest part of the Boats did not see the Mole, but went on shore through a raging surf, which stove all the Boats to the left of it.

For the detail of their proceedings, I send you a copy of Captain Troubridge's account to me, and I cannot but express my admiration of the firmness with which he and his brave associates supported the honour of the British Flag.

Captains Fremantle, Bowen, and myself, with four or five Boats, stormed the Mole, although opposed apparently by 400 or 500 men, took possession of it, and spiked the guns; but such a heavy fire of musketry and grape-shot was kept up from the Citadel and houses at the head of the Mole that we could not advance, and we were all nearly killed or wounded.[11]

The raid proved to be a disaster. The defenders included thousands of militia, their morale was high and their arms effective. Troubridge tried to bluff the Spaniards into surrender by threatening to burn the town, but in the end was only able to negotiate an honourable withdrawal after promising to cease to attack the Canaries. The only bright side to the whole affair was the courtesy with which the Spaniards treated their defeated enemy. Nelson was badly wounded by a musket ball and had to have his right arm amputated. According to the account in *The Naval Chronicle*,

the shock caused him to fall to the ground, where for some minutes he was left to himself, until Mr Nisbet [Josiah] missing him, had the presence of mind to return, when after some search in the dark, he at length found his brave father-in-law weltering in his blood on the ground, with his arm shattered, and himself apparently lifeless. Lieutenant Nisbet having immediately applied his neck hankerchief as a tourniquet to the Admiral's arm, carried him on his back to the beach; where, with the assistance of some sailors, he conveyed him into one of the boats, and put off to the *Theseus* under a tremendous, though ill-directed fire from the enemy's battery.

The next day after the Rear Admiral had lost his arm, he wrote to Lady Nelson; and in narrating the foregoing transaction, says 'I know it will add much to your pleasure, in finding that your son Josiah, under God's providence, was instrumental in saving my life'.[12]

He was invalided home, where he spent the next eight months struggling with pain and depression. Fanny overcame her repugnance, and learnt to dress his wound with care. Nelson showed great devotion to her, and insisted that she be invited to join him at official functions. In the twentieth century, his career would have been at an end, but in fact his greatest triumphs were just about to begin. He was ashore, in Bath recovering from the injury, when General Napoleon Bonaparte set in motion his campaign to conquer Egypt, and open the way for recovery of French power in the Far East.

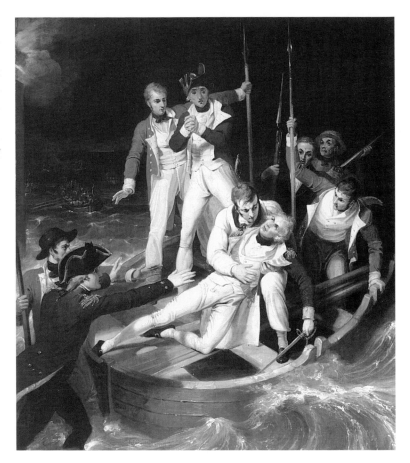

Nelson wounded at Tenerife, 24 July 1797, by Richard Westall (1765-1836). (National Maritime Museum, London: BHC 0498)

Camperdown

The French, having failed twice to carry the war to Britain by invasion, had decided to make another attempt. The navy of the Netherlands, which had capitulated in 1795, was to escort an invasion force over to southern England. Nelson was not himself involved in this campaign, but the tactics Admiral Duncan employed at the Battle of Camperdown in the North Sea in October 1797 were an important milestone in the establishment of the ideas Howe had developed. There is a clear connection between Howe's victory at the Glorious First of June, Jervis's at Cape St Vincent, Duncan's at Camperdown, and Nelson's own tactics at Trafalgar. Cutting the enemy fleet was definitely in favour as a solution to the problem of holding the enemy in battle, disorganising his tactical plan, and cre-

10. 24 July 1794, *Wynne*, p278; and Nelson to Sir Andrew Hamond, 8 September 1797, Naish, p280.

11. 'A Detail of the Proceedings of the Expedition Against the Town of Santa Cruz, in the Island of Tenerife', Nelson Papers, DLN II pp425-28.

12. *NC* 3 p179; see Nelson to his wife, 5 August 1797, Naish, p332 and DLN II p436.

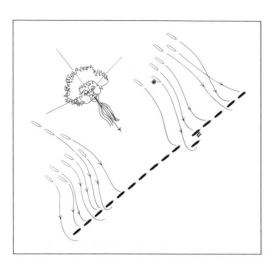

The battle of Camperdown. Admiral Duncan deployed his fleet in two divisions which attacked the Dutch in line abreast, overwhelming and cutting through Admiral de Winter's van and rear.
Nelson's plan of attack at Trafalgar, which he did not carry out, was similar to Duncan's except that the windward line was to attack in line ahead and direct its effort at the centre.

ating the opportunity for superior British shiphandling and gunnery to prevail. The failure of the invasion attempt was also important as it led directly to the Egyptian campaign.

There was no difficulty in ensuring interception of Admiral de Winter's fleet in the North Sea, but the recent mutiny at the Nore did raise serious questions about British morale. When Admiral Duncan met the enemy, however, his men showed by their determined fight against resolute foes that professional pride and national feeling had not been destroyed.

When the Dutch fleet was sighted to leeward forming a close-hauled line, Admiral Duncan ordered his two divisions to shorten sail in order to come into close order in line ahead, in reverse order. He then bore down in line abeam and cut through the enemy fleet in four places. To ensure that his fleet reached the enemy line in good order, so that their gunnery would be most effective, Duncan made extensive use of flag signals to correct station keeping. In the close action which followed, superior British gunnery, and effective mutual support, determined the outcome.[13] Nine of the fifteen Dutch ships of the line, which were significantly smaller than their British opposite numbers, surrendered. It was a victory on an unparalleled scale, but the record was to be far surpassed by Nelson in less than two years.

The battle of Camperdown, 11 October 1797, by George Chambers, 1803-1840. Nelson was not at this battle, but Admiral Duncan's tactical ideas are an important step to those Nelson developed and used at Trafalgar. (National Maritime Museum, London: BHC 0502).

The Nile Campaign

The brilliant success of Napoleon's operations in northern Italy had established his reputation, and forced Austria to sue for peace. That had left Britain as the only enemy of France, but on his return from Italy Napoleon visited the camps around Boulogne where the Army of England was massed and advised the government that there was no prospect of taking an army across the Channel without command of the sea. He had been placed in command of the Army of England, but after Camperdown the incentive for continuing in command was small. By the coup of 9 Thermidor, 27 July 1794, Robespierre had been driven from power, and executed, but the new constitution of the Directory had not created political stability. Napoleon again sought to pursue his career at a safe remove from Paris, and promoted the idea of the Egyptian expedition, with himself in command. His idea was adopted by the government which was just as pleased to have him out of the way.

This was to be Napoleon's most romantic adventure. With a mixture of idealism and cynicism, he set out not only to conquer, but also to enlighten. He took with him in his army leading members of the French Academy who were to study every aspect of Egyptian archaeology, and natural history. Amongst their achievements was to be the discovery of the Rosetta stone with an inscription in Greek, Demotic and Heiroglyphs, which enabled scholars to begin the translation of ancient Egyptian texts.

Anxious to make a quick start because the annual flooding of the Nile in August would necessarily put an end to the movement of armies, Napoleon set in motion preparations at Marseilles, Toulon, Genoa, Corsica and Civitavecchia, and on 9 May 1798 he arrived at Toulon where he was accommodated onboard Admiral Brueys suitably-named flagship, *L'Orient*. Two days later the armada sailed, made up of thirteen ships of the line, seven frigates, and nearly 300 transports. The van was commanded by Vice Admiral Blanquet,

General Napoleon Bonaparte on campaign in Italy. It was in Italy that Napoleon established his reputation for brilliance as a general. Andrea Appiani's portrait, however, was more influenced by the Revolutionary image of Napoleon's early years. It was this image, the hope of those who longed for an end to European monarchy, which inspired Beethoven's early works. Nelson never shared this view. His mother who died when he was a child had taught him to hate all Frenchmen, and his later service in the Mediterranean brought him in contact with refugees from Revolutionary guillotines. (British Museum: BM 1926.4.12.80)

and the rear by Rear Admiral Villeneuve, and Admiral Genteaume acted as Brueys's chief of staff. It took four weeks for the fleet to make its way to Malta. There, with the help of a popular insurrection, Napoleon took possession, abolishing the ancient warrior order of the Knights of St John and installing a French garrison. In a week, he set about the reformation of the island and its institutions, plundered its treasury and library, and departed. Avoiding the more direct route, course was made towards the coast of Crete. On the night of 22–23 June signal guns were heard, which some thought might be those of a British fleet, but it was not until 1 July when Alexandria was in sight that Napoleon learnt that the Royal Navy had reached the Levant ahead of him.

13. Tunstall/Tracy, pp219–222.

Thomas Hardy, who was to see action in all three of Nelson's great battles, and be his flag-captain at Trafalgar. Published 1 November 1794 by B Crosby. (National Maritime Museum, London: PAD 8252)

Napoleon felt free to move his army about the Mediterranean because the Royal Navy had no base east of Gibraltar. Never very astute about the strengths and limitations of naval forces, Napoleon did not consider the possibility of a detachment from Admiral the Earl of St Vincent's squadron off Cadiz as a serious obstacle.

None of the British envoys or agents had been able to discover what was the intended destination of the force being prepared in French-controlled ports, but the First Lord, Earl Spencer, expressed to St Vincent the belief on 29 April 'that the appearance of a British Squadron in the Mediterranean is a condition on which the fate of Europe may at this moment be stated to depend'.[14] It says a great deal for the reputation Nelson had gained that he was entrusted with this responsibility. His wound having healed enough for him to apply for employment, he had been ordered to join St Vincent, who had been urging upon the Government the desirability of returning to the Mediterranean. On Nelson's joining, and before receiving Earl Spencer's letter, St Vincent ordered him to sail for the Gulf of Lyons. This caused tremendous resentment with the other rear admirals, Sir Peter Parker and Sir John Orde, both of whom were his senior. Nelson flew his flag in *Vanguard* commanded by Sir Edward Berry, and his squadron consisted of *Orion* commanded by Sir James Saumarez and the *Alexander* under Alexander Ball, and two frigates. When the Admiralty dispatch sug-

An engraving by Nicholas Pocock purporting to represent the Agamemnon *disabled and under tow by* Alexander *commanded by Captain Ball. In fact, Nelson's disabled flagship was the* Vanguard, *and the danger occurred not during the storm, but afterwards when there was a nearly flat calm but the swell was driving the dismasted* Vanguard *onto the shore. (National Maritime Museum, London: PAF 5876).*

gesting that Nelson should be put in command, and with word that reinforcements were being sent out from England, arrived St Vincent immediately determined to reinforce Nelson with ten further ships of the line under Thomas Troubridge who had done so well at the St Valentine's day battle. He sent a brig, *Mutine,* under the command of Thomas Hardy who was to be with Nelson in all of his great battles, to inform him.

As so often happened in eighteenth-century naval warfare, it had proved to be impossible to prevent the sailing of the enemy, or even to mark its progress. Wind and weather could be counted on by a patient commander to force blockading ships off station. This time, the elements went further and all but wrecked *Vanguard* on the coast of Sardinia, due perhaps to inattention on the part of Captain Berry who had never previously commanded a ship of the line. *Alexander* took *Vanguard* in tow when the wind died, but in the calm which followed the storm the heavy swell put both ships in danger. Nelson shouted through the speaking trumpet that Ball should cast off, but he refused to do so and succeeded in towing the *Vanguard* clear.[15]

Dismasted though she was, *Vanguard* was ready again for sea in two days. During those days, however, the French fleet had got away. Worse, the captains of the British frigates had made their own way to Gibraltar because they believed that Nelson would have to return there for repairs. Without frigates for scouts, Nelson's squadron made a small footprint on the sea, and had little chance of finding Napoleon. Troubridge joined from Cadiz with the expected reinforcement of ten 74-gun ships of the line, and Nelson set off in what was to be an epic pursuit. As there was no British base, he made his way to Naples to take on water, by force if necessary, and to ask after news of the French from Sir William Hamilton. Although the Neapolitan court could not risk open support for a British fleet, its sympathies were clearly hostile to the French republic, and with Sir William's help supplies were quietly made available.

Sir William had no certain news of the

Sir William Hamilton by David Allen. (British Museum)

French armada, but guessed it might be off Malta. If he did not find them there, Nelson guessed that they would be bound for Alexandria with the objective of getting troops to India where Tippo Sahib was fighting to drive out the British East India Company.[16] The squadron made a frustratingly slow passage through the Strait of Messina, and then off Cape Passaro Nelson learnt from a Genoese ship that Napoleon had already taken Malta, and departed. His orders were not to let the French get to westward of him, where they would be a threat to St Vincent's force off Cadiz. His conviction that Napoleon must have gone east, therefore, required great moral courage. 'With the opinion of those Captains in whom I place great confidence,' (Ball, Berry, Darby, Saumarez) he explained to St Vincent, he decided that Egypt was the more likely destination. Had Sicily been the French objective there would have been clear evidence of it from passing merchantmen.[17] Nevertheless, as Sir James Saumarez put it in his journal:

14. Earl Spencer to Admiral St Vincent, 29 April 1798, *Spencer,* II p438.

15. 'The Friend', Essay IV, *Coleridge,* I p548.

16. Nelson to Earl Spencer [15 June 1798], and to George Baldwin, Consul at Alexandria, 26 June 1798, DLN III pp31 and 37.

17. Nelson to St Vincent, DLN III pp38-41; see Nelson's questionnaire and replies, 22 June, Naish, pp407-09.

Some days must now elapse before we can be relieved from our cruel suspense; and if, at the end of our journey, we find we are upon a wrong scent, our embarrassment will be great indeed. Fortunately, I only act here *en second*; but did the chief responsibility rest with me, I fear it would be more than my too irritable nerves would bear.[18]

The tension affected Nelson so greatly that he felt as though a belt were tight around his chest, making it an agony to breath.

Had Nelson had frigates with him he could scarcely have avoided falling in with the French armada on its way, but as it happened he passed them by without making contact, and without knowing for sure that he was not on a wild goose chase. When he arrived off Alexandria on 29 June and found no sign of the French he was in a terrible dilemma. Had he been a less driving admiral, he might have stayed off the mouth of the Nile for a day or two and intercepted the French when they arrived two days later. However, what he actually did was to press on eastward to look into the ports of the Levant, and then, when he had exhausted hope of finding the French there, worked all the way back west to Syracuse in southeastern Sicily. There he could obtain no news, but at least the squadron could take on supplies. To support his later request that Emma be pensioned by the Government, Nelson later claimed that she had obtained a letter from the Queen ordering the governor to open his port to the British fleet, but in any case Nelson had orders to take what he wanted by force if necessary. The strain on him was immense, but he resolutely turned his fleet eastward again, and three days later it was learnt from a captured French merchantman that Napoleon's armada had been seen off Crete sailing southeastward. This was soon corroborated from another source. By 1 August Nelson was once again off Alexandria, looking at the French transports filling the harbour and safe behind batteries now manned by the French army.

'When the reconnoitring ship made the sig-

nal that the enemy [battlefleet] was not there', Saumarez wrote, 'despondency nearly took possession of our minds. I do not recollect ever to have felt so utterly hopeless or out of spirits as when we sat down to dinner.' Within half an hour, however, *Zealous* had found Brueys moored in Aboukir Bay close west of the Rosetta entrance to the Nile. 'As the cloth was being removed, the officer of the watch hastily came in, saying, "Sir, a signal has just now been made that the enemy is in Aboukir Bay". All sprang to their feet, and only staying to drink a bumper to our success, we were in a moment on deck.'[19]

One of *Goliath*'s midshipman, the Honourable George Elliot, son of Nelson's friend the Earl of Minto, claims to have been the first to actually sight the French fleet.

I, as signal-midshipman, was sweeping round the horizon ahead with my glass from the royal-yard, when I discovered the French fleet at anchor in Aboukir Bay. The *Zealous* was so close to us that, had I hailed the deck, they must have heard me. I therefore slid down by the backstay and reported what I had seen. We instantly made the signal but the under toggle of the upper flag at the main came off, breaking the stop, and the lower flag came down. The compass-signal, however, was clear at the peak; but before we could recover our flag, *Zealous* made the signal for the enemy fleet; whether from seeing our compass-signal or not I never heard. But we thus lost the little credit of first signaling the enemy, which as signal-midshipman, rather affected me.[20]

Napoleon had made an easy conquest of Egypt, at the battle of the Pyramids turning the firepower of late eighteenth century infantry against the Mameluke slave-warriors who were armed and equipped as light cavalry. It was too late to affect that issue, but the ambition to proceed to the conquest of India could only become a reality if the Mediterranean could be kept open. This Nelson was more than willing to prevent.

18. *Saumarez*, I p207.

19. *Saumarez*, I p207.

20. Fraser, *Sailors*, p86

21. Nelson to Berry, quoted in Southey, p164.

22. Edward Berry, 'Engagement of the Nile', *NC* 1799; *Saumarez*, I p210.

Nelson's Tactics

The Battle of the Nile set a new, and much higher, standard for the conduct of naval actions. Unlike the achievements of earlier generations, especially of French admirals like d'Estaing, victory was not won by complex manoeuvre: the French fleet was found at anchor, and the only tactical manoeuvre of the British fleet in the entire engagement was its attack on the head of the line in relatively loose order. It would be a misunderstanding of the fundamentals of tactics, however, to suppose that tactical concepts played no part in the battle. Nelson's precipitous attack was based on a careful assessment of the most effective means of overcoming the enemy gunners. He was certain of the outcome. He insisted that the boldest measures were the safest, and only admitted that 'who may live to tell the story' could not be foretold.[21]

As Sir James Saumarez and Sir Edward Berry both described it in their accounts of the Nile campaign, Nelson had had his captains onboard virtually daily to discuss the tactical methods he would use in different situations, and the probable movements of the enemy. Saumarez wrote one day of his having 'passed the day onboard the *Vanguard*, having breakfasted and stayed to dinner with the admiral'.[22] They discussed tactics for the manoeuvre battle they were hoping and expecting, as well as tactics for the engagement at anchor which actually occurred.

Berry was careful not to reveal any details of Nelson's tactical plans, but he did write that, had Nelson 'fallen in with the French at sea, that he might make the best impression upon any part of it that might appear the most vulnerable, or the most eligible for attack, he divided his force into three sub-squadrons, viz.'

Vanguard,	*Orion,*	*Culloden,*
Minotaur,	*Goliath,*	*Theseus,*
Leander,	*Majestic,*	*Alexander,*
Audacious,	*Bellerophon,*	*Swiftsure,*
Defence,		
Zealous.		

Captain Sir Edward Berry (1768-1831), by John Singleton Copley (1737-1815). Captain Berry was flag-captain of Nelson's flagship at the Nile, HMS Vanguard, *and wrote an account of the battle and Nelson's methods of command.* (National Maritime Museum, London: : BHC 2554)

In itself, this indicates a radical departure from traditional line tactics, but as yet his attitude to tactical command was orthodox. In a general order which Nelson issued on 8 June, the day that Troubridge joined him with reinforcements, he warned his fleet that,

As it is very probable the enemy may not be formed in regular order on the approach of the squadron under my command, I may in that case deem it most expedient to attack them by separate divisions; in which case, the commanders of divisions are strictly enjoined to keep their ships in the closest order possible, and on no account whatever to risk the separation of one of their ships. The captains of the ships will see the necessity of strictly attending to close order; and, should they compel any of the enemy's ships to strike their colours, they are at liberty to judge and act accordingly, whether or not it may be most advisable to cut away their masts and bowsprits; with this special observance, namely, that the destruction of the enemy's armament is the sole object. . . .

The commanders of divisions are to observe that no consideration is to induce them to separate in pursuing the enemy, unless by signal from me; so as to be unable to form a speedy junction with me; and the ships are to be kept in that order that the whole squadron may act as a single ship.[23]

The importance Nelson attached to impetus is evident, but at the same time it is clear that he did not at this stage in his career believe that the tactical initiative of his captains, their seamanship and gunnery, was an entirely adequate compensation for deficiencies of squadron tactics.

Berry states that Nelson's tactical objective was firstly the destruction of the transports, and the army they carried.

Two of these sub-squadrons were to attack the ships of war, while the third was to pursue the transports, and to sink and destroy as many as it could. The destination of the French armament was involved in doubt and uncertainty; but it forcibly struck the Admiral, that, as it was commanded by the man whom the French had dignified with the title of the 'Conqueror of Italy', and as he had with him a very large body of troops, an expedition had been planned, which the land force might execute without the aid of their fleet, should the transports be permitted to make their escape, and reach in safety their place of rendezvous; it therefore became a material consideration with the Admiral so to arrange his force, as at once to engage the whole attention of their ships of war, and at the same time materially to annoy and injure their convoy.[24]

No indication was given as to where on the French battle line Nelson intended to concentrate the blows of his divisions. As it happened, the battle of the Nile was to be fought in confined waters, against an anchored enemy, but that eventuality had also been discussed.

23. *Saumarez*, I pp212-3.

24. Edward Berry, 'Engagement of the Nile'.

ENGLISH LINE OF BATTLE AT THE NILE

Ships		Guns
Culloden	*T Troubridge, Captain*	*74*
Theseus	*R W Miller, Captain*	*74*
Alexander	*Alex J Ball, Captain*	*74*
Vanguard	*Rear-Admiral*	
	Sir Horatio Nelson KB,	
	Edward Berry, Captain	*74*
Minotaur	*Thomas Louis, Captain*	*74*
Leander	*T B Thompson, Captain*	*74*
Swiftsure	*B Hallowell, Captain*	*74*
Audacious	*David Gould, Captain*	*74*
Defence	*John Peyton, Captain*	*74*
Zealous	*Samuel Hood, Captain*	*74*
Orion	*Sir James Saumarez,*	
	Captain	*74*
Goliath	*Thomas Foley, Captain*	*74*
Majestic	*G B Westcott, Captain*	*74*
Bellerophon	*Henry D E Darby, Captain*	*74*
La Mutine, *Brig*		
		Total 1,012

FRENCH LINE OF BATTLE AT THE NILE

Ships		Guns
Le Guerrier	*Captain Trulet, Snr*	*74*
Le Conquérant	*Captain Dalbarade*	*74*
Le Spartiate	*Captain Emereau*	*74*
L'Aquilon	*Captain Thévenard*	*74*
Le Peuple Souverain	*Captain Raccord*	*74*
Le Franklin	*Admiral Blanquet,*	
	First Contre-Admiral,	
	Captain Gillet	*80*
L'Orient	*Admiral Brueys, Admiral*	
	and Commander-in-Chief,	
	Captain Casabianca	*120*
Le Tonnant	*Captain Dupetit-Thouars*	*80*
L'Heureux	*Captain Etienne*	*74*
Le Timoléon	*Captain Trullet, Jnr*	*74*
Le Mercure	*Captain Cambon*	*74*
Le Guillaume Tell	*Admiral Villeneuve,*	
	Second Contre-Admiral,	
	Captain Saulnier	*80*
Le Généreux	*Captain Le Joille*	*74*
Frigates		
La Diane	*Admiral Decrès,*	
	Captain Soleil	*48*
La Justice	*Captain Villeneuve,*	*44*
L'Artemise	*Captain Estandlet*	*36*
La Sérieuse	*Captain Martin*	*36*
		Total 1,190

The Battle of the Nile

The French battle squadron had not entered the harbour because Admiral Brueys believed the approach was too difficult for large ships. He chose to moor in Aboukir Bay but had not made the most of his position, perhaps because he was convinced that the British would not attack. All the same, it was a naturally strong disposition. Inshore the bay is shoal, and at its southwestern end there is a small islet on which the French had established a small battery. The fleet were ordered at anchor with this battery guarding the head of their line, but at a distance of nearly two miles. The shoal extended only about a mile from the island, so that there was nearly a mile of clear water inshore of the van ship. The prevailing onshore wind made any approach under sail hazardous. However, Brueys had neglected to make some of the most obvious provision for fighting at anchor. His ships were anchored by the bow only, and without springs on their warps. In consequence, they could not be swung to bring their guns to bear, and they had had to be anchored far enough from the shoals to allow room for the ships to swing. The British captains were quick to discover that, where there was room for a French ship to swing, there was also room for a British ship of the line to pass by inshore of the French line.

The French had sighted the British squadron at about 2:00pm, and Brueys gave orders to recall working parties from ashore, and to stow hammocks. He considerably out-gunned Nelson's thirteen 74s and a 50-gun ship, having nine 74s stiffened by three 80s, and the immense *L'Orient* in the centre with 120 guns. He also had seven frigates, which makes the lack of forward reconnaissance by the French fleet inexcusable. When first sighted, the British were not in any battle formation, and Brueys apparently concluded that they would not attack immediately. He considered sailing to meet them at sea, but rejected the idea, perhaps because he was short of sailors, but more likely because he thought it unlikely Nelson

Vice Admiral Francis Paul, Count de Brueys, by Alexander Lacauchie, engraver, and published by Rigo freres. (National Maritime Museum, London: PAD 0113).

would risk his fleet making an attack into a bay on the leeward shore towards the end of day. There was also a risk of collision and disorganisation if he attempted to beat out of the bay in any sort of battle order, and in the dark he could not expect to be able to make the most effective use of his three-decker. Having made his decision, Brueys ordered each ship to run a cable to the ship next astern, and to put a spring on the anchor hawse. According to the account of Rear Admiral Blanquet, a translation of which Nelson saved amongst his papers, few ships carried out this order. Certainly the cables did not prevent British

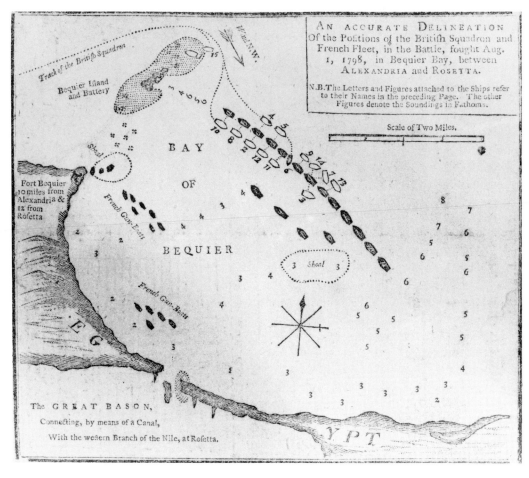

ships passing through the French line in several places. Brueys then ordered the fleet to lay out an anchor to the south-southeastward so that they could swing to engage the British, which was done in time to fire on the advancing ships.[25]

Brueys evidently presumed that the only approach the British could take was into the bag of the bay and then along the line of soundings until their leading ship came up to engage his rear. In this way, the approach would expose the attacker to the minimum of fire. In anticipation of this attack, he had stationed his heavier ships in the centre and rear. The fact that the wind on the evening of 1 August would not have allowed that approach, reinforced his conviction that no attack would be made.

Nelson did not leave the French much time to strengthen their defences. Saumarez later wrote that

although our squadron was not collected, – the *Alexander* and *Swiftsure* being at a considerable distance from having been detached to reconnoitre the port, and the *Culloden* a great way off from having had a prize in tow, – Sir Horatio deemed it of such importance to make an immediate attack on the enemy, that he made sail for them without waiting for those ships.[26]

A cautious commander might well have been intimidated by the natural dangers of a coast which was not well charted and with which he was not familiar. There were no frigates to go ahead to take soundings, so there was a very real risk of grounding, perhaps under fire. However, the daily tactical discussions Nelson had had with his captains had included action against an anchored enemy. Something could be inferred about depths from the position taken by the enemy fleet.

25. 'Translation of the French Rear-Admiral Blanquet's Account of the Battle of the Nile', DLN III pp67-71.

26. Saumarez to his wife, 2 August 1798, *Saumarez* I p232.

27. Nelson to Howe, 8 January 1799, DLN III p230.

28. See Hood's Instructions of 25 December 1793, KEI/S/11(c), signal 54 'To prepare for battle; when it may be necessary to anchor with a bower or sheet cable in abaft and springs, etc.'; and a private signal book of 1796 with this signal entered in pencil, TUN/20.

Nelson wrote to Lord Howe after the battle that his plan was to concentrate on 'the enemy's van and centre, the wind blowing directly along their line. I was enabled to throw what force I pleased on a few ships. This plan my friends readily conceived by the signals (for which we are principally, if not entirely, indebted to your Lordship)'.[27] For it to be carried out successfully, it was necessary that the French be spaced far enough apart that each could be engaged by two British, or that it be possible for some of the British ships to pass inshore of the French line. In fact, Brueys had permitted both these weaknesses, and it also appears that he had not ensured that his ships took the precaution of loading their inshore guns. How much Nelson could see from a distance of several miles must be uncertain, but probably he committed his squadron to action without being certain of the arrangements Brueys had made.

For the enemy line to be brought under continuous and effective gunfire it was necessary that the British fleet should itself anchor. Nelson had issued a second memorandum on 8 June warning his captains that 'As the wind may probably blow along the shore when it is deemed necessary to anchor and engage the enemy at their anchorage, it is recommended to each line-of-battle ship of the squadron to prepare to anchor with the sheet-cable in abaft and springs, etc'.[28] If they had anchored from the bow in the usual way, ships would have inevitably swung around when fetching up, exposing bow and stern to raking fire. The use of a stern anchor and spring would permit the British ships to swing to engage their enemy through an arc of virtually 180°. The cable on each ship was led through one of the stern windows, and made fast to the mizzen mast.

The British approach in a rough, irregular line ahead, invited the French to rake their

English plan of the battle of the Nile. (National Maritime Museum, London; PAD 4026)

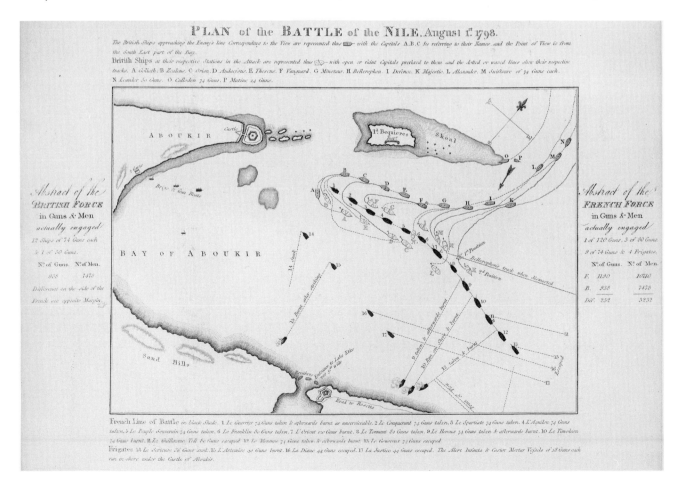

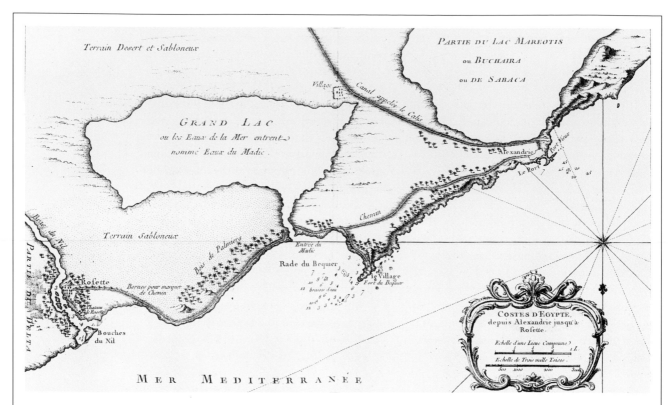

The Coast of Egypt

from Jacques Nicolas Bellin's *Petite Atlas Maritime* (5 volumes, 1764). Although this chart is limited in its detail, it provided Captain Thomas Foley with much more information than was provided in *The English Pilot* which had been published by the Hydrographer to the King, John Seller, in 1677. He was thus best able to lead the fleet into the shoal waters behind Aboukir Island.

The passage in the 1677 pilot is of interest:

> South of Rosetti is a great Bay called Mady or Medy Bay [Aboukir], where there runneth also a great stream from another Arm of the River Nile, into this Bay.
>
> Before this Bay lies an Island, behind which is good Riding, and good Ground; and if you are forced to remove from Rosetti, then you may run into the Bey of Mady, behind the foresaid Island, and come to an anchor in six or seven fathom water.

Four Leagues to the Southward of Rosetti, lies Cape Becur, between these two lies the foresaid Island before the Bay of Mady.

> Between Cape Becur and that Island, you cannot sail with great ships, except you are very well acquainted, for the Ground is very foul, some Rocks lie above, and some under Water; the Turks sometimes with small ships sail through, but to the Northward of the Island is a broad and good passage.
>
> Upon Cape Becur, standeth a Castle, called Apokera [Aboukir], which when you first get sight of, is like a Sail.
>
> From Apokera, or Cape Becur, to Alexandria, the Coast reacheth S.W. by S. about four Leagues; this Land is high and full of Trees.

(British Museum: BL K MAR I 12).

bows and shoot down their masts, spars and rigging. As it grew dark the French should have been at a tremendous advantage because they would know where their own neighbours were, so they would have no danger of firing into a friend. They should have been able to subject the British to a devastating cross-fire. The French fleet, however, was not fully worked up. Although the cables they laid out enabled them to open fire on the approaching British, their gunnery was poor.

The British ships came up in no sort of order, but by the time they came within firing distance the leading ships had taken up an *ad hoc* line ahead. Nelson's signals to his fleet were few:

No. 9 (to *Alexander* and *Swiftsure*) leave off chase;

No. 53 (general) prepare for battle;

No. 54 (general) prepare for battle, when it

29. The time noted in the logs of the fleet for the explosion of *L'Orient* vary from 9:37 to 11:30. *Logs*, Introduction, p5.

30. Bellin's *Petite Atlas Maritime*. 5 vols, 1764.

may be necessary to anchor with a bower or sheet cable in abaft, and springs, etc.;

No. 45 and No. 46 [hoisted together] (general) engage enemy's centre, and engage enemy's van;

No. 31 (general) form line of battle ahead and astern of the Admiral as most convenient;

No. 34 (general) alter course one point to starboard in succession; No. 66 (general) make all sail (after lying by), the leading ship first;

No. 5 [with red pendant] (general) engage the enemy closer.

There were great differences between the times being kept by the different ships, but the leading ship of the British attack, *Goliath*, recorded that it commenced action at 6:15pm.[29] The sun set about 7:00pm, and last light would be an hour later.

Brueys tried to lead the British onto the shoal by sending a brig to reconnoitre, and then to flee back taking a route through water too shallow for ships of the line. The bait was not taken. Nelson hailed Captain Samuel Hood of the *Zealous* to inquire what depth he was in, and Hood undertook to bear up and lead around the shoal taking soundings. Nelson himself dropped back to direct the approach of the rest of the fleet, and presumably to avoid the danger that the flagship might itself run aground. All but one ship safely negotiated the rocky shoal, but Troubridge in *Culloden* was a little astern of the fleet because he had been towing a prize, and in his hurry to catch up he had the mortification to go hard aground. By the most strenuous effort he managed to get her off, but with underwater damage, the loss of his rudder, and only after the battle had been fought and won.

The first ship round the end of Aboukir shoal was the *Goliath* commanded by Thomas Foley who had been flag captain in *Britannia* at the battle of Cape St Vincent. He had managed to steal ahead by having his studding sails hoisted and ready to break out when Nelson

made his signal, and he was better equipped to pioneer the route because he had an atlas which showed the bay and which was based on a survey done within the last forty years.[30] It was he who noticed that the French ships were spaced at 500 feet, and who judged that it should be possible to pass inshore of the head of their line. Elliot, the midshipman who claimed to have been the first to sight the French, called his attention to the buoy on *Le Guerrier*'s anchor which was the usual 200 yards from her stem. Between the buoy and the ship there was bound to be enough water, although there was a risk that the French line might be close to the bank. Elliot also heard Foley say that

he should not be surprised to find the Frenchman unprepared for action on the inner side; and as we passed her bow I saw he was right. Her lower-deck guns were not run out, and there was lumber, such as bags and boxes, on the upper-deck ports, which I reported with no small pleasure. We first fired a broadside into the bow. Not a shot could miss at the distance. The *Zealous* did

Sir James Saumarz, Nelson's second-in-command at the Nile. This picture was made by 'Jean' in 1838 from a miniature in possession of his family which had been made when he was 45; engraved by William Greatbach, and published by Richard Bentley. (National Maritime Museum, London: PAD 3473).

the same, and in less than a quarter of an hour this ship was a perfect wreck, without a mast, or a broadside gun to fire.[31]

In so interpreting Nelson's orders, Foley was using the sort of judgment Nelson appreciated. He knew the value of tactical cohesion, but by opening the engagement on the unexpected side, and taking the enemy between fires, Foley was making the most of the tactical opportunity. Nelson later wrote to Lord Howe: 'I had the happiness to command a Band of Brothers; therefore, night was to my advantage. Each knew his duty, and I was sure each would feel for a French ship.'[32] Captain Saumarez, for one, did not agree with the wisdom of doubling the enemy because of the very real danger of firing on friends, which he claimed was in fact to happen during the battle: 'a fact too notorious to be disputed'. The darkness greatly increased the danger. When Saumarez visited Nelson in the morning following the battle he began to express his regret that it had not been conducted with better squadron discipline. Nelson, however, was to cut him short: 'Thank God there was no order'.[33] Nelson's tactics always emphasised the importance of using overwhelming concentration of power to destroy enemy morale and gun-deck organisation. To do so bold measures were acceptable despite their danger.

Hood was directly behind Foley, and later

wrote that as they approached the enemy, they shortened sail gradually. 'The van ship of the enemy being in five fathoms water I expected the *Goliath* and *Zealous* to stick on the shoal every moment, and did not imagine we should attempt to pass within.'[34] Captain Miller of the *Theseus* believed that Saumarez in *Orion* actually took the ground briefly before breaking free.[35] Four British ships were able to pass inshore of the head of the French line, and a fifth passed between the first and second ships. The battery on Aboukir island fired as the ships approached, but it had only four guns and a mortar. A French frigate, *Sérieuse*, tried to block the gap. One of *Goliath*'s crew, the cooper John Nicol whose battle station was in the magazine where he was quite unable to see any of the action, wrote in his memoirs that 'Captain Foley cried, "Sink that brute, what does he there?" In a moment she went to the bottom, and her crew were seen running into her rigging'.[36] But Saumarez recorded that it was his ship, *Orion*, which sunk the frigate with one double-shotted broadside. She ran herself aground and her masts went by the board, leaving her as a sea mark showing the limits of deep water.

The standard procedure from the time Admiral Boscawen issued a chase signal following the night action of Lagos Bay 1759 was that the first ship of the *ad hoc* British line should bring too alongside the closest ship of

The battle of the Nile, 1 August 1798, by Thomas Luny (1759-1837). (National Maritime Museum, London: BHC 0512)

the enemy, and that the following ship should pass its disengaged side and anchor alongside the next. *Goliath*, however, failed to drop her anchor in time. She carried on to the next ship, giving three cheers and firing a broadside into *Le Guerrier* as she passed. The British seamen believed that the cheering was even more intimidating to the enemy than was the broadside. According to Elliot, the French tried to imitate the British cheer. It was a dismal failure, reducing the British sailors to shouts of laughter.

Hood saw what had happened, and himself anchored alongside *Le Guerrier*.

I commenced [such] a well-directed fire into her bow within pistol shot a little after six that her fore mast went by the board in about seven minutes, just as the sun was closing the horizon; on which the whole squadron gave three cheers, it happening before the next ship astern of me had fired a shot and only the *Goliath* and *Zealous* engaged. And in ten minutes more her main and mizzen masts [went]; at this time also went the main mast of the second ship, engaged closely by the *Goliath* and *Audacious*, [*Le Guerrier*] but I could not get her commander to strike for three hours, though I hailed him twenty times, and seeing he was totally cut up and only firing a stern gun now and then at the *Goliath* and *Audacious*. At last being tired of firing and killing people in that way, I sent my boat on board her, and the lieutenant was allowed . . . to hoist a light and haul it down to show his submission.[37]

Captain Miller later wrote to his wife:

In running along the enemy's line in the wake of the *Zealous* and *Goliath*, I observed their shot sweep just over us, and knowing well that at such a moment Frenchmen would not have the coolness enough to change their elevation, I closed them suddenly, and, running under the arch of their shot, reserved my fire, every gun being loaded with two and some with three

round-shot, until I had *Le Guerrier*'s masts in a line, and her jib-boom about six feet clear of the rigging; we then opened with such effect, that a second breath could not be drawn before her main and mizzen masts were gone.[38]

He then put *Theseus* alongside *Le Spartiate*, until Nelson brought *Vanguard* along her other side, when Miller gave 'up my proper bird to the Admiral', and engaged *L'Aquilon* and *Le Conquérant*. *Orion* came up astern, but Saumarez distrusted his stern anchor and let go the bower. Swinging head to wind, she opened fire with her starboard battery on *Le Peuple Soverain*.

Vanguard was the first British ship to stay on the outer side of the enemy, probably because by then there were plenty inside to insure engagement from both sides, and perhaps also because in the failing light and increasing smoke from the black powder, Nelson did not want subsequent ships exposed to the navigational hazards of passing inside the enemy line.

Ships brought-up as best they could, and not always precisely where they wanted. Anchoring, and by the stern, is always a test of seamanship even when not under fire. *Bellerophon* found herself alongside the 60-gun starboard battery of *L'Orient*, and was heavily battered for an hour before other ships came to her support. She was dismasted and wrecked, with 200 officers and men killed or wounded. Eventually her cable was cut and she drifted away to leeward. *Majestic* was also unfortunate in her anchoring, and took a heavy beating from *L'Heureux* without being able to give as much as she took. Captain Westcott was killed. Eventually she got clear, and then anchored to advantage off the bow of the next ship.

According to John Nicol of *Goliath* there were many foreigners serving the guns, including a company of Austrian grenadiers who had been rescued from Napoleon and had volunteered for service. There were also several women in the ship who carried ammunition to the guns. One died of wounds she received,

31. Fraser, *Sailors*, pp100-101.

32. Nelson to Howe, 8 January 1799, DLN III p230.

33. *Saumarez*, I, pp227-29.

34. Samuel Hood to Viscount Hood, 10 August 1798, *Logs*, II p 21.

35. Miller's Narrative, in a letter to his wife, DLN VII pCLIV.

36. John Nicol, Mariner, *Life and Adventures of . . .*, Edinburgh: William Blackwood; and London: T Cadell, 1822, pp185.

37. Samuel Hood to Viscount Hood, 10 August 1798, *Logs*, II p22.

38. Miller's Narrative, in a letter to his wife, DLN VII pCLIV.

and another gave birth to a son during the action. The gunner's wife brought wine to relieve the thirst of her husband and Nicol.[39]

Nelson was amongst the wounded, receiving a heavy blow on the head over his bad eye that cut a rectangular flap of flesh away from his forehead and blinded his good eye with the flow of blood. The blow was to give him headaches for the rest of his life and may well have been responsible for his emotional imbalance in the following months. Staggering, he exclaimed: 'I am killed. Remember me to my wife . . .' However, Berry caught hold of him and helped him to the cockpit by which time he had recovered so much as to refuse to take precedence over the more seriously wounded and dying men. When his wound had been bound up, he tried to get his secretary, or his chaplain to take dictation, but neither could concentrate on the task in hand. Taking the pen himself in his left, and only, hand, he began his famous dispatch while the sounds of cannonade was still loud:

> Almighty God has blessed his Majesty's arms in the late battle, by a great victory over the fleet of the enemy, whom I attacked at sun set on the 1st of August off the mouth of the Nile. . . .[40]

He later lamented to Lord Howe, however, that his injury had prevented him ensuring that no French ships escaped:

> . . . Had it pleased God that I had not been wounded and stone blind, there cannot be a doubt but that every ship would have been in our possession. But here let it not be supposed, that any Officer is to blame. No; on my honour, I am satisfied each did his very best.[41]

It was after 8pm when the *Alexander* and *Swiftsure* arrived, safely passing to seaward of the stranded *Culloden*. *Leander* 50 had been attempting to help *Culloden* float off the shoal, but now joined the arrivals. Together, the three made for *L'Orient*. *Alexander*, Captain Ball, anchored inside the enemy line,

sandwiching *L'Orient* against *Swiftsure* on the outside. *Bellerophon*'s identification lights had gone by the board during her unequal fight with *L'Orient*, and *Swiftsure* nearly fired into her as she drifted away. Just in time Captain Hallowell recognised her for a British ship, and took her place abreast the *L'Orient*. When a shot cut the cable of *Le Peuple Souverain* so that she drifted away and left a gap between *L'Orient* and *Franklin*, Captain Thompson was able to place the small *Leander* where he could direct a raking fire into both. Brueys had his legs shot off, but continued to direct action from a chair with tourniquets on the stumps, until he was cut nearly in half by another shot. He refused to be moved, and died on his quarterdeck.

Even before Brueys died, *L'Orient* had caught fire on her poop. Ball's account, according to Coleridge, was that the fire was caused by an incendiary device he had made and which one of *Alexander*'s lieutenants threw into *L'Orient*. Apparently Ball had prepared his ship thoroughly for the use of incendiaries:

> All the shrouds and sails of the ship, not absolutely necessary for its immediate management, were thoroughly wetted and so rolled up, that they were as hard and as little inflammable as so many solid cylinders of wood; every sailor had his appropriate place and function, and a certain number were appointed as the firemen, whose sole duty it was to be on the watch if any part of the vessel should take fire.[42]

Other accounts suggest that the fire on *L'Orient* burnt out of control because the crew had been engaged in painting ship, or because inflammable chemicals being used by the academicians had been stored onboard.

The flames could not be extinguished, and it became obvious that she must blow up. Ships began to cut their cables to get clear, and in the confusion several of the French van, according to Rear Admiral Blanquet, fired into each other.[43] Captain Hallowell, on the other hand, refused to move because he reasoned that the

39. John Nicol, *Life and Adventures of . . .*, pp186-187.

40. Edward Berry, 'Engagement of the Nile', p20.

41. Nelson to Howe, 8 January 1799, DLN III p230.

42. *Coleridge* I p549.

43. 'Translation of the French Rear Admiral Blanquet's Account of the Battle of the Nile', DLN III pp67-71.

44. Miller's Narrative, in a letter to his wife, DLN VII pCLIV.

45. *Coleridge* I p549.

explosion would arch over his ship. The heat was so intense that the pitch was bubbling out from between the planks, but he placed sentries at the cable with orders to shoot anyone who tried to cut it, ordered *Swiftsure*'s gunports closed, and placed fire parties through the ship. Men began to throw themselves into the sea from *L'Orient*, but Commodore Casabianca apparently refused to leave because his son had earlier had a leg shot off and was below in the orlop. About 10pm *L'Orient* blew up with a tremendous force which killed all but seventy of her 1,010 men. With her sank Napoleon's cash box, and the immensely valuable loot taken from the Knights of Malta.

Captain Miller wrote that such a sight would 'formerly have drawn tears down the victor's cheeks; but now pity is stifled as it rose by the remembrance of the numerous and horrid atrocities their unprincipled and bloodthirsty nation had and were committing.'[44]

This was the climax of the battle. All firing apparently stopped for some ten minutes. *Alexander* had her sails set alight by the explosion of *L'Orient* but Ball was able to get them extinguished. By then his men were so exhausted that the first lieutenant requested that they be permitted to sleep at their guns. According to the account that Coleridge later published, permission was granted.[45] The re-

Battle of the Nile: destruction of L'Orient, 1 August 1798, by Mather Brown (1761-1831). (National Maritime Museum, London: BHC 0510)

Destruction of L'Orient *at the battle of the Nile, engraving published by J & J Cundee, 1813.* (National Maritime Museum, London: PAD 7692)

markable thing was that after twenty minutes when Ball ordered them to stand to their guns again, they all leapt to their feet and recommenced firing into the nearest French ship, which was slow to respond because her gunners were also asleep.

When gradually firing resumed, it was clear that the battle was all but over. *Le Franklin* had lost her main and mizzen masts, and suffered so heavily that only a few guns continued firing. When the flagship blew up, she was covered with flaming wreckage, which was extinguished, but finally at 11pm or thereabouts she surrendered. As the ships at the head of the French line were now all subdued, Nelson sent his signal lieutenant, Capel, in a boat to urge the captains to move along the line. When he boarded *Goliath* which was severely disabled aloft to urge her to move clear so that *Audacious* could advance, Foley immediately ordered the cable cut and was able to set enough sail to give her steerage way. *Theseus* found herself looking at the broadsides of three French ships, but they did not fire, and

Captain Miller was careful to hold his own until support came up. Eventually he hove his anchor and slipped to leeward, his men falling asleep on the deck beneath the capstan bars.

In the morning John Nicol 'went on deck to view the state of the fleets, and an awful sight it was. The whole Bay was covered with dead bodies, mangled, wounded and scorched, not a bit of clothes on them except their trousers'.[46] The British fleet had captured seven ships of the line. Three others had been burnt, besides *L'Orient*. The frigate *Sérieuse* had been sunk; another, *L'Artémise*, first struck her flag then ran herself aground where her crew set her on fire. The 80-gun *Le Tonnant* with 1,600 men crowding her decks, and the frigates *L'Heureux* and *Le Mercure*, had slipped their cables to avoid the explosion but had run aground. They tried to bluff Nelson into providing a merchant ship to take them to France, but *Theseus* moved into position to engage the hulk, and *Tonnant* promptly surrendered.

Rear Admiral Villeneuve had moved his 80-gun flagship, *Le Guillaume Tell*, during the night, and now he got under way and made to windward out of the bay with *Le Généreux* and *Le Timoléon*, but the last failed to wear and ran herself onto the beach where her crew set her on fire and escaped. Villeneuve, who would later meet Nelson at Trafalgar, was accompanied by two frigates, *La Diane* and *La Justice*. *Theseus*, *Alexander* and *Majestic* opened fire on the fleeing ships, and Hood pursued them for a while, but as no other ship could join him, Nelson ordered his recall.

Nelson made arrangements to land the French wounded, 3,105 in number, so that they could be cared for by their own surgeons at Alexandria. He retained 200 prisoners, officers and technicians, and he calculated that 5,235 of the enemy were killed or missing. British casualties were 218 killed and 677 wounded. As always, once gunnery disorganised the enemy gun decks and reduced their capacity to reply they had begun to take disproportionate casualties.

One of Nelson's first orders on the morning of 2 August was to arrange services of thanksgiving throughout the fleet, which apparently greatly impressed 'the minds of the prisoners – the demoralised citizens of the French republic'. Captain Sir John Ross, who arranged Saumarez's papers for publication, wrote that he understood 'that they did not fail to express their astonishment and admiration at a scene of that kind under such circumstances'.[47] On the other hand, John Nicol noticed that the prisoners were not complacent as they had been during the American war, but, 'while thankful for our kindness', were 'sullen, and as downcast as if each had lost a ship of his own'. The revolution, with its promise of social change, had apparently made its mark on them.[48]

Nelson's official dispatch, which he had begun shortly after he was wounded in the midst of the battle, was both dramatic and brief. He made little mention of individual officers, other than Captain Westcott who had been killed, and Lieutenant Cuthbert who had so ably carried on the fighting of his ship, Hood for his endeavour to pursue the fleeing ships after the battle, and Berry for his support

on board *Vanguard*. This was a break with tradition, and hard on individual officers such as Saumarez who as second-in-command would normally have been mentioned. But the selection of individual names could be invidious, as Howe had discovered after the Glorious First of June. Nelson's own discontent with the little recognition he had received for his part in the sieges of Bastia and Calvi did not influence him. He simply wrote:

nothing could withstand the Squadron your Lordship did me the honour to place under my command. Their high state of discipline is well known to you, and with the judgment of the captains, together with their valour, and that of the officers and men of every description, it was absolutely irresistible. Could any thing from my pen add to the character of the Captains, I would write it with pleasure, but that is impossible.[49]

In reply to Earl Howe's congratulations, Nelson wrote: 'I have the happiness to command a Band of Brothers; therefore night was my advantage. Each knew his duty, and I was sure each would feel for a French ship.'[50] Nelson did exert himself to obtain a Nile gold medal for Troubridge even though *Culloden* had not fired a shot, a fact which considerably irritated Saumarez.

Two copies of the victory dispatch letter were sent. One was carried by Sir Edward Berry onboard the 50-gun *Leander*, but she had the misfortune to run into *Le Généreux* with 74 guns and a crew strengthened to 900 with survivors of the Nile. After a hard struggle in which Captain Thompson was himself hit four times and Berry was also wounded, her surrender was inevitable. The second copy had been sent to Naples in *Mutine* under the command of Lieutenant Capel, and Nelson brought Hardy to be captain of *Vanguard*. A more reliable ship master, Hardy was also temperamentally suited to the difficult task of flag captain. The partnership between him and Nelson was to last with little interruption until the latter's death at Trafalgar.

46. John Nicol, *Life and Adventures of . . .*, pp187-188.

47. *Saumarez* I p224.

48. John Nicol, *Life and Adventures of . . .*, pp187-188.

49. Edward Berry, 'Engagement of the Nile'.

50. Nelson to Howe, 8 January 1799, DLN III p230.

Tarnishing Glory

The news of the victory was greeted with absolute delight at the Court of Naples, especially by the Queen who was the sister of the executed Marie Antoinette. The Egyptians were no less rapturous, even though their country was still occupied by the French and was to remain in French control until they were defeated by British soldiers under the command of Sir Ralph Abercromby in March 1801. Nelson was quick to send a dispatch to the East India Company governor at Bombay, sending Lieutenant Duval who had the languages and diplomatic connections needed to travel overland to the Persian Gulf. The company was so pleased to be spared the expense of military preparations to meet Napoleon that they voted Nelson a purse of £10,000.

M. Poussielgue, Comptroller-General of the Finances of the Army of Egypt, believed that Nelson's victory would have the most wide-ranging consequences:

> The fatal engagement ruined all our hopes; it prevented us from receiving the remainder of the forces which were destined for us;

it left the field free for the English to persuade the Porte to declare war against us; it rekindled that which was barely extinguished in the heart of the Austrian Emperor; it opened the Mediterranean to the Russians, and planted them on our frontiers; it occasioned the loss of Italy and the invaluable possessions in the Adriatic which we owed to the successful campaigns of Bonaparte, and finally it at once rendered abortive all our projects, since it was no longer possible for us to dream of giving the English any uneasiness in India. Added to this was the effect on the people of Egypt, whom we wished to consider as friends and allies. They became our enemies, and, entirely surrounded as we were by the Turks, we found ourselves engaged in a most difficult defensive war, without a glimpse of the slightest advantage to be obtained from it.[51]

The actual results were somewhat less comprehensive, certainly in Italy, but were dramatic enough. The effect of the victory was unfortunate for King Ferdinand I of Naples

The Nile Medal struck by Alexander Davison, Nelson's prize agent. This engraving was made for publication in the Anti-Jacobin Review and Magazine, *March 1799.* (National Maritime Museum, London: PAD 3960)

NELSONIAN MEDAL.

REAR-ADMIRAL LORD NELSON OF THE NILE

EUROPE'S HOPE AND BRITAIN'S GLORY

R. Cleveley.

ALMIGHTY GOD HAS BLESSED HIS MAJESTY'S ARMS

VICTORY OF THE NILE
AUGUST.1.1798.

R. Cleveley.

Engraved (by Permission of Alexander Davison, Esq. for the Anti Jacobin Review & Magazine, March 1.1799.

whom Nelson encouraged to take the offensive. With Royal Naval support, he entered Rome on 29 November and drove out the French. His little initiative soon collapsed, however, his army being incapable and corrupt, and Naples was itself occupied by a French army without a battle. The Court had to be withdrawn to Palermo. The royal treasure was secretly carried out to *Vanguard*, and then Nelson and Emma Hamilton led the King and Queen and their family to the waterfront through a secret passages, where they embarked at dead of night to avoid the interference of the King's loyal subjects. Sir William's collection of art and antiquities was also embarked on a storeship which was later wrecked on the Scilly Isles. The passage of the royal party to Palermo was through one of the worst storms Nelson ever experienced, during which a young prince died in Emma's arms.

The citadel at Valetta did not fall to its Maltese besiegers, stiffened by British soldiers and the Royal Navy under Alexander Ball, until September 1800, and Egypt for another six months. On the other hand, the victory led to the Porte and Russia entering into understandings with the British government. The Royal Navy reestablished itself in the Mediterranean by seizing Minorca, and under the energetic leadership of Captain Sidney Smith, assisted the Turkish defence of Acre against Napoleon.

Nelson's reaction to his victory made him ridiculous. When he had arrived back in the Straits of Messina the King, Queen and the Hamiltons had themselves rowed out several miles to meet him. The welcome then, and in the subsequent months, quite turned his head. In extenuation, he was absolutely exhausted, had mountains of paper work to get through daily, and the Hamiltons and the court made him very welcome. It is also possible that his head wound had affected his self-control. Certainly, he was very unwell during the year he lived with the Hamiltons, and suffered continually from headaches.

Nelson, like most of the captains, had written his wife a stirring account of his heroics, but instead of flattering his vanity she continued to express concern about his safety. His letters to her about how good Emma was being to him, and to her Josiah who was being 'wonderfully improved', were tactless in the extreme. Her repeated, perhaps only half-serious, suggestions that she should come out to be with him were flatly rejected. All his friends thought he was behaving badly. The *Naval Chronicle* was expressing the general feeling in the service when it wrote, in capitals: 'LORD NELSON'S SEVEREST TRIAL IS YET TO COME! his present elevation has drawn upon him, the eyes of all men; and those of envy ever wakeful will steadily observe, whether the great Conqueror of the modern hydra, excels the demigod of Greece, by rising superior to the delusive snares of Prosperity.'[52] His parson father wrote a letter to a friend which warmly supported Horatio, but also betrays his concern for him.

My great and good Son went into the world without fortune, but with a heart replete with every moral and religious virtue. These have been his compass to steer by; and it has pleased God to be his shield in the day of

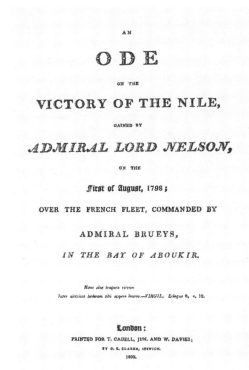

51. Poussielgue, E, *Lettre de M. Poussielgue*, Paris: 1845. p28 (Loose Translation).

52. *NC* 3 p185–86.

Two portraits of Emma, Lady Hamilton, by Sir Thomas Lawrence, artist and publisher, and Charles Knight, engraver. (National Maritime Museum, London: PAD 3239, 3240)

Long before she became Sir William Hamilton's wife, and even longer before she met Nelson, Emma had at one time been reduced to earning her living posing in the nude, when her beauty had attracted a strong following. As a not-quite respectable married woman she continued to develop her skills as a model, which she referred to as her 'Attitudes'. This engraving, by Frederick Rehberg, artist, and George Shepheard, engraver, was published in a book of Lady Hamilton's Attitudes *by Random & Stainbank.* (National Maritime Museum, London: PAD 3219)

battle, and to give success to his wishes to be of service to his Country. His Country seems sensible of his services; but should he ever meet with ingratitude, his scars will cry out, and plead his cause.[53]

In March 1799 the French Directory ordered Admiral Bruix, Minister of the Marine, to hoist his flag at Brest and with the forces there enter the Mediterranean and attempt to bring Napoleon and his army back to France. This created an operational crisis for the Royal Navy, in the midst of which Nelson defied his orders to concentrate with Admiral Lord Keith, the new commander-in-chief Mediterranean, at Minorca, and instead conveyed a Neapolitan army to successfully retake Naples. Fortunately Bruix was unable to affect anything, and returned to Brest with the Spanish fleet under the command of Admiral Gravina, who found himself trapped there until the Treaty of Amiens brought a brief period of peace in 1802.

The outcome was for the best, although the

King of Naples exacted a terrible revenge on the quislings, and Nelson thoroughly approved. He was implacable towards the desperate appeals of fleeing Neapolitans whom he prevented from sailing to France, and turned over to the executioners. Considering his usual humanity, this can only be explained by his obsession with royalty, the awful example of the French Revolution besides which the brutality of King Ferdinand paled into insignificance, his head wound, and the moral decay produced by his life with the Hamiltons. As a reward for his services he was made a Sicilian duke, of Brontë, and adopted the style without his sovereign's permission. Hallowell, the Canadian captain of the

53. *NC* 2 p192.

The capture of the Guillaume Tell, *30 March 1800, by Nicholas Pocock, sketch in graphite and print of finished picture.* (National Maritime Museum, London: PAD 8765, PAF 5879)

Lord Nelson's Coat of Arms. (National Maritime Museum, London: PAD 3997)

transport. He later made one more excursion to Malta, with the Hamiltons, and it was on that trip that he and Emma became lovers. He was all but ordered home, and made his way there through central Europe, with the Hamiltons, and greeted everywhere as the hero of the hour.

His weaknesses, as well as his strengths, endeared him to the public. Lieutenant Cavel had been pumped by the London press when he arrived with Nelson's dispatches, and England was wild in its rejoicing. King George III made him a baron with the style of Lord Nelson of the Nile and Burnham Thorpe in Norfolk where he had been born, and awarded him a pension of £2,000 per year for his own life and those of his two successors. There was considerable surprise that he was not made a viscount. The annihilating scale of Nelson's victory deserved greater recognition. However, it was a problem that Nelson was a comparatively junior flag officer, and not the commander-in-chief of a station.

Napoleon was to give Nelson ample opportunity to recover his professional reputation, and to earn higher distinction. Napoleon had ended his Egyptian adventure by defeating a Turkish army landed at Aboukir, and then had crossed the Mediterranean under the noses of the Royal Navy. After three lucky escapes, which perhaps Nelson might have prevented had he been paying closer attention to his naval duties, Napoleon returned to France hard on the heels of the news of his victory. He had snatched triumph from humiliation and frustration, and was the hero of France. Soon, he was also to be its political leader. He was drawn into a conspiracy led by Sieyès, one of the Directors, and took a prominent role in the coup d'état of 18 Brumaire (November 1799). A plebiscite confirmed the autocratic powers of the newly reconstituted French Republic, and Napoleon was made its 'First Consul'. As early as August 1798, nine days after the Battle of the Nile, Nelson had forwarded to Earl Spencer captured letters including one from Napoleon which led Nelson to warn that the Corsican general seemed to want 'to be the Washington of France'.[54]

Swiftsure, perhaps thinking of the traditional exhortation: 'remember Caesar, thou too are human', presented Nelson with a coffin made from the mainmast of *L'Orient*. To his great credit, Nelson was delighted and had it placed upright behind his chair in *Vanguard*'s cabin.

Nelson, however, had greatly exceeded the latitude that a junior flag officer should take, and without the extenuating circumstances of immediate tactical necessity. Keith had to intervene, but could not control Nelson's weakness. Together they patrolled towards Malta, where Nelson was delighted to be able personally to participate in the capture of *Le Généreux*, in revenge for the loss of the *Leander*. By then Berry, who had been in *Le Généreux* as a prisoner, was again Nelson's flag captain. Before Berry was able to bring *La Guillaume Tell* to book, however, Nelson had returned to Palermo and hoisted his flag on a

54. Nelson to Earl Spencer, 9 August 1798, DLN III pp98-99; Napoleon to Joseph, 7 Thermidor 1798, Add MS 23,003.

Part IV

COPENHAGEN

THE BATTLE of Copenhagen was the central act of a naval raid on the largest scale against the states of the Baltic region, whose ostensible neutrality was increasingly shifting to a pro-French position. It was ordered by the British Government because of the vital necessity of preserving the capacity of the Royal Navy to defend Britain against invasion, and to influence affairs on the continent. Nelson's victory at the Nile had been the culmination of a classic campaign to contain French potential for power projection across the sea. In contrast, Copenhagen was operationally a British offensive, especially when seen from the point of view of the Baltic states. In strategic terms, however, the operation was essentially defensive because it was needed to preserve access to the naval *matériel* upon which Britain depended for survival, and the legal regime at sea which made British sea power a means of confronting Bonapartism.

London was determined not to let the Baltic situation get out of hand again as it had in the war against the American revolution. Every means had to be tried to stop the flow of naval stores to French and Spanish dockyards, and to ensure that the Royal dockyards were supplied. No less important was the need to ensure that British trade remained profitable. In January 1798 there had been a clash with a Swedish convoy, and in December 1799, when a Danish frigate tried to prevent the search of a Danish convoy, shots were fired. A more serious skirmish occurred in July 1800 when a Danish frigate and her convoy were captured after a violent exchange.[1] The Danish minister Count Bernstorff protested vigorously, but London's response was to send a fleet to the Sound. The Danish court appealed to the mad Tsar Paul for support and in early 1801 occu-

Rear Admiral Sir Horatio Nelson (1758-1805), painted in 1801 by John Hoppner (1758-1810). (National Maritime Museum, London: BHC 2897)

pied Lübeck and Hamburg, closing the Elbe to British trade.

A convention was patched up, but British naval superiority was not so clearly established that its capacity to impose unwanted controls on Baltic trade was beyond question. In 1800 the Royal Navy had 546,000 tons of shipping, but France and Spain together had 431,000 tons. This made the 265,000 tons controlled by Russia, Sweden and Denmark in the Baltic a considerable force if it could be consolidated operationally.[2] In August 1800 Tsar Paul formally proposed to Prussia, Denmark and Sweden that they jointly resist attempts by belligerents to blockade Baltic trade. When he learnt about the British squadron sent to the Baltic, Paul seized all British property in Russia. He soon released it, but renewed his orders, despite the treaty he had concluded with Britain at the formation of the Second Coalition which provided security to British nationals, when he found that London would not assist his ambitions for Russia to become a Mediterranean power.

1. ADM 1/4186.

2. Jan Glete, *Navies and Nations*, II p376, table 23:35.

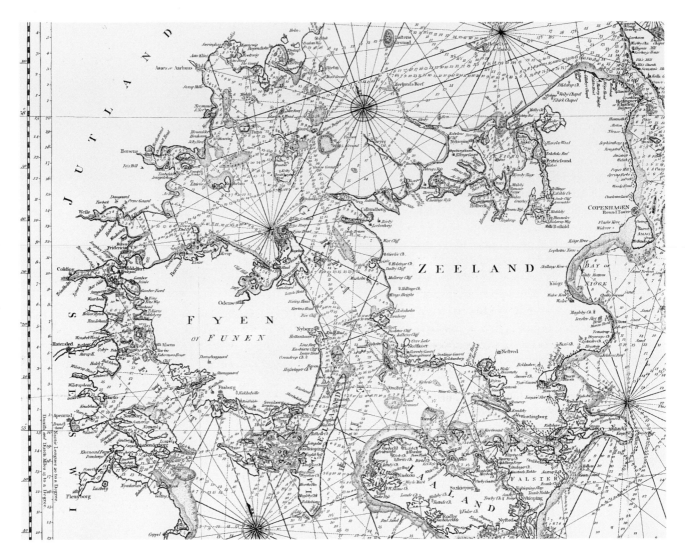

The approaches to the Baltic. Chart of 1794. (British Museum: BL 1069(72))

3. Carysfort Papers, Elton Hall, quoted by Dudley Pope, in *The Great Gamble*, London: Ramage Company Ltd, 1972, p65

4. State Papers, Denmark, FO 22/40, December 1880.

5. Circular letter from the Duke of Portland, 14 January 1801, ADM 1/4186, State Letters.

6. Nicholas Tracy, *Manila Ransomed: The British Expedition to the Philippines in the Seven Years War*, Exeter: Exeter University Press, 1995.

Tsar Paul had been elected Grand Master of the Knights of St John after their defeat by Napoleon, and he imagined that the defeat of the French garrison of Valetta citadel would lead to his securing Valetta harbour for the Russian navy. Although valuing Russia's capacity to dominate eastern Europe, and Russian naval and military forces which were being encouraged to play useful roles in the Italian theatre, London had no wish to have Britain's position as naval arbiter prejudiced by the Russian navy acquiring a permanent base in the Mediterranean. There was also a real possibility that Malta in Tsar Paul's hands would be open to the French navy. Paul had come under Napoleon's influence, and was anything but a reliable ally.

On 14 December 1800 Sweden and Russia signed a convention undertaking to stop trade in contraband, and to prevent interference with any other trade. Contraband was narrowly defined as guns, ammunition and military hardware. Naval stores were not included, but Tsar Paul's shift from an anti- to a pro-French policy was so pronounced that he rigorously embargoed the shipping of naval stores and grain to Britain. Napoleon responded to the embargo Paul placed on British ships in Russian ports by ordering French warships to stop operating against Russian merchantmen. He declared that the French Republic was already at peace with Russia. Paul sent a plenipotentiary to Paris, and was drawn into Napoleon's plans against Britain.

He urged Napoleon to put pressure on Portugal and the United States to join the League.

The League was ostensibly directed against the exercise of power by any belligerent, but Britain had most to lose because of her strategic dependence on naval power, and because it was only the French and Spanish navies which would benefit from free trade in naval stores. Napoleon encouraged the reappearance of the League, which if nothing else could be counted on to divide the coalition of forces joined against France, of which Russia was one. The fact that the Baltic states had not protested when in 1797 the French Directory had ordered privateers to seize any ship carrying British manufactures, even as part of the ship's equipment, and had not objected when in 1798 neutral ships were seized to provide transport for the Egyptian expedition, clearly defined the League as anti-British.

The threat to British interests was so great that London took decisive action. Lord William Grenville, the Foreign Secretary, warned the British ambassador in Berlin, the Earl of Carysfort, that 'the object of such a confederacy will not be attained but by a struggle in which Great Britain, contending for her very existence, will exert the utmost efforts'. In the hope of persuading Prussia not to join the League, he warned that the record of French behaviour in central Europe suggested that, should France succeed in defeating Britain at sea, the trade of the Baltic states would be no better off, and probably in a worse predicament.[3] To William Drummond, British representative at the Court of Denmark, Grenville wrote:

> In all the Courts of Europe they speak openly of a confederacy between Denmark and some other powers, to oppose by force the exercise of those principles of maritime law on which the naval power of the British Empire in a great measure rests, and which in all wars have been followed by the maritime states, and acknowledged by their tribunals.

A 'plain, open and satisfactory answer' was demanded.[4] When Count Bernstorff provided no more than an attempt to justify the restoration of the system of 1780, London moved swiftly to resolve the threat, by force if necessary. The Admiralty began to prepare a fleet for Baltic service, and instructions were sent to British admirals and governors throughout the world to seize any ships belonging to Russia, Denmark or Sweden.[5] Rear Admiral Duckworth in the West Indies was ordered to capture all the Danish and Swedish islands.

The Baltic Force Assembles

The Admiralty Board appointed Admiral Sir Hyde Parker to take command of the Baltic force. It was an unfortunate choice. Parker came from an old naval family. His father had sailed before the mast in Admiral Anson's *Centurion* when he circumnavigated the world between 1740 and 1744, and had made an early reputation as a captain in the operations to capture Manila undertaken by Admiral Cornish in 1762, during which he had captured a great galleon.[6] The younger Hyde

Vice Admiral Sir Hyde Parker (1714-1782), by James Northcote, artist, and H R Cook, engraver. Published 30 November 1808 by Joyce Gold. (National Maritime Museum, London: PAD 2916)

Parker's career had been less glorious, but he had made a good impression in the American war when he had forced the passage of the North River above New York. His earlier refusal to take action against a rebel army occupying New York, for fear of the injury which the citizens would suffer, may have been more significant. Twenty years later, he was an old man although only 61. His latest command had been at Jamaica, where he had grown rich on the captures made by his captains, but had quarrelled so violently with his second-in-command, Vice Admiral Richard Bligh, that he had, quite wrongly, sent him home. On his own return home he married a girl of 18 who was referred to unkindly in the fleet as 'Batter Pudding'. He had little taste for adventures of a colder kind in the dark and icy Baltic.

Parker's appointment can only be explained by the fact that he was given Nelson as a subordinate. The combination of the hero of Europe with a taste for battle and a poor repu-

Horatia Nelson (1801-1881). Nelson's only child, Horatia was smuggled out to be raised by a nurse so as to protect Emma's already compromised reputation. (National Maritime Museum, London: BHC 2886)

tation as a courtier, with a steadying senior admiral, must have appeared a sensible one to the First Lord, Lord Spencer. In November 1800 the Earl of St Vincent, now C–in–C Channel, had expressed to the Secretary of the Admiralty, Evan Nepean, his opinion that Nelson could not be trusted with 'a separate command'. 'He cannot bear confinement to any object; he is a partisan; his ship always in the most dreadful disorder, and [he] never can become an officer fit to be placed where I am.'[7]

Soon after Nelson's appointment in January 1801 the prime minister, William Pitt, resigned. St Vincent was asked by the new premier, Henry Addington, to replace Spencer as the First Lord. Nelson's close friend Troubridge was brought in as a member of the Admiralty Board. There is little evidence to suggest that the new board regretted putting Nelson in a subordinate position. It is possible, however, that Addington, who was on good terms with Nelson, would have given him the supreme command had he come to office before Parker's appointment was made.

Nelson had offered his services to the Admiralty as soon as he returned to England. This was not a good time in his life. The quarrel with his wife Fanny cannot have been easy on the conscience of a man with such strong religious convictions, and the knowledge that his brother officers all thought he was making himself ridiculous was painful. Emma was about to give birth to his daughter, Horatia, who had apparently been conceived onboard *Foudroyant* during the cruise Nelson had made with her to Malta. She was teasing him with the idea that Sir William was about to receive as a guest the Prince of Wales who was a notorious womanizer. His remaining eye was troubling him. It may be that he privately agreed with his friends who thought it would be well to get away to sea. On 1 January 1801 he was promoted to Vice Admiral and thirteen days later he left home, leaving Fanny for good. Whether or not his head wound had occasioned the lapse in his self-control at Naples, his loyalty had now been transferred to Emma and he was incapable of going back.

Initially he was appointed to the Channel

Fleet under the Earl of St Vincent, and hoisted his flag on the *San Josef*, the ship he had captured from the Spaniards, with Hardy as his flag captain. This may have been part of a cover story the Admiralty tried to establish, planting notices in the newspapers suggesting that Nelson was to be sent to the Dardanelles to chastise Russia.[8] The *San Josef*, a three-decker, was of too deep draft to be used in the Baltic. Nelson, however, had been warned that he should probably soon be moved into a smaller vessel. He was not kept waiting long for serious work. On 1 February he informed Emma that he had been ordered to change his ship for the *St George*, which had a draft shallow enough for the Baltic. After a brief leave during which he saw his new daughter, he sailed north to Yarmouth, where he arrived 6 March.

Pitt resigned because he was committed to the emancipation of the Catholics following the union of Ireland with England. George III refused to implement an agreement, which he believed violated his coronation oath, that Catholics would be entitled to take office. A relatively smooth transition was arranged, but the very quality which made Addington a successful Speaker, his accommodation of differing points of view, made his grasp of power uncertain. His first move, reasonably enough, was to make another effort to prevent the expansion of the war by sending an emissary by way of Hamburg to Copenhagen in response to an opening from the Prince of Hesse who was father-in-law to the Danish Crown Prince Frederick. The Crown Prince was effective sovereign of Denmark because of the imbecility of the king, Christian VII. Nicholas Vansittart, the recently appointed Joint Secretary of the Treasury who was entrusted with this mission, was instructed to offer Denmark an alliance, with a guarantee of a fleet of twenty sail-of-the-line to defend her against Russian resentment, in return for abandoning the League.

Very quickly, Addington and the new Foreign Secretary Lord Robert Hawkesbury were persuaded by a letter from the Danish Minister, Count Bernstorff, that Denmark would not be deflected from the pro-Russian policy without resort to force. When faced with the reality that the strategic power of the Royal Navy could only be secured by a confrontation with the Baltic states, the new administration quickly grasped the nettle.[9] However, their purpose remained firm only until after the departure of the fleet. On 17 March, before the guns started firing at Copenhagen, Addington was to make overtures to Napoleon for a peace treaty.

In the circumstances, Parker's aversion to discomfort and risk-taking was more strategically dangerous than would have been any impetuousness on the part of Nelson, especially because Nelson in fact was always a careful judge of technical difficulties. The speed with which Grenville had reacted to the news of the formation of the League had made it possible for the fleet to deal with Denmark before the ice was out of the harbours of Carlskrona, Reval and Kronstadt. Quick action would prevent the conjunction of the Russian and Swedish fleets with that of Denmark, and could make possible the destruction in detail not only of the Danish fleet, but of the Russian squadron at Kronstadt before the ice cleared enough to let it join that at Reval. A warning from Drummond that there was a possibility that the Netherlands would join the League further increased the need for quick action.[10] All this was put at risk by Parker's reluctance to get to sea.

To get the fleet ready for sea, St Vincent exercised an iron authority to break collective action on the part of the shipwrights in the Royal Dockyard, who demanded an 100 per cent increase in their already high wages. He had their delegates and all the leaders peremptorily dismissed. He had to be very nearly as firm with Parker.

St Vincent had written on his appointment that he had 'known many a good admiral make a wretched First Lord of the Admiralty. I will, however, support Commanders-in-chief upon all occasions, and prohibit any intrigue against them in this office'. Knowing his crusty old chief as he did, Nelson was careful to avoid the appearance of going behind

7. St Vincent to Nepean, *Naval Miscellany* II, p329.

8. *The Times* 13 January 1801.

9. Drummond to Grenville, 7, 14 February 1801; Vansittart's instructions; Bernstorff to British Government, 27 January 1801; Hawkesbury to Drummond 23 February No. 1; FO 22/40.

10. Drummond to Grenville, 20 January 1801, FO 22/40 no 4.

William Domett (1754-1828), Hyde Parker's Captain of the Fleet, later a Rear Admiral, as shown, and ultimately a full Admiral, by Robert Bowyer, artist, and William Ridley and William Hall, engravers. Published 31 January 1806 by Joyce Gold. (National Maritime Museum, London: PAD 3395)

Parker's back, and it is evident that he had a high regard for Parker personally although the latter was ill at ease with his brilliant junior. Nelson wrote a guarded letter warning that Parker 'is a little nervous about dark nights and fields of ice'. When Parker made it clear that he did not want to do anything so decisive as to discuss the forthcoming campaign with Nelson, and William Domett, his Captain of the Fleet made it clear that not all was right, Nelson made an indirect approach to the Board through Troubridge. His letters proved effective, peremptory orders were issued to Parker to sail, and St Vincent followed it up with a personal letter warning that any delay 'would do you irreparable injury'.[11] As the *Morning Post* put it, Parker was forced to 'leave his *sheet anchor* behind him'.[12] The ball his wife had organised had to be cancelled.

The fleet which had been brought together for the Baltic contained two three-deckers, Parker's *London* and Nelson's *St George*. There were eleven 74-gun third rates, and seven 64s with six sloops and frigates, besides small craft of which the most important were the bomb vessels which would provide Parker with the means to demolish the dockyard at Copenhagen if the threat alone did not prove sufficient. Several of the ships were still to the southward when Parker sailed. Unfortunately he left their orders at Yarmouth, rather than sending them to the Admiralty to be forwarded, or sending a dispatch boat to Sheerness. When Rear Admiral Totty arrived in *Invincible* it was wrecked with great loss of life on one of the bars off the harbour entrance. Captain Foley was more fortunate, and was eventually able to join the fleet off the Danish coast in the 74-gun *Elephant* on which Nelson was to fly his flag during the battle.

They carried with them 600 soldiers of the 48th regiment, under the command of Lieutenant-Colonel William Stewart. He proved to be a thoroughly efficient and aggressive soldier quite after Nelson's own heart, and the journal he kept of the expedition provides a valuable insight into its events and personalities.[13] The soldiers were paid as supernumeraries, giving them the status of marines which enabled them to be employed about the ships, and to receive a share of any prize money.

Parker had been given the help of several talented people. The Reverend Alexander John Scott, later to become famous because of his account of Nelson's death at Trafalgar, joined Parker's flagship as a translator. Captain Nicholas Tomlinson joined as a volunteer. He had been serving in the Imperial Russian Navy, but had resigned and returned home when it looked as if there might be war between Britain and France. He was exceedingly well informed about Baltic naval affairs, and advised the Admiralty that at Copenhagen, Kronstadt and Reval the roadstead was so open that fleets could not be adequately protected by batteries. Nelson was also provided with an expert on Baltic navigation, another Briton who had been in service in the Imperial Russian Navy. Captain Frederick Thesiger had had a distinguished career, but had resigned because of dissatisfaction with service under Tsar Paul, and had escaped when he was denied a passport and his back pay.

Only after receiving the order to sail did Parker issue his captains with orders of sailing and of battle. Domett had prepared drafts, which Parker only now looked at. Why he did so can only be surmised, but he placed a 64-gun ship and a 50 together in the van under Nelson instead of the two 74s that Domett, and Nelson, considered appropriate. When Domett protested, Parker told him to place a 74 between them, but a 64 ought not have been placed in the van, and a 50 was unsuitable for the line. When facing a superior enemy, which Parker was unlikely to have to do, a 50 might have to take a place in the line but the more common practice was to use them as a reserve to reinforce the line as required. Of course, Parker could always have ordered the smaller vessels to fall out of the line, but even so, there was little reason to place them even nominally in the van. In the Baltic Parker could expect to need the smaller ships because of their shallower draft.[14] In the event, and perhaps fortunately, he did not have to fight a fleet action at sea.

The 'Gunboat' Phase

Soon after the fleet cleared Yarmouth, Parker received his instructions to make a settlement with the Danish Government, either by 'amicable arrangement, or by actual hostilities'. Vansittart was to conduct the diplomacy, and he was to give them 48 hours to withdraw from the League or face the consequences. Parker was 'to make such a disposition of the ships under his command as in his judgment may appear most likely to ensure the success of the attempt it will be his duty to make (should all proposals for conciliation fail) to destroy the Arsenal . . . with the whole of the shipping in that port'. Once the threat from the Danish fleet had been eliminated, Parker was to attack the Russians at Reval, and follow up with an attack on the Swedish fleet at Kronstadt.[15]

The task was formidable, and could only become more formidable by delay, but Parker was not a man for vigorous measures. Despite favourable winds Parker made a slow and careful passage to the Sound, and Vansittart's meeting with Bernstorff took place before the fleet was even in sight of the Danish coast. Whether the Danes would have been intimidated by the sight of Parker's ships lying to anchor close off-shore cannot be known, but as it was, Bernstorff was unimpressed and preferred to parade his contempt for Britain in letters meant to be read by Napoleon. The news of Pitt's resignation, and that King George was seriously ill, helped to convince that the British establishment was determined to make peace with Napoleon, and that it would be safe to call their bluff. He did not allow for the possibility that Addington would vacillate, and commit forces to taking strong measures only a few weeks before he made peace overtures.

Danish constitutional development was behind that of Britain. Although the king was a cipher because of his imbecility, Crown Prince Frederick controlled both foreign and defence policy. His advisors could acquire considerable influence, however, as the Bernstorff family had for two generations. It was the Crown Prince who made the decisions, but Bernstorff ensured that Vansittart never had an audience.

Danish foreign policy customarily regarded Britain as a friend and trading partner. It was Russia which had been the focus of attention in Copenhagen because of the Tsars' longstanding ambitions in the Baltic, and the British were convinced that it was fear of Russia which lay behind the Danish pro-Russian policy. Drummond had earlier reported his conviction that 'this Court [of Denmark] is under the greatest dread and embarrassment, and already repents of its rash appeal to Russia last Autumn'. The regret was not lessened by the sudden decision of the mad Tsar Paul to expel the Danish ambassador and recall his own. This was occasioned by a declaration by the Danish court that it would take no part against Britain, but the inner story only became known to Nelson after the attack on Copenhagen had been made. Bernstorff, however, had been the chief advocate of the League with Russia, and was careful to keep a line of retreat open to France. Drummond reported that he was incoherent in his anger with Britain, because his own political influence was threatened.

The revolution in France, and Napoleon's conquests in central Europe, had added fear of and admiration for France to the fear of Russia. Tsar Paul's newfound admiration for Napoleon was the last straw. Bernstorff's policy was one of appeasement, and Danish politicians were eager to appear well in the light of the rising French sun. They were committed to their new pro-Russian and pro-French alignment, and it was difficult in Copenhagen to appreciate that Danish policy was converting Britain into the most immediate danger of all.[16]

Having been too late to support Vansittart's first meeting with Bernstorff, Parker compounded the fault. Instead of immediately running past the batteries of guns at Elsinore

11. St Vincent to Lord Keith, 21 February 1801, J S Tucker II p175; Nelson to St Vincent, 1 March 1801, DLN IV p291, and to Troubridge 4-11 March, *Naval Miscellany* I pp415-19; St Vincent to Parker, 11 March 2:30pm, *St Vincent* I pp86-87.

12. *Morning Post*, 31 January 1801.

13. Colonal Stewart's Journal, DNL IV pp299-312.

14. Nelson to Troubridge, 13 March 1801, *Naval Miscellany* I p420.

15. Dundas to Admiralty, 23 February 1801, ADM 1/4186.

16. Drummond to Grenville, 6 and 20 January 1801, FO 22/40 nos. 2 and 4; Minutes of a Conversation between Count Bernstorff and Messrs. Drummond and Vansittart, 14 March 1801, Add MS 38537; Drummond to Hawkesbury, 14 March 1801, FO 22/40.

where the Kattegat narrows into the Sound a few miles north of Copenhagen, Parker sent a frigate, *Blanche*, ahead on 19 March to Elsinore Roads to take the last ministerial note from Hawkesbury to Drummond and Vansittart, to be delivered to Bernstorff in its original English. All this time Nelson had been kept in the dark about Parker's orders, and his plans to carry them out, but what be observed made him skeptical that they would be effective. To Troubridge Nelson had written on the 16th that he believed the place for the British fleet during the negotiations was directly outside Copenhagen where that 'fellow' would have seen 'our flags waving every moment he lifted his head', and the threat of action against the Danish fleet and dockyard could not be ignored.[17] To his prizes agent Davison he wrote

All I have gathered of our first plans, I disapprove most exceedingly; honour may arise from them, good cannot. I hear we are likely to anchor outside Cronenburgh Castle, instead of Copenhagen which would give weight to our negotiation: a Danish minister would think twice before he put his name to war with England, when the next moment he would probably see his master's fleet in flames, and his capital in ruins; but out of sight is out of mind, is an old saying. The Dane should see our flag waving every moment he lifted his head.[18]

The belief that Kronborg castle at Elsinore could prevent any fleet reaching Copenhagen was a contributing factor to the Danish conviction that they had little to fear from Britain. In reality, its batteries were only able to command the western half of the channel. Only if the Swedish battery on the eastern side of the channel at Halsingborg cooperated with Kronborg did the passage become at all dangerous, and in fact the Swedes had few guns mounted. Sweden had once been united with the Danish crown, but she was now an independent state, and it was far from certain that she would cooperate. Although they were joined by the League in defence of neutral rights, the commitment had been entered into without much expectation that it could lead to serious blows. Sweden was not seeking conflict.

The fleet was still above the battery when Drummond forwarded Hawkesbury's note, and Bernstorff continued to act as though he believed the British to be bluffing, or at any rate offering no immediate danger. The note was returned with the acid comment that it should have been written in French, as was the diplomatic custom, and with it came the passports for Drummond and Vansittart to permit their departure. They had done what they could. At Elsinore they boarded *Blanche* together with British nationals who thought it best to leave.

Nelson wrote Troubridge shortly before reaching the anchorage off the Koll at the southern end of the Kattegat where it narrows into the Sound that he had 'not had a bulkhead in the ship since last Saturday. It is not so much their being in the way, as to prepare people's minds that we are going at it, and that they should have no other thought but how they may best annoy their enemies'.[19] Parker's mind was not similarly fortified, and the reports of Danish preparations that Vansittart and Drummond brought intimidated him. To their untrained civilian eyes the threat seemed formidable. Because he had not sent *Blanche* to Copenhagen, but only as far as Elsinore, he had denied himself the intelligence she could have acquired of the Danish defences of the capital. But Captain Hamond had been well placed to observe the batteries at Elsinore, and Lieutenant McCulloch, who had carried the dispatches, had made the trip to Copenhagen and had had opportunity to make observations. Parker did not send for them to make a report. His fears were increased by the reluctance of his civilian pilots to take the fleet past Elsinore.

Nelson believed that Parker had decided to wait in the Kattegat for the Danes to come out and fight. Late on the 23rd, however, he was asked to came onboard Parker's flagship, *London*, for a conference with the Commander-in-Chief and Vansittart. No notes

17. Nelson to Troubridge, 16 March 1801, *Naval Miscellany* I pp420-21.

18. Nelson to Davison, 16 March 1801, Egerton MSS Add 2240, f 62 No. 28; Clarke and M'Arthur (1840) II p386; DLN IV p294.

19. Nelson to Troubridge, 20 March 1801, *Naval Miscellany* I p421-22.

20. Vansittart to Nelson, 8 April 1801, Morrison p556.

21. Nelson to Troubridge, 29 March 1801, *Naval Miscellany* I p424-25; Domett to Lord Bridport, 4 May 1801, Add MS 35201, Bridport Papers.

22. *Historical Memoir of Sir Robert Waller Otway*, London, 1840 p20.

were kept. Nelson warned that the lateness of the season meant that there was a real threat that the Russian and Swedish fleets would join the Danish before it ventured into the Sound to challenge the British. He also was able to ascertain from questioning Vansittart that the defences of Copenhagen were less formidable from the south. His preference was for running the battery of Elsinore, and then rounding to off Copenhagen to attack the tail of the Danish line, as eventually he was to do.

But Parker had become so intimidated by the prospect that he grasped at the straw presented by Captain Murray's recent survey of the Great Belt to prefer the 200-mile circuitous route which would eventually make it possible to approach Copenhagen without passing Elsinore. Nelson apparently accepted the plan without making a strong protest, and perhaps even encouraged it, because he felt that otherwise Parker was determined to remain where he was. The route through the Belts was less disadvantageous if ultimately the British fleet were to leave the Danes and sail directly to deal with the Russians, as Nelson recommended. When Vansittart reported to Addington, the latter said he fully supported Nelson in his position.[20]

Nelson, probably incorrectly, blamed Domett for favouring the Belts route, but when on the morning of the 25th the fleet tacked away from its anchorage and it became apparent the route it was taking, Domett became alarmed. He later wrote to Lord Bridport that he pointed out to the Admiral that if the fleet did pass through the Belts and reach Kioge Bay

south of Copenhagen it would be impossible for the larger ships to get north to Copenhagen because southerly gales reduced the depth of water. The attack would have to be made by 64s and smaller, and the Danes would know that under no circumstances could they be reinforced.[21] He credited himself with persuading Parker to change his mind. London's captain, Robert Waller Otway, later made virtually the same claim, based on the same argument. Parker, he told his biographer, was not 'a man to persevere in an error when pointed out'.[22]

In fact Parker did not immediately change the fleet's heading, but he did send Otway to ask Nelson onboard London, and Nelson brought Captain Murray with him. Nelson had been drafting a letter to Parker explaining why the Sound was a better route, and he now read it to him. Time was of the essence. The Danes were getting stronger every day, and the probability of being supported by the Russians and Swedes increasing. He warned the old man he had

almost the safety, certainly the honour of England more entrusted to you than ever yet fell the lot of any British officer: on your decision depends whether our country shall be degraded in the eyes of Europe or whether she shall rear her head higher than ever: again do I repeat, never did our country depend so much on the success of a Fleet as on this. How best to honour our Country and abate the pride of her Enemies, by defeating their schemes, must

The British fleet passing up the Sound, 28 March 1801, with a view of Copenhagen below, by Robinson Kittoe who was secretary to Rear Admiral Thomas Graves who was second-in-command under Nelson during the action. (National Maritime Museum, London: PAH 4028)

be the subject of your deepest consideration as commander-in-chief; and if what I have to offer can be the least useful in forming your decision, you are most heartily welcome. . . . The measure may be thought bold, but I am of opinion the boldest measures are the safest.[23]

Nelson's tact and rhetoric was successful. His offer to take a detachment of ten ships to attack the Russians while the main fleet dealt with the Danes was rejected, but eventually Parker agreed to the route down the Sound. The fleet put about, and by sunset was anchored a few miles south of their previous day's position.

Parker's aloofness from Nelson, which perhaps had been occasioned by the public's much greater estimation of the junior admiral, virtually disappeared after the decision had been made. It was now agreed that Nelson should command a squadron of shallower draft ships to make the attack on the Danish position, and on the 27th he transferred his flag into *Elephant* commanded by Tom Foley.

Parker visited him in his new ship shortly after his own arrival, which is a clear indication that he had become more comfortable with his subordinate.

The fleet's progress continued, nonetheless, to be almost glacial. It was the 29th before Parker reached Elsinore, where he entered into negotiations with the governor of the castle, who eventually made it clear that he would fire on the British fleet if it came into range. This Parker warned would be taken as a declaration of war. In the exchange of letters an opening was made, authorised directly by the Crown Prince, for a renewal of the ministerial proposal of which Parker had a copy. The governor made time by using couriers to carry his letters, instead of transmitting them by shutter telegraph between Elsinore and the capital.[24] Instead of doing so, however, he simply invited the Danes to make a proposal of their own. Had Nelson been informed of the contents of the letters it is hard to believe that he would not have made better use of the opportunity to negotiate from a position of strength. His conduct throughout this cam-

Copenhagen, passage of the Sound, by Robert Dodd (1748-1815). (National Maritime Museum, London: BHC 0522)

paign revealed that he was far more than just a fire-eating admiral.

While the messengers were hurrying up and down the road between Elsinore and Copenhagen, the bomb vessels under the direction of Captain Murray were taking up their position to enfilade the Danish batteries. On the morning of the 30th the fleet finally made the passage to Copenhagen. It was fired on, but the Swedes did not open fire from their shore. They, and the Prussians, had already begun the scramble to distance themselves from the League, which was looking less like safe policy as the days passed. In consequence Parker was able to make his way without loss from the guns at extreme range. Most of the British ships did not return fire. The bomb vessels showered the batteries with mortar fire, but as Colonel Stewart wrote, 'as is usually the case in sea bombardments, little or no damage was afterwards found to have been done by our shells'.[25]

Nelson's Tactics

By ten o'clock on the night of 30 March Parker was anchored close north of Copenhagen, and he, Nelson, Rear Admiral Thomas Graves, Captain Domett, and Colonel Stewart boarded Captain Riou's frigate *Amazon* to reconnoitre the enemy position. There are similarities between the tactical problem facing the British fleet at Copenhagen, and that which Nelson had so decisively mastered at Aboukir Bay. In both cases, the British had to attack an anchored line of enemy warships, reinforced by shore batteries. In both cases, the navigational difficulties were considerable, and only partly charted. Copenhagen harbour enters the Sound at an oblique angle and the coast is fringed with mud-flats. Off shore a middle ground restricted the anchorage to a quarter mile width, and forced an approach from north or south. Along this inner channel, south of the harbour mouth, the Danish fleet lay moored in line ahead. In the harbour entrance, and in the fairway were moored four two-deckers, two of them hulked, a frigate and two 18-gun brigs.

Midshipman William Millard of *Monarch* wrote that

The appearance of the enemy was not a little terrific. A long line, consisting of eighteen ships of all descriptions, several of them line-of-battle ships, was moored on a flat before the town, flanked on their right by a battery upon the Isle of Amak, and on their left by two large batteries on artificial islands mounting eighty-eight [sic] pieces of cannon (24-pounders); these are called the Crown Islands, and are very formidable from their strength and situation. Between these and the shore was moored a second line of hulks and men-of-war to protect that approach to the town.

The Danish position was stronger than had been that taken by the French in Aboukir Bay, because of the great Trekroner ('Three Crowns') battery built on piles at the mouth of the harbour and armed with sixty-eight brass 36- and 24pdrs. The timber bulwarks were backed by thick earth berms and there were furnaces for heating the shot red hot. Its only weakness was that the gunners had no overhead protection from shell fire, so that if the lines of blockships were put out of action, allowing bomb vessels to be brought into range, it would be vulnerable. A smaller fort enfiladed the Trekroner to protect it from assault, and on shore there were batteries which had the Roads at the fairly long range of between 1,500 and 2,000 yards. The Danes had an arsenal behind them, and a city, so that they were able to draft additional men into ships to replace casualties. The time wasted by Parker had enabled them to strengthen their position considerably.

23. Nelson to Admiralty, Admiral's Despatches, Baltic Fleet, ADM 1/4 f. Ha 48a; Clarke & M'Arthur (1840) II p387. DLN IV pp294-298.

24. Millard, *Macmillan's Magazine*, June 1895, pp81-93.

25. Clarke & M'Arthur (1840) II p392.

List of ships present at Copenhagen

NELSON'S COMMAND

La Désirée *(frigate)*	40	Captain H Inman
Polyphemus	64	Captain J Lawford
Russell	74	Captain W Cuming
Isis	50	Captain J Walker
Bellona	74	Captain T B Thompson
Edgar	74	Captain G Murray
Ardent	64	Captain T Bertie
Glatton	54	Captain W Bligh
Elephant	74	Vice Admiral Lord Nelson, Captain T Foley
Ganges	74	Captain T F Fremantle
Monarch	74	Captain J R Mosse
Defiance	74	Rear Admiral Sir T Graves, Captain R Retalick
Amazon *(frigate)*	38	Captain E Riou
Blanche *(frigate)*	36	Captain G E Hamond
Alcmene *(frigate)*	32	Captain S Sutton
Arrow *(sloop)*	30	Captain W Bolton
Dart *(sloop)*	30	Captain J F Devonshire
Zephyr *(sloop)*	14	Captain C Upton
Otter *(sloop)*	14	Captain G MacKinley
Agamemnon	64	Captain R D Fancourt
7 bomb vessels		

DANISH

Provesteenen	56	Captain Lassen
Wagrien	48	Aide-de-Camp Risbrigh
Rendsborg	20	Captain Lieutenant Egede
Nyborg	20	Captain Lieutenant Rothe
Jylland	48	Captain Brandt
Svaerdfisken	20	Lieutenant Somerfeldt
Kronborg	22	Lieutenant Hauch
Indfodsretten	64	Captain Thura
Hayen	20	Captain Moller
Elven	6	Lieutenant Holstein
Gerner Radeau	24	Captain Willemoes
Dannebroge	62	Commodore Fischer, Captain F Braun
Aggershuus	20	Lieutenant Fasting
Charlotte Amalia	26	Captain Kofod
Holsteen	60	Captain Ahrenfeldt
Saelland	74	Captain Harboe
Hjelperen	20	Captain Lieutenant Lilienskiold

Three Crowns Battery, mounting 160 guns
A frigate ready for sea
Two ships of the line ready for sea
Two ships of the line
Two gun brigs
Armed schooners and vessels

Apart from the shore batteries, however, the firepower of the Danish fleet was less than that of the 74s, 80s, and 110-gun ships Vice Admiral Brueys commanded at the Nile. The smaller Danish units, the pontoons and floating batteries, mounted only nine to twelve guns on a side, although they were considerable forces because they were so low to the water that they were difficult for a ship of the line to engage at close range. Because they had no deckhead, their crews could work the guns without crouching, and were less exposed to injury from splinters. Originally the floating batteries had been placed slightly further from the channel, staggering the line, but when it was seen how many ships the British had the line was straightened so that the hulks would be less exposed. The strong crews of the Danish ships, reinforced to more than full complement and fighting not only under the eye of their sovereign but in defence of homes which could easily be seen any time they looked over their shoulders, were what made the guns of the Danish fleet a formidable force. The head of the Danish line to the northward was strongest, with four 64s close to the Trekroner battery. Two 74s and three 64s were spaced along the rest of the line.

The Crown Prince's control of the military was exercised directly, without the appointment of a commander in chief for the navy. Command of the ships in the Roads had been given to Commodore Johan Olfert Fischer, whom Nelson had met when they were both serving in the West Indies in 1786 and 1787. Captain Steen Bille had been put in command of the squadron defending the entrance of the harbour, and also controlled the light vessels supporting Fischer's ships. The Crown Prince expected to exercise overall command from the shore.

The Danish defence plan had a major weakness. It relied entirely upon defending the position without any manoeuvering, even of the most obvious and undemanding kind. Like Brueys, Commodore Fischer had made no provision for swinging his ships so that they could fire down the channel at an advancing enemy. It is difficulty to believe that an attack

26. For example, see the orders to Colonel Draper, 21 January 1762, CO 77/20.

27. Nelson to Spencer, 17 January 1801, DLN IV, pp274-5.

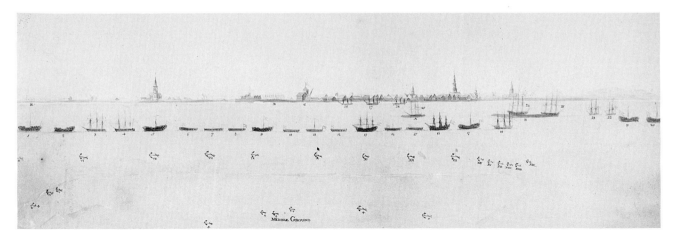

would have succeeded had he done so, or if the lines had been moored across the channels rather than along them, if it is remembered how difficult were the navigational problems. Steen Bille had placed his ships in the harbour entrance with even less regard to effective gunnery. Two of them were so clearly in the middle of the channel that it invited attacking British ships to pass north of them where they would be screened from the guns of the Trekroner battery. The Danish navy had evidently learnt nothing from reading accounts of the battle of the Nile.

Neither did the Danes use their flotilla to harass the British during their approach. They pulled up all the buoys marking the channel, but did not keep guard boats patrolling at night to prevent them being replaced. Perhaps if Crown Prince Frederick had given command of the fleet to a naval officer the defence would have been more active: as it was, the British were able to conduct the attack at the time and place of their choosing.

The Danish defence plan had assumed that the attack would be from the north, possibly with a diversionary attack around the Middle Ground. Even after Nelson moved the attack force to its final anchorage at the southern end of the shoal, the Danes apparently continued to believe that the attack would come from the north where Parker lay with the larger ships. This misjudgment, however, hardly explains the failure to ensure that the batteries of the moored ships could be used to best effect.

Spencer had told Nelson in January that

consideration was being given to providing a landing force of 10,000 men, and there is little doubt that a spirited action by such an army could have taken possession of the Danish arsenal, perhaps without heavy losses. However, there had been a serious impediment. The general best capable of undertaking the command of the landed solders was considered to be Major-General John Simcoe, but Hyde Parker had quarrelled with Simcoe, and with several other senior officers, during his command at Jamaica. In the Seven Years War the army and navy had learnt to cooperate well, and it had become common practice to place in the instructions sent to commanders the caution that 'the Success of this Expedition will very much depend upon an Entire good Understanding between Our Land and Sea Officers'.[26] Later experience had amply confirmed that any incompatibility between navy and army commanders would be fatal to success. Nelson had advised both Spencer and St Vincent that, as the admiral and the general were unable to cooperate, it would be better to do the job without troops. In consequence the operation against the Danish fleet would have to be a naval affair with only a limited provision for the use of soldiers.[27] The 600 men of the 48th regiment were available should it be necessary to storm one of the batteries, and were deployed in flat-boats towed by the ships of the line. In the event, they were not employed.

Parker's orders called for him to destroy the fleet and arsenal, if that was necessary to

View of the battle of Copenhagen, 2 April 1801, by Robinson Kittoe. (National Maritime Museum, London: PAH 4029)

coerce the Danes. Copenhagen was very vulnerable to bombardment from the Sound. It would only have been necessary to defeat the southernmost units of the Danish fleet to have been able to bring bomb vessels within range. Subsequently accusations were made that Nelson threatened to bombard the town itself, but clearly that was never in his mind, nor was ever intended.

Parker recorded in his journal that he found the enemy's line more formidable than he had expected, but Nelson's opinion was that the Danish defences were only formidable 'to those who are children at war, . . . with ten sail-of-the-line I think I can annihilate them; at all event', he added in a letter to Emma, 'I hope to be allowed to try'.[28] Nelson perceived, as he had anticipated, that he needed to attack the Danish position from the south, at the rear of the Danish line. Parker dictated orders for Nelson to take the ships under his command for the purpose of making the attack, but before finally committing himself he made another reconnaissance the next day, and summoned a council of war made up not only of himself, Nelson, and Rear Admiral Thomas Graves, but Captains Domett, Fremantle, Foley, Murray and Riou and Colonel Stewart. Colonel Stewart later wrote:

> During this Council of War, the energy of Lord Nelson's character was remarked: certain difficulties had been started by some of the members, relative to each of the three Powers we should either have to engage, in succession or united, in those seas. The number of Russians was, in particular, represented as formidable. Lord Nelson kept pacing the cabin, mortified at everything which savoured either of alarm or irresolution. When the above remark was applied to the Swedes, he sharply observed, 'The more numerous the better'; and when to the Russians he repeatedly said; 'So much the better, I wish they were twice as many; the easier the victory, depend on it'. He alluded, as he afterwards explained in private, to the total want of tactique among the Northern Fleets; and to his intention, whenever he

should bring either the Swedes or Russians to Action, of attacking the head of their Line, and confusing their movements as much as possible. He used to say: 'Close with a Frenchman, but out-manoeuvre a Russian'.

Parker asked the Council whether in their opinion an attack should be made, and according to Domett, Rear Admiral Graves was decidedly against. Domett, as youngest officer, had previously given his opinion that an attack should be made, and of course Nelson was strongly for doing so. The upshot was that Parker decided to accept Nelson's offer, but gave him twelve ships instead of the ten he requested, and all the small craft.[29]

Thomas Fremantle, his old friend and veteran of Tenerife who was personally in charge of the landing craft, grabbed the chance to get his ship, *Ganges*, added to the striking force.[30] Hardy joined *Elephant* as a volunteer. The remaining ships of the squadron included *Edgar* under Murray who was a close friend, and would later be Nelson's chief of staff in the Mediterranean. Another Nile veteran, Sir Thomas Thompson, commanded *Bellona*. Captain Bertie of the *Ardent* had been in the East Indies with Nelson as a young man. Riou had proved himself an exemplary frigate captain, and *Glatton* (56) was commanded by that superb seaman but ineffective leader, William Bligh who had survived mutiny in the Pacific and an epic voyage in an open boat. *Glatton* was a converted merchant ship with an experimental armament of 42- and 68pdr carronades on her gun decks.

The operational objective was to clear the way for a bombardment of the naval dockyard by engaging and defeating the line of moored warships and batteries. In this way, if the Danish government could not be intimidated into complying with British demands that they separate themselves from the Russian alliance, they could at all events be rendered unable to interfere with British trade control. The greatest weakness of the plan was that the ships remaining directly under Parker's command played no effective part in the

28. Parker's Journal, 6 April, ADM 1/4, f6, Ha 55, ff217-19; Nelson's letter book—to Lady Hamilton, 30 March 1801, Morrison, No. 551 I p132.

29. C & M (1840) II 394 and DLN IV 303; Domett to Lord Bridport, 4 May 1801, Add MS 35201, Bridport Papers.

30. Fremantle to Marquis of Buckingham, 4 April 1801, *Wynne* p315.

31. Clark and M'Arthur (1840) II pp266-67, DLN IV p312.

32. DLN IV, p304; C & M (1840) II p397.

action. It was intended that they should support Nelson's thrust from the south by engaging the Trekroner from the north, but they were moored too far away, and Parker did not think to bring them closer. Although a south-westerly breeze could bring Nelson's force into action a quarter of an hour after it left its anchorage, it would oblige Parker's ships to cover 23 miles tacking. Clearly Nelson thought he was lucky to have got orders to make the attack with the forces he controlled, and felt it best not to worry Parker with the thought that he should move closer to the 'very formidable' Danish defences.

To attack from the south, Nelson needed a northerly breeze to take his ships south past the middle ground, and then a southerly to take him up the Danish line. In this respect, he was extremely fortunate. At 7am on 1 April he reconnoitered the outer channel in *Amazon*, and then went onboard *London* to receive last-minute instructions from Parker. The channel had been surveyed and buoyed in the previous nights. Mr Ferguson, surgeon in the *Elephant*, wrote that

> As *his* was the invigorating spirit of the Council that planned the attack, so in the execution *he* only could have commanded success. During the interval that preceeded the Battle, I could only silently admire when I saw the first man in the world spend the hours of the day and night in Boats, amidst floating ice, and in the severest weather; and wonder when the light showed me a path marked by buoys, which had been trackless the preceeding evening.[31]

At 2:30pm he signalled his squadron to sail and by nightfall it was safely anchored off the southern end of the middle ground. During the night the wind shifted to the south, and he was able to attack in the morning.

'As soon as the Fleet was at anchor,' wrote Stewart,

> the gallant Nelson sat down to table with a large party of his comrades in arms. He was in the highest spirits, and drank to a leading

wind, and to the success of the ensuing day. Captains Foley, Hardy, Fremantle, Riou, Inman, his Lordship's Second in Command, Admiral Graves and a few others to whom he was particularly attached, were of this interesting party; from which every man separated with feelings of admiration for their great leader, and with anxious impatience to follow him to the approaching Battle.[32]

This was his last opportunity to pass on his tactical plans in person, and the fact that he was able to do so is testimony to the passivity of the Danish defence. He was also able to send Captain Hardy to sound the channel in the King's Deep where Fischer's ships lay, and place buoys.

He did not depend entirely on verbal instructions, however, or leave his captains with the great tactical responsibility which had been appropriate when acting in haste against the French at Aboukir. He spent the rest of the evening writing orders with his left hand and with the help of Thomas Foley and Edward Riou. With the Danes in fixed and observable positions, it was possible for him to be quite meticulous in assigning tasks to his captains, and he did so. There was no possibility that the Danes would be able to discount the tactical surprise Nelson had achieved by moving to attack the rear of their line. Haste was only

Thomas Allen, Nelson's Servant, painted by John Burnet (1784-1868) c1832 when Allen was a pensioner at Greenwich Hospital. (National Maritime Museum, London: BHC 2510).

Plan of Attack by the British Squadron under the command of Vice Admiral Lord Nelson against the Danish line of defence off Copenhagen, 2nd Day of April 1801. (National Maritime Museum, London: PAD 4062)

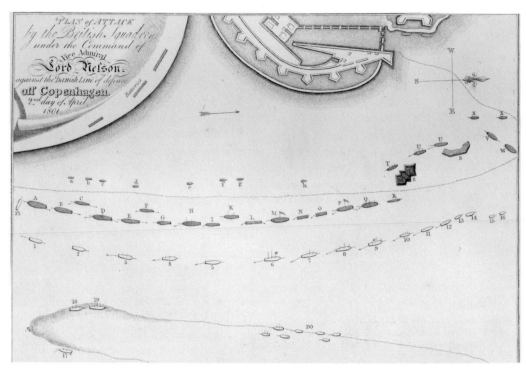

Plan of the battle of Copenhagen, by John Ninham, engraver, and I D Downes, publisher. (National Maritime Museum, London: PAD 4063)

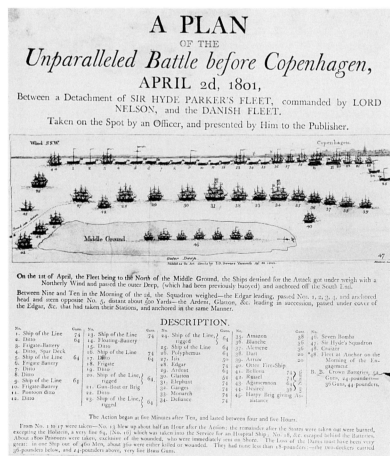

necessary because of the expected change of the wind. 'From the previous fatigue of this day', Stewart continued,

and of the two preceding, Lord Nelson was so much exhausted while dictating his instructions, that it was recommended to him by us all, and, indeed, insisted upon by his old servant, Allen, who assumed much command on these occasions, that he should go to his cot. It was placed on the floor, but from it he still continued to dictate.

He only went to sleep at 1am, leaving six clerks to copy out the letters. At 7.37am the captains of the squadron were signalled, using the new Admiralty Day Signal Book of 1799, and each received a copy of his own orders.

The pilots, who had been ordered on board *Elephant*, were very unhappy about taking ships of the line up the narrow channel under fire. They were more used to the smaller Baltic traders, and they were right to be concerned. Hardy had discovered that the channel was deepest near the Danish line, but the pilots could not be persuaded. Nelson later wrote caustically that he had 'experienced the misery of having the honour of our country entrusted to a set of pilots who had no other thought than to keep the ships clear of danger, and their own silly heads clear of shot'. Stewart wrote in his journal: 'Not a moment was to be lost; the wind was fair, and the signal made for action. Lord Nelson urged them to be steady, to be resolute, and to decide.' Alexander Briarly, the master of the *Bellona* who had piloted *Audacious* at the Nile, eventually declared himself ready to lead the squadron in, and was transferred to *Edgar*. The rest fell in line.[33] The signal was made to weigh anchor in succession at 9:30am according to Nelson's journal, or 10:00am according to *Elephant*'s master's log.

The plan was that the leading ship, *Edgar*, should make her way along the Danish line firing into each ship until she reached the fifth, the 64-gun ship *Jylland*. She was to anchor there, and the two succeeding ship were to follow, pass her on the disengaged side, and anchor in succession, *Ardent* alongside the frigate *Kronborg* and a battery, and *Glatton* alongside the 64-gun *Dannebroge*, Fischer's flagship under the command of Captain Ferdinand Braun. By the time they did so, the first four Danish ships would have endured the broadsides of three ships of the line in passing, and they were then to be closely engaged by numbers four and five in the British line, *Isis* and *Agamemnon*, which were to anchor opposite the Danish number two, a hulked 64, and number one, the 74-gun *Provesteenen*. The frigate *Désirée* was to follow *Agamemnon* and take a position to rake number two, and the remaining ships

33. Nelson to St Vincent, 29 September 1801, DLN IV pp499-500; Colonel Stewart's Journal, DNL IV pp299-312; and Master Briarly's log, ADM 52/2396.

A Plan of the battle of Copenhagen, July 4th 1804, J Nelles, engraver, R Colburn, publisher.

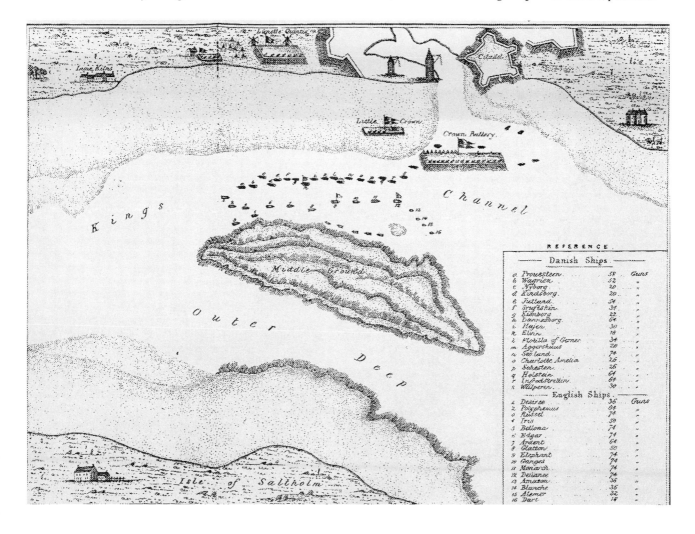

Battle of Copenhagen, 2 April 1801, by Nicholas Pocock (1740-1821). (National Maritime Museum, London: BHC 0525)

were to sail up the disengaged side of the anchored British line, firing when they could, and anchor in succession in reverse order beyond the *Glatton*. This should have eventually brought the last ship, *Polyphemus*, to the head of the Danish line.

If and when the first four Danish ships were subdued, *Isis* and *Agamemnon* were to cut their cables and pass on to engage the Trekroner battery. Flat boats were ready to carry soldiers to storm it. Seven bomb vessels were detailed to take positions close to the middle ground where they could fire shells over the British ships at the Danish ships and into the arsenal. Captain Riou's frigates and sloops were to pass all the way up the line and support the ships attacking the battery. Nelson had ordered his captains to prepare to

anchor by the stern, with springs on their warps so that they could swing to engage.

Perhaps surprisingly, he did not order his ships to take the Danish line on both sides, as had happened at the Nile. He did not know whether there was enough depth of water to permit this, and the fact that the Danish ships were moored, and not lying to a single anchor as the French had done in Aboukir Bay, meant that they could have been placed right at the edge of a bank. In fact, there was deep water on both sides of the Danish line. Nelson did not explain his reasons for preferring to confine the attack to the outer side of the Danish line, but an important consideration was the batteries along the shore. To seaward of the Danes, these batteries were partly masked, and were at considerably greater range.

Battle of Copenhagen, 2 April 1801, by Robert Dodd (1748-1815). (National Maritime Museum, London: BHC 0530)

The Battle

Midshipman Millard in the *Monarch*, wrote about the awful moments before the battle:

> As soon as reports had been delivered from all parts of the ship that everything was prepared for action, the men were ordered to breakfast. As the gunners' cabin, where I usually messed, was all cleared away, I went into the starboard cockpit berth, . . . When we left the berth [after eating], we had to pass all the dreadful preparations of the surgeons. One table was covered with instruments of all shapes and sizes; another, of more than usual strength, was placed in the middle of the cockpit: as I had never seen these produced before, I could not help asking the use of it, and received for answer 'that it was to cut off legs and wings upon'. One of the surgeon's men (called Loblolly Boys) was spreading yards and yards of bandages about six inches wide, which he told me was to clap onto my back. My reader will be surprised and perhaps a little shocked at the conversations, or more properly dialogues, which passed between the surgeons' mates and the midshipmen as the latter went on deck to quarters. . . .
>
> A man-of-war under sail is at all times a beautiful object, but at such a time the scene is heightened beyond the powers of description. We saw [*Edgar*] pressing on through the enemy's fire and manoeuvering in the midst of it to gain her station; our minds were deeply impressed with awe, and not a word was spoken throughout the ship but by the pilot and the helmsman, and their communications being chanted very much in the same manner as the responses in our cathedral service, and repeated at intervals, added very much to the solemnity.[34]

The Danes were unable to fire on the head of the line until they drew opposite the rear of their own, but it did not take long for the *Edgar* to come under fire as she worked her way up the Danish line to her position opposite the *Jylland*, where she anchored at 11am. Murray had ordered his gun crews to hold their fire until the ship reached its intended station, so that the first carefully loaded and double shotted broadside should be reserved for the ship they had to defeat. Because the pilots were unwilling to take their ships as close to the Danish line as Nelson had intended, *Ardent* had to pass between *Edgar* and the Danish ship to take her station. Then *Glatton* took the third station, opposite *Dannebroge* on which was flying Olfert Fischer's pendant.

At this point, however, the friction of war intervened. Nelson's old ship, the 64-gun *Agamemnon*, was unable to weather the middle ground. Warned of her danger by a signal from Nelson, she anchored out of range of the enemy, and despite strenuous efforts to warp clear was unable to get around the end of the shoal against wind and current. She never got into action. Nelson ordered *Polyphemus* to take her station astern of the *Isis*, to deal with the *Provesteenen*, the last ship in the Danish line, and the first to be reached by the British advancing from the south. This meant that the light craft engaging the Trekroner at the other end of the line would have less support. In the best tradition of mutual support, Captain James Walker also took independent action in response to *Agamemnon*'s inability by anchoring *Isis* short of his position so that he could engage both his own objective, *Wagrien*, and *Agamemnon*'s, *Provesteenen*. The captain of the frigate *Désirée*, Henry Inman, was under orders to place herself athwart *Provesteenen*'s bow, which in consequence came under a very heavy fire indeed.

The conviction of the pilots that the deepest water must be near the Middle Ground, despite Hardy's survey, brought a further abrupt change in Nelson's plan. As *Bellona* passed up the disengaged side of *Isis*, she ran aground on a spur of the Middle Ground and was unable to get off. Throughout the action she was only able to fire at relatively long range through the gaps between the British ships.

34. Millard, *Macmillan's Magazine*, June 1895, pp81-93.

Captain Sir Thomas B Thompson (1766-1828): engraving published 1 August 1805 by George Engleheart, artist, William Ridley, engraver, and Joyce Gold, publisher. Captain Thompson was commander of the Bellona *which ran aground at the battle of Copenhagen.* (National Maritime Museum, London: PAD 3399)

Her position, however, allowed her to engage both the *Provesteenen* and *Wagrien*, raking the latter's bows. Although she was less affected by return fire, because of her distance, her casualty list was to be a long one. Her captain, Sir Thomas Thompson, had his leg shot off early in the action, and two of her guns blew up, killing their crews, seriously wounding scores of men, and bringing down deck beams. She suffered eighty-three men either killed or wounded. Her guns may have been badly cast, and exploded when they overheated, or in the excitement of the action they may have been loaded with two cartridges, or three shot.

Nelson was next astern in *Elephant*. Her pilot was convinced that the deeper water must be on the side furthest from the Danish line, and he wanted to take *Elephant* past the grounded *Bellona* on her disengaged side. That, of course, was the standard tactical practice, but it would have been disastrous had he done so, because Nelson's flagship would have grounded. Nelson overruled the pilot, and

Elephant moved up the line to take *Bellona*'s place ahead of *Glatton*, also engaging the *Dannebroge*. Despite the evidence he had now seen that the deeper water was nearer the Danes, Nelson could not overcome the reluctance of the pilot to place *Elephant* as close to the enemy as he wanted her to be. This, *Agamemnon*'s inability to get into action at all, and *Bellona*'s grounding were both galling and worrying. *Elephant*'s surgeon, Dr Ferguson, wrote that Nelson's 'agitation during these moments was extreme: I shall never forget the impression it made on me. It was not, however, the agitation of indecision, but of ardent, animated patriotism panting for glory, which had appeared within his reach, and was vanishing from his grasp.'[35] Standing in the gangway, Nelson hailed each passing ship in his squeaky Norfolk drawl giving the captains new positions.

Fremantle in *Ganges* followed in Nelson's wake inshore of *Bellona*, and took his new position ahead of the flag engaging the *Saelland*. *Russell*, however, was unable to navigate through the thickening gun smoke, and grounded close astern of *Bellona* where she was also able to open an effective but distant fire. *Monarch* passed up the line firing at every ship or battery in succession and finally took a position opposite the *Sohesten* and *Charlotte Amalia*. 'When the ship came to,' wrote Millard,

> I was on the quarter-deck, and saw Captain Mosse on the poop; his card of instructions was in his left hand, and his right was raised to his mouth with the speaking-trumpet, through which he gave the word, 'Cut away the anchor'. I returned to my station at the aftermost guns; and in a few minutes the Captain was brought aft perfectly dead. . . . He was then laid in the stern walk, and a flag thrown over him. Colonel Hutchinson turned round and exclaimed with tears in his eyes, 'poor man, he has left a wife and family to lament him'.[36]

The last ship, *Defiance,* carrying Rear Admiral Graves's flag, passed *Monarch* and let go her

35. Clarke and M'Arthur, (1840) II pp266-7.

36. Millard, *Macmillan's Magazine* 1895 pp81-93.

37. Nelson to Lindholm and reply, 22 April and 2 May 1801, DLN, IV p344-347.

anchor from the stern at 11:30am engaging the *Holsteen*, which had been intended for *Monarch*, and *Indfodsretten*, abreast the Trekroner battery which immediately opened fire on her. Riou led the frigates past *Defiance*, and in succession *Amazon, Alcmene, Blanche, Dart, Arrow* and *Cruizer* took up positions at the head of the line where they came under heavy fire from the battery. The shortening of the line due to the grounding or incapacity of three ships increased the exposure of the frigates. There were two fireships with the squadron, *Otter* and *Zephyr*, but in a close action like this the risk of fire spreading was so great that they could not be used. Most of the crew of *Otter* boarded the *Dart* to help man her guns.

It was a dogged slogging match. Being outnumbered, several of the British ships suffered heavily from raking fire. So too did *Provesteenen*, being fired into by the four ships concentrated at the end of the Danish line, and raked by *Désirée*. On three occasions her gun crews had to be called to put out fires which had been started. *Dannebroge* was also set on fire, by *Glatton*'s heavy carronades firing incendiary carcases. About 1:30pm. Fischer shifted his pendant to *Holsteen*, and then to the Trekroner battery. Subsequently,

when Fischer angered him by making false statements about the course of the battle, Nelson scathingly wrote:

> In his letter he states that, after he quitted the *Dannebroge*, she long contested the battle. If so, more shame for him to quit so many brave fellows. *Here* was no manoeuvering: *it was* downright fighting, and it was his duty to have shown an example of firmness becoming the high trust reposed in him.[37]

However, Fischer had been wounded in the head, and was not blamed by his own service. The gunners on the Danish ships were not easily to be driven from their posts by the British broadsides, and new drafts of men from shore helped to keep the surviving guns firing.

British gunnery did not slacken, and morale remained good. One of the army lieutenants stationed onboard *Monarch* for eventual service ashore repeatedly started a cheer, which Midshipman Millard remarked was 'of more importance than might be imagined, for the men have no other communication throughout the ship, but know whcn a shout is set up, it runs from deck to deck, and that their

The battle of Copenhagen, 2 April 1801, by J T Serres. (British Museum)

comrades are, some of them, in good spirits'.[38] This unflinching determination was all the more remarkable because Nelson's account of British casualties in the battle were 254 dead and 689 wounded, which were numbers greater than those suffered by the victors in any battle except for the Glorious First of June, and Trafalgar. When later in the action Millard had to go to the main-deck he found

not a single man standing the whole way from the main-mast forward, a district containing eight guns on a side, some of which were run out ready for firing; others lay dismounted, and yet others remained as they were after recoiling.

Lieutenant Yelland had taken over when Captain Mosse was killed:

How he escaped unhurt seems wonderful. [Millard recalled] several times I lost sight of him in a cloud of splinters; as they subsided I saw first his cocked hat emerging, then by degrees the rest of his person, his face smiling, so that altogether one might imagine him dressed for his wedding day.

The British squadron could not hope to manoeuvre under such fire in such confined waters, and had to prevail or suffer defeat where they were. The difficulty of their position is enough to explain Nelson's sharp rejoinder to a lieutenant who spoke despondently about the grounding of *Bellona* and *Russell*. As the day wore on, however, it would have become evident to Nelson that the British were more than holding their own. Parker was less well-placed to make that judgment, but he should have been able to judge the danger of trying to move ships damaged aloft under fire through the narrow channels. When, about the time Fischer had to shift his flag, Parker made his notorious signal to 'Discontinue Action' he was clearly inspired by sympathy rather than judgment.

Parker, aboard *London,* had been vainly beating to windward all morning trying to bring his ships into action against the northern

end of the Danish line. He could see the two ships aground, and the frigates taking terrible punishment from the Trekroner battery which he ought to have been engaging himself. Perhaps his age robbed him of the capacity to be inactive under terrible stress. Domett begged him to delay sending the message, but eventually Parker determined to do so. He thought it would be moral cowardliness not to give Nelson permission to withdraw. But the signal was not in fact permissive, and it was made 'general' so that every ship in the fleet ought to obey it without waiting for Nelson to repeat it.

Rear Admiral Graves wrote later to his brother that 'If we had discontinued the action before the enemy struck, we should have all got aground and been destroyed.'[39] Captain Nicholas Tomlinson, who was later asked by St Vincent to write an account of the action, was of the same opinion:

The events of the Battle and the consequences that would have resulted from an obedience to the Signal to discontinue the Action which was made from the *London,* and repeated with guns, are too well-known to require any comment.[40]

Captain Otway got permission from Parker to take a boat and tell Nelson that the order should be treated as permissive, but in fact he could not get to the *Elephant* in time. Graves had no choice but to repeat the signal, but he hoisted it where his sails would obscure Nelson's seeing it, and later claimed that all the other halyards were broken.

When *Elephant*'s signal lieutenant asked Nelson whether he should repeat Parker's signal, he said only to acknowledge it. 'He then called after him, "Is No. 16 [for close action] still hoisted?". The Lieutenant answering in the affirmative, Lord Nelson said: "Mind you keep it so."'

He now walked the deck considerably agitated, [Stewart recorded], which was always known by his moving the stump of his right arm. After a turn or two, he said to me in a

38. Millard, *Macmillan's Magazine*, June 1895, pp81-93.

39. Rear Adm Graves to John Graves, 3 April 1801, *Logs* II pp101-3.

40. Tomlinson to Nepean, 4 June 1801, *Tomlinson Papers* p310.

41. Colonal Stewart's Journal, C & M (1840) II p403; DLN IV p309.

42. Fremantle to Marquis of Buckingham, 4 April 1801, *Wynne* p315.

quick manner, 'Do you know what's shown on board of the Commander-in-Chief – No. 39?' On asking him what that meant he answered: 'Why, to leave off Action.' 'Leave off action!' he repeated, and then added, with a shrug, 'Now, damn me if I do.' He also observed, I believe to Captain Foley: 'You know, Foley, I have only one eye – I have a right to be blind sometimes.' and then with an archness peculiar to his character, putting the glass to his blind eye, he exclaimed, 'I really do not see the Signal'.

Where Riou was stationed at the head of the line he could not see Nelson's flagship, but he could see *London* clearly, and could also see Graves's repeat of Parker's signal. An exceptionally skillful and determined officer, he was nonetheless far too junior to disobey the orders of the Commander-in-Chief. He not only repeated the signal himself, but acted on it. Turning to withdraw, *Amazon* and the other small craft were exposed to raking fire from the Trekroner battery. Stewart recorded the report that Riou

> was sitting on a gun, was encouraging his men, and had been wounded in the head by a splinter. He had expressed himself grieved at being thus obliged to retreat, and nobly observed, 'What will Nelson think of us?'. His Clerk was killed by his side; and by another shot, several of the Marines, while hauling on the main-brace, shared the same fate. Riou then exclaimed, 'Come, then, my boys, let us die all together!'. The words were scarcely uttered, when the fatal shot severed him in two.[41]

Lieutenant John Quilliam, who was to serve as first lieutenant on *Victory* at Trafalgar, took over command and got *Amazon* away.

Shortly after this time, the Danish fire began to slacken. Fremantle later commented that he attributed the good fortune of *Ganges* losing only six seamen 'to the bad gunnery of our opponents, and beating them most completely in less than an hour'. However, most of the Danes had fought stubbornly. When

Captain Edward Riou (1758-1801), by Samuel Shelley, artist and publisher, and James Heath, engraver. During the few weeks that Nelson knew Riou before his death at the battle of Copenhagen, he strongly impressed him with his abilities. Hyde Parker's famous signal of recall, which Nelson ignored but which Riou could not, was blamed for exposing him to impossible odds. (National Maritime Museum, London: PAD 3056)

Fremantle boarded the Danish vessels he found the carnage exceeded anything he had ever heard of: 'the *Ça Ira* or Nile ships are not to be compared to the massacre on board them. The people generally were carpenters, labourers and some Norwegian seamen.'[42] The failure of the Crown Prince, or the naval commanders, to move some of Steen Bille's ships from the harbour entrance to bring Nelson's ships between fires had made their defeat inevitable. All of Nelson's ships were capable of further action, and continued Danish resistance would only have enabled Parker's ships to get into action. At 2:00pm two floating batteries sank trying to escape into the harbour, but a frigate succeeded. Half an hour later the Danish fire all but stopped. Lieutenant Benjamin Sproule of *Polyphemus* recorded in his log that

> the fire was kept up between us and the enemy [*Provesteenen* and *Wagrien*] without

any intermission until 45 minutes past 2, when the 74 abreast of us ceased firing, but not being able to discern she had struck, our fire was kept up 15 minutes longer; then we could perceive the people making their escape to the shore in boats. We ceased firing and boarded both ships and took possession of them.[43]

Either some of the drafts brought onboard to work the Danish guns did not understand that the fight was over when their officers surrendered their ships, or in fact they had not surrendered but were unable to replace the flags which had been shot away. Boats' crews from *Elephant* and *Glatton* were fired on as they attempted to take possession of *Dannebroge*, and in consequence firing recommenced from their main batteries. The Danish flagship was reduced to a shambles, drifted away, and finally blew up with her crew still on board. Out of a total Danish crew list of 5,234 men, 370 were killed and 665 wounded.[44]

Truce

Nelson was always humane to the victims of war, and determined to put an end if he could to the firing. He drafted a letter to the Crown Prince to be carried under a flag of truce by Captain Sir Frederick Thesiger who could speak Danish, taking the time to get it properly sealed with wax and his coat of arms so that there should be no hint that he was in haste.

Rear Admiral Sir Thomas Graves (1747?-1814), by James Northcote (1746-1831). (National Maritime Museum, London: BHC 2722)

Prince Frederick sent back one of his own staff, Captain Lindholm, to ask what was Nelson's object, to which he replied that it was 'humanity', so that the wounded Danes could be taken ashore. When this was reported ashore, the Danish batteries ceased to fire. Fischer later claimed that Nelson's victory was far from complete, and that the offer of a truce had ulterior motives. This led Nelson to write a very angry letter to Lindholm, for the Crown Prince's information. Lindholm's reply made it clear that Frederick appreciated Nelson's purpose:

> As to your Lordship's motives for sending a Flag of Truce to our Government, it can never be misconstrued, and your subsequent conduct has sufficiently shown that humanity is always the companion of true valour.[45]

Nelson had sent for Graves to instruct him to lead the squadron out past the shoals: 'It was beautiful to see how the shot beat the water all round us in the boat', Graves wrote to his brother. Colonel Stewart says that

> previous to the boat's getting on board [with Captain Lindholm], Lord Nelson had taken the opinion of his valuable friends, Freemantle and Foley, the former of whom

had been sent for from the *Ganges*, as to the practicability of advancing with ships which were least damaged, upon that part of the Danish line of defence yet uninjured. The opinions were averse from it; and, on the other hand, decided in favour of removing our fleet, whilst the wind yet held fair, from the present intricate channel.[46]

It appears from the logs of the ships on both sides of the battle that Stewart's memory was at fault about the timing: the withdrawal did not begin until firing had ceased.

Because of the damage the ships had suffered aloft, they had great difficulty sailing clear. The difficulty experienced in doing so underlined the probable consequence of making the attempt at the time of Parker's recall. *Ganges* ran foul of *Monarch*, and the latter was unable to wear without boats towing her head around. Millard wrote that:

Our decks were choked with disabled guns; nearly half our complement were either killed or wounded; and there was not fore or aft one single brace or bowline that was not shot away, so that the sails could not possibly be directed one way or the other, but hung on the caps as when we first anchored. The consequences were that the *Ganges* came directly on board us, upon the larboard quarter, her jibboom passing over the quarter-deck, and her spritsail yard grappling with our main and mizzen rigging. Both ships were now alike, ungovernable, and both were drifting fast towards the Crown Islands. To their perpetual shame be it spoken, they took advantage of our distress, and opened their fire again upon us.[47]

Elephant ran hard aground, had to lighten ship, and lay out a borrowed anchor and cable before she could haul herself off. As Nelson's battered ships worked themselves clear, those with Parker at last reached the scene of action and moved into the vacated stations opposite the Danish line.

Possession was taken of most of the prizes,

Rear Admiral Sir Robert Waller Otway (1770-1846), by an unknown painter. (National Maritime Museum, London: BHC 2926)

but one, probably the *Saelland*, rehoisted her flag in the night and tried to warp into harbour. The boats crew sent to take possession was fired on. At Nelson's advice, Parker sent Captain Otway, who got his coxswain to go aloft and take in the Danish flag while he was talking to the ship's officers. This sleight of hand enabled him to persuade Commodore Fischer that the ship had indeed struck.[48] Her cable was immediately cut, she drifted clear and was taken in tow. Shortly after, Nelson himself came aboard the ship flying Fischer's flag, and renewed his acquaintance.

At sunset Captain Lindholm was sent out to Parker by the Crown Prince to enquire what were his terms, and Parker gave him a copy of those Hawkesbury had given to Vansittart to deliver before the battle. In reply Prince Frederick sent a verbal offer the next morning to mediate between Britain and Russia. This was probably no more than an opening gambit. Recognising his limitations as a negotiator, Parker deputed Nelson to go ashore and try and resolve the conflict. He took with him Thesiger and Hardy, and he was surprised by his welcome from the Danish people, many of whom had family members killed, injured, or missing 'My reception was too flattering',

43. Lt Sproule's log, *Polyphemus, Logs* II p115.

44. Dudley Pope, *The Great Gamble*, p417.

45. Nelson to Lindholm and reply, 22 April and 2 May 1801, DLN, IV pp344-7.

46. Clarke & M'Arthur (1840) II p407; Pope p417.

47. Millard, *Macmillan's Magazine*, June 1895 pp81-93.

48. Nelson to Parker, 3 April 1801, DLN IV p331; Otway p23-87; Pope p432.

This engraving of Nelson by Simon de Koster is inscribed on the copy in the National Maritime Museum: 'This is the best likeness which I have ever seen of Lord Nelson—Jan 1801—Nov 1801.' (National Maritime Museum, London: PAD 3772)

Nelson wrote to Troubridge, 'and landing at Portsmouth or Yarmouth could not have exceeded the blessings of the people; even the Palace and stairs were crowded, and huzzas, which could not have been very grateful to Royal ears.'[49]

Colonel Stewart's account was more restrained:

> The populace showed a mixture of admiration, curiosity, and displeasure. A strong guard secured his safety, and appeared necessary to keep off the mob; whose rage, although mixed with admiration at his thus trusting himself amongst them, was naturally to be expected.[50]

He walked to the palace and was received by the Prince in person, with only Captain Lindholm present. On the way in he

saw Count Bernstorff for a moment, and could not help saying he had acted a very wrong part in my opinion, in involving the two Countries in their present melancholy situation, for that our Countries ought never to quarrel.[51]

He eventually persuaded Prince Frederick that the League must work to injure Britain, that it would have been impossible for Denmark once a part of it to have refused to cooperate with a Russian fleet acting against Britain, and that British control of trade was in fact in Denmark's economic interest because it gave her a disproportionate share in supplying the needs of British commerce and the British navy. He readily agreed to Nelson's suggestion that reconciliation should begin with 'a free entry of the British Fleet into Copenhagen, and the free use of everything we may want from it', but was non-committal with the second condition that 'whilst this explanation is going on', the Court of Denmark should make 'a total suspension of your treaties with Russia'.

Nelson wrote that night to Troubridge that he believed he had told Prince Frederick 'such truths as seldom reach the ears of Princes. HRH seemed much affected'.[52] His diplomacy proved to be more effective than he expected, but the Danes did not immediately concede the British demands. Captain Lindholm was sent twice to negotiate with Parker, who was anything but an effective diplomat but in the end sent them away with even stiffer terms. When the Danish court continued to temporise, he sent Nelson to negotiate once again.

Dundas's instructions to the Admiralty had noted that it probably would be impossible to destroy the Arsenal and shipping in Copenhagen without damaging the city, and when Parker confirmed Nelson's suggestions, he warned that unless they were complied with he would have to continue his attack on the Arsenal 'without regard to the preservation of the Town'. Nelson summarised to Addington the considerations which he felt would determine the outcome of his discussions, and what he had achieved:

1st. We had beat the Danes. 2nd. We wished to make them feel that we are their real friends, therefore have spared their Town, which we can always set on fire; and I do not think if we burnt Copenhagen it would have the effect of attaching them to us; on the contrary they would hate us. 3rd. They understand perfectly that we are at war with them for their treaty of Armed Neutrality made last year. 4th. We have made them suspend the operations of that treaty. 5th. It has given our Fleet free scope to act against Russia and Sweden; 6th, which we never should have done, although Copenhagen would have been burnt, for Sir Hyde was determined not to have Denmark hostile in his rear. Our passage over the Grounds [the shoals south of Copenhagen] might have been very seriously interrupted by the batteries near Draco. 7th. Every reinforcement, even a Cutter, can join us without molestation, and also provisions, stores &c. 8th. Great Britain is left with the stake of all the Danish property in her hands, her Colonies, &c., if she refuses peace. 9th. The hands of Denmark are tied up; ours are free to act against her confederate Allies. 10th. Although we might have burnt the City, I have my doubts whether we could their ships.[53]

When the Danes muttered to themselves in French, thinking Nelson would not understand, that they might have to renew hostilities, he immediately retorted that the British fleet was ready to do so that very night. Finally, the Crown Prince agreed to the British terms, although he cut the duration of the truce from sixteen to fourteen weeks.

During the discussion Prince Frederick had been privately informed that Tsar Paul had been assassinated, but the British did not learn the news for several weeks. Nelson had made it clear that the reason he wanted a protracted truce was not just to permit a negotiation in London of the trade dispute, but also to enable the British fleet to destroy the Russians. However, he was not to be called on to fight another battle. The Swedes kept safely behind the rocks and batteries of Carlskrona, and expressed every desire to accommodate matters with Britain. On 22 April while the fleet was laying off the Swedish dockyard, Parker received a letter from the Russian ambassador in Copenhagen informing him of the death of Tsar Paul, and expressing 'the Emperor Alexander's desire to be on the same friendly footing with Great Britain as formerly'.[54] Parker replied that he would suspend hostilities against Russia until he received instructions from London, and returned to Kioge Bay south of Copenhagen. Here Nelson asked for, and received, permission to return to England to recover his health.

Command-in-Chief

This was not to be quite the end of Nelson's service in the Baltic. The sequel makes it clear that he was motivated by more than an immature thirst for action. Before he was able to depart from Kioge Bay on the voyage home, dispatches were received from London relieving Sir Hyde of the command of the British fleet. Colonel Stewart had reached London with Parker's report on the armistice, and Nelson's letters to the Prime Minister and to St Vincent. Stewart was asked to give a first-hand account of everything which had happened, and the upshot was that Parker was immediately sent an order to hand over command to Nelson and return home.[55]

The fleet generally felt that Parker had been unkindly used. He had angered those who had fought in the action by ignoring tradition and giving the honour of carrying his victory dispatch to Otway, a deserving officer who was one of his protégés but had never been in any danger. Too many of his promotions to

49. Nelson to Troubridge, 4 April 1801, *Naval Miscellany*, I p426.

50. Clarke & M'Arthur (1840) II p409.

51. Nelson to Addington, 4 April 1801, DLN IV pp332-336.

52. Nelson to Troubridge, 4 April 1801, *Naval Miscellany*, I p426.

53. Nelson to Addington, 9 April 1801, DLN IV pp339-341.

54. Parker's Journal, ADM 50/65.

55. Nelson's Commission, Add MS 34934, Nelson Papers, Official Correspondence, ff43-45B.

replace casualties were also his own people, rather than such highly deserving officers as Lieutenant Yelland who had fought *Monarch* so bravely. He was also inconsiderate of the financial interests of the officers who had been in the battle, ordering all but one of the prizes burnt. He had certainly proved far too elderly and indolent to conduct the business of the British fleet in the Baltic, and the consequence had been the death of many men. However, he nonetheless retained the affections of many. Fremantle wrote his wife Betsey: 'The insult of the Admiralty to my friend Sir Hyde is scarcely to be named without feeling detestation to the person who occasioned his recall in such a way as *Treason only* could have rendered necessary.'[56] After his return to England, Nelson went out of his way to comfort Sir Hyde, and to persuade him not to expose himself by requesting an enquiry or making published statements.

There is no question, however, but that Nelson had proved himself in every way to be more capable of undertaking the diplomatic as well as the tactical leadership required. Parker was not the man to carry out the orders which had just been sent to him to discover at first

hand the willingness of the Russians to put themselves on a footing of peace with Britain, or to oblige them to.[57]

As soon as he assumed command, and Parker had sailed for England, Nelson took the fleet to Reval. The Russian squadron had already sailed, but Nelson anchored the fleet, and communicated with the Russian government. Despite leaving behind the bomb vessels and fire ships, his intentions were misunderstood and he was asked to leave the harbour. The manner in which he took this 'insult', by treating it as a misunderstanding and sailing immediately, was very well received by Tsar Alexander who sent a message to Nelson at sea. In Colonel Stewart's words,

it expressed an anxious wish that peace should be restored on the most solid basis; and in a particular manner invited Lord Nelson to Petersburgh [sic], in whatever mode might be most agreeable to himself.[58]

The Russian foreign minister, Count Pahlin (or Panin) advised that the Tsar had ordered the lifting of the embargo on British ships.

Home

56. Fremantle to his wife, 21 May 1801, *Wynne* pp330-31.

57. Admiralty Secretary to Parker, 17 April 1801, Add MS 34934, Nelson Papers, Official Correspondence, ff43-45B.

58. Colonel Stewart's Journal, DLN IV p393.

59. Macready pp6-7.

Nelson was back in England on 1 July, and was given command of the forces arrayed against the flotilla assembled around Boulogne for the invasion of England. It was felt at the Admiralty that his presence amongst the anti-invasion force was essential to keep the populace from panicking, but Nelson thought that his old friends were also trying to keep him away from the Hamiltons. He put up a paper outlining the principles which must govern the defence which is a model of its kind, but, as he had been at Tenerife, he was unlucky in the combined-arms operation he planned to pre-empt French action. A raiding force he sent to destroy the transports on 15 August 1801 was repulsed. This was humiliating, but in fact

there never was much prospect of the French army crossing to England without command of the Channel. Napoleon's advice in 1798 that control of the sea was a necessary precondition for success remained sound.

In March 1802 Addington concluded the Treaty of Amiens with the French, buying peace with the return of almost all of the conquests made by British arms. The defeat of Denmark, the breaking of the League of Armed Neutrality, the new spirit of cooperation with Russia, had all been important gains. However, the outcome of Addington's peace mission was more determined by Napoleon's great victory over the Austrians at Marengo in June 1801 which forced Emperor Francis II to

sign the treaty of Lunéville putting an end to the 'Second Coalition' against France. The cost of the war was becoming a great burden to Britain, but in fact Britain's financial position was very much stronger than was that of France, as was to become apparent during the short peace.

The improbability of the peace being enduring was all too apparent, but St Vincent set about laying up the fleet with a thoroughness which was characteristic. Nelson who had been rewarded with a step in the peerage to viscount, supported the peace in the House of Lords with a speech, mostly because of his friendship for Addington. He soon learnt that he was a complete ignoramus in politics, and on his last visit to England in 1805 he told Pitt, who by then was back in power and who was also a friend of Nelson's, that he intended to keep a low profile in the Lords.

Nelson and the Hamiltons took the chance presented by the peace to make a trip into the west of England and the Welsh borders, partly to get away from the snubs to which they were subjected in London. Nelson was so uneasy about his treatment of Fanny that he did not even attend his father's funeral because he was afraid she would be there. The Reverend Edmund Nelson had been greatly saddened by Horatio's behaviour, and had continued to correspond with Fanny and visit her, and she herself had hastened to his deathbed. An actor, Charles Macready, who met Nelson in Birmingham remarked that he looked 'melancholy'. 'The extremely mild and gentle tones of his voice impressed me most sensibly.'

> I should not omit to mention that in the hall of the hotel were several sailors of Nelson's ships waiting to see him, to each of whom the great admiral spoke in the most affable manner, inquiringly and kindly, as he passed through to his carriage, and left them, I believe, some tokens of his remembrance.[59]

Emma's own insecurity was expressed by a chorus of unjust bitterness aimed at Fanny, and she continued with her overwhelming flattery of Nelson. He basked in it, but assured Fanny that she was not at fault. The house he purchased at Merton was made into a shrine to him, filled with pictures of him and mementos of his victories. Sir William found the noise and confusion a heavy burden to bear during his last months of life, but did not move back to his own rented house because he wished to avoid hurting his friend.

Lord Nelson's Villa at Merton, published 1 March 1806 by Gyford, artist, Aml Warren, engraver, and J Stratford, publisher, and intended for D Hughson's Description of London. (National Maritime Museum, London: PAD 3980)

Memorandum by Lord Nelson, on the defence of the Thames, etc.

Besides the stationed Ships at the different posts between the North Foreland and Orfordness, as many Gun-vessels as can be spared from the very necessary protection of the Coast of Sussex and of Kent to the westward of Dover, should be collected, for this part of the Coast must be seriously attended to; for supposing London the object of surprise, I am of opinion that the Enemy's object *ought* to be the getting on shore as speedily as possible, for the dangers of a navigation of forty-eight hours, appear to me to be an insurmountable objection to the rowing from Boulogne to the Coast of Essex. It is therefore most probable (for it is certainly proper to believe the French are coming to attack London, and therefore to be prepared) that from Boulogne, Calais, and even Havre, that the Enemy will try and land in Sussex, or the lower part of Kent, and from Dunkirk, Ostend, and the other Ports of Flanders, to land on the Coast of Essex or Suffolk; for I own myself of opinion that, the object being to get on shore somewhere within 100 miles of London, as speedily as possible, that the Flats in the mouth of the Thames will not be the only place necessary to attend to; added to this, the Enemy will create a powerful diversion by the sailing of the combined Fleet, and the either sailing, or creating such an appearance of sailing, of the Dutch Fleet, as will prevent Admiral Dickson [Commander-in-Chief in the North Sea] from sending anything from off the great Dutch Ports, whilst the smaller Ports will spew forth its Flotilla,–viz. Flushing, &c. &c. It must be pretty well ascertained what number of small Vessels are in each Port.

I will suppose that 40,000 men are destined for this attack, or rather surprise, of London; 20,000 will land on the west side of Dover, sixty or seventy miles from London, and the same number on the east side: they are too knowing to let us have but one point of alarm for London. Supposing 200 Craft, or 250, collected at Boulogne, &c., they are supposed equal to carry 20,000 men. In very calm weather, they might row over, supposing no impediment, in twelve hours; at the same instant, by telegraph, the same number of troops would be rowed out of Dunkirk, Ostend, &c. &c. These are the two great objects to attend to from Dover and the Downs, and perhaps one of the small Ports to the westward. Boulogne (which I call the central point of the Western attack) must be attended to. If it is calm when the Enemy row out, all our Vessels and Boats appointed to watch them, must get into the channel, and meet them as soon as possible: if not strong enough for the attack, they must watch, and keep them company till a favourable opportunity offers. If a breeze springs up, our Ships are to deal *destruction*; no delicacy can be observed on this great occasion. But should it remain calm, and our Flotilla not fancy itself strong enough to attack the Enemy on their passage, the moment that they begin to touch our shore, strong or weak, our Flotilla of Boats must attack as much of the Enemy's Flotilla as they are able–say only one half or two-thirds; it will create a most powerful diversion, for the bows of our Flotilla will be opposed to their unarmed sterns, and the courage of Britons will never, I believe, allow one Frenchman to leave the beach. A great number of Deal and Dover Boats to be on board our Vessels off the Port of Boulogne, to give notice of the direction taken by the Enemy. If it is calm, Vessels in the channel can make signals of intelligence to our shores, from the North Foreland to Orfordness, and even as far as Solebay, not an improbable place, about seventy or eighty miles from London.

A Flotilla to be kept near Margate and Ramsgate, to consist of Gun-boats and Flat-boats; another Squadron to be stationed near the centre, between Orfordness and North Foreland, and the third in Hosely Bay. The Floating Batteries are stationed in all proper positions for defending the different Channels, and the smaller Vessels will always have a resort in the support of the stationed Ships. The moment of the Enemy's movement from Boulogne, is to be considered as the movement of the Enemy from Dunkirk. Supposing it calm, the Flotillas are to be rowed, and the heavy ones towed (except the stationed Ships), those near Margate, three or four leagues to the north of the North Foreland; those from Hosely Bay, a little approaching the Centre Division, but always keeping an eye towards Solebay; the Centre Division to advance half-way between the two. The more fast Rowing boats, called Thames Galleys, which can be procured the better, to carry orders, information, &c. &c.

Whenever the Enemy's Flotilla can be seen, our Divisions are to unite, but not intermix, and to be ready to execute such orders as may be deemed necessary, or as the indispensable circumstances may require. For this purpose, men of such confidence in each other should be looked for, that (as far as human foresight can go) no little jealousy may creep into any man's mind, but to be all animated with the same desire of preventing the descent of the Enemy on our Coasts. Stationary Floating Batteries are not, from any apparent advantage, to be moved, for the tide may prevent their assuming the very important stations assigned them: they are on no account to be supposed neglected, even should the Enemy surround them, for they may rely on support, and reflect that perhaps their gallant conduct may prevent the mischievous designs of the Enemy. Whatever plans may be adopted, the moment the Enemy touch our Coast, be it where it may, they are to be attacked by every man afloat and on shore: this must be perfectly understood. *Never fear the event.* The Flat Boats can probably be manned (partly, at least) with the Sea Fencibles (the numbers of fixed places of whom I am entirely ignorant of), but the Flat Boats they may man to be in grand and sub-divisions, commanded by their own Captains and Lieutenants, as far as is possible. The number of Flat Boats is unknown to me, as also the other means of defence in Small Craft; but I am clearly of opinion that a proportion of the small force should be kept to watch the Flat-boats from Boulogne, and the other in the way I have presumed to suggest. These are offered as merely the rude ideas of the moment, and are only meant as a Sea plan of defence for the City of London; but I believe other parts may likewise be menaced, if the Brest fleet, and those from Rochfort and Holland put to sea; although I feel confident that the Fleets of the enemy will meet the same fate which has always attended them, yet their sailing will facilitate the coming over of their Flotilla, as they will naturally suppose our attention will be called only to the Fleets.

Part V

THE BATTLE OF TRAFALGAR

THE BATTLE of Trafalgar was tactically and strategically the most decisive naval battle of the war against the French Revolution and Empire. It is a controversial action because Nelson's tactics were unorthodox and dangerous, and only justified by the outcome. Nelson's dictum that 'the boldest measures are the safest', has left generations of naval historians breathless. Some admire the subtlety of his method, others are shaken by the dangers he faced down, but all have to concede that they worked. The battle was strategically decisive because it put an end for good to the threat of invasion of the British Isles, it ensured that it would be Britain and not France which could use naval forces to influence the course of history in the Mediterranean, and it ensured that British seaborne trade would be able to pay for the coalitions of European states formed to defeat Bonapartism. In this, the final achievement of his career, Nelson lost his own life.

The camps at Etaples, Boulogne, Wimereau, Calais and Dunkirk had been broken up after the signature of the Treaty of Amiens, and Napoleon rhetorically asked the British ambassador, Lord Whitworth,

how could it be supposed that after having gained the height on which he stood, that after having raised himself from little more than a common soldier to the head of the most powerful country on the Continent, he would risk his life and reputation in such a hazardous attempt [as an invasion of England], unless forced to it by necessity, when the chances were that he and greatest part of the expedition would go to the bottom of the sea?[1]

When in May 1803 Britain declared war, however, acting precipitously so as to enable the Royal Navy to capture at sea many French seamen who were thus denied to the French

1. Oscar Browning, ed., *England and Napoleon in 1803: being the despatches of Lord Whitworth and others*, London: Royal Historical Society, 1887, p80.

This 'Accurate Representation of the Floating Machine invented by the French for Invading England' shows something of the hysteria surrounding the invasion threat in 1805. (National Maritime Museum, London: A5505)

Three of the twenty-seven Martello towers erected along the Kent coast between Folkestone and Dungeness to protect the flat lands of Romney Marsh, an ideal spot for landing, against a Napoleonic invasion. In fact, they were not begun until the summer of 1805 by which time Napoleon's invasion force had left Boulogne for Austria. By the time they were completed in 1808 any real threat of invasion had evaporated. (Photo: John Mannering)

Marine, Napoleon's preparations for invasion were renewed. The victor of Marengo and absolute ruler of France could not regard with complacency the idea that Britain was beyond the reach of French arms, and 'a descent was the only means of offence he had'. One hundred and twelve thousand soldiers were encamped near the embarkation ports, with reserves behind them, and nearly 2,000 boats were made ready to transport them. On 18 May 1804 the French Senate proclaimed Napoleon Emperor of the French, and two months later he insisted on witnessing a rehearsal of the embarkation. He would not be dissuaded by Admiral Bruix, commanding the naval forces in the Channel, who objected that the weather was dangerous, and between 50 and 100 soldiers were drowned. Nevertheless, he could not believe that he would fail. On 2 December he crowned himself Emperor in Notre Dame Cathedral.

St Vincent, who had to face a parliamentary enquiry into his handling of the Admiralty, scornfully dismissed the threat of invasion. His confidence was not misplaced, but the threat of invasion did have wide operational

and strategic significance. Napoleon's control of the Dutch navy continued to be a factor, and when Spain declared war on Britain in December 1804 another thirty-two Spanish ships of the line were added to the forces Napoleon controlled. This revived the prospect of his being able to overwhelm the Royal Navy in the Channel.

The peace of Amiens had been especially welcome in Spain which had watched with concern British efforts to encourage revolt in the Spanish empire, and Napoleon's humiliation of the Pope. But the imbecile King Charles IV could not distance himself from Napoleon who obliged him to reinstate the disgraced Godoy as his minister, to cede Louisiana to France, which Napoleon then sold to the United States, and to declare war on Portugal. By a treaty of 9 October 1803, Spain was required to enforce on Portugal a strict neutrality which inevitably led to conflict with Britain. A tribute was exacted from Spain by Napoleon, and eventually Pitt sanctioned an ill-considered effort to intercept a small Spanish treasure fleet so that the specie it carried should not reach France. The operation was badly conceived, because not enough force was sent to justify the Spanish commander surrendering without a fight. In the action which followed, one of his ships blew up with great loss of life and treasure. Even following this tragedy, Spanish sentiment was still against France, but after holding out against French pressure for several months, the Spanish government declared war.

This time, there was to be no repeat of the strategic withdrawal of the British Mediterranean fleet to the Atlantic as there had been in 1796. The diplomatic consequences were clearly unacceptable. The threat imminent in Napoleon's camps and flotillas could in the long term be just as dangerous if they prevented support being offered to England's few allies. In the Baltic, Russia, Prussia, Sweden and Denmark were all more or less vulnerable to Napoleon's forces, but their politics could be influenced by naval power, and especially by the power to control maritime trade. In the Mediterranean, Britain's few friends depended upon the support they could receive from the Royal Navy, and from seaborne forces.

The Kingdom of Naples continued to hold out against the Revolution, but an army corps under General Gouvion St Cyr had moved into Neapolitan territory at Taranto where it threatened Naples, and was also well-placed to renew the French interest in the Levant. It was to be a plan developed during the early months of 1805 to dispatch a British army under Lieutenant-General Sir James Craig, to relieve the garrison at Malta and use the veterans in a joint operation with a Russian army based on Corfu to insure the independence of Naples, which in the end set the scene for the battle of Trafalgar. The offensive move to Malta was important in persuading the Tsar to act against France, whilst the movement of Anglo-French forces to Naples tied down French forces in Italy, which encouraged the Austrian Emperor Francis II to join the third coalition.

With the resumption of hostilities, Nelson had been given command of the Mediterranean squadron, and hoisted his flag as Vice Admiral of the Blue. Nominally his base was Malta, but that island was too distant from Toulon for the fleet to spend any time there. Much to his irritation, he was relieved of responsibility for the Atlantic coast of Spain, a

The Victory *off Stromboli, by Nicholas Pocock.* (National Maritime Museum, London: PAF 5885)

separate command being established based on Gibraltar. This was given to Sir John Orde. The two were not well suited as a team. In 1798 Orde had been so angry when Nelson had been given command of the detachment which defeated Brueys at the Nile that he had had to be sent home.

Month after month the watch was kept, by the ships under Nelson's command before Toulon and Cartagena, by Sir John Orde's off the western ports of Spain, and by squadrons off Ferrol and Rochefort, all of which were backed by the Western Squadron under Admiral Cornwallis closely blockading Brest. Nelson's care for the health of his men was a vital factor in his ability to keep on station at such a long distance from home. For nearly two years he did not step ashore from the *Victory*, and for much of the time his squadron operated out of the Magdalena anchorage in northern Sardinia.

There was little prospect of any enemy squadron coming out if it would be immediately confronted by a Royal Navy squadron. The blockades had to be at once distant and at the same time skilfully deployed so that the enemy once out could be pursued with a good chance of intercepting it before it could do any harm, or return to its base. Much depended upon the accidents of weather, and upon a correct anticipation of the enemy's intentions. The political tasks were as important as the tactical. The

regular presence of a British ship of war in Naples harbour was important if the court, which once already had owed their lives to Nelson's ships, was to resist French bullying.

After the death in August 1804 of Admiral Latouche-Tréville, France's most distinguished sailor and the man who had organised the defences of Boulogne, command of the squadron at Toulon was given to Vice Admiral Pierre de Villeneuve. Following his defeat at Trafalgar, he was met by Midshipman Hercules Robinson of the *Euryalus* who described him as 'a tallish thin man, a very tranquil, placid, English-looking Frenchman', fashionably dressed in 'a long- tailed uniform coat, high and flat collar, corduroy pantaloons of a greenish colour, with stripes two inches wide, half boots with sharp toes, and a watch chain with long gold links'.[2] Villeneuve was one of the French aristocracy who had been rewarded for their willingness to serve the Republic by rapid promotion. He had served with Admiral Suffren, whose tactical skills had been unparalleled in the pre-revolutionary navy, before his service under Brueys and his escape at the end of the Battle of the Nile. He had been given command of the Mediterranean fleet before the age of 40. Those British officers who met him after his defeat were surprised by their discovery that he was 'gentlemanly' and 'well-bred', and 'a very good officer'. The Spaniards also found that he was a man they could respect.

When on 17 January 1805 Villeneuve got out of Toulon with eleven ships of the line, Nelson was unable to react in time. His frigates found him at the Magdalena anchorage and reported that the French were sailing south-southwest. His more immediate concern was for the safety of Sardinia and Sicily, and he sailed at once against a heavy gale. When he failed to intercept the French there, he sailed eastward to Greece, and then Alexandria. Villeneuve, however, had found that his seamen were too raw after months of harbour service, and eventually he put back into Toulon. He begged Napoleon to relieve him of his responsibility, but his request was refused.

Amiral Pierre Charles Jean-Baptiste Silvestre, Comte de Villeneuve (1763-1806). British officers who met Villeneuve found they had to make an exception to their prejudices against Frenchmen. (Musée de la Marine, Paris: 85905)

Napoleon's Invasion Directives

It was at this point, with Nelson's force back at its Sardinian anchorage, that Napoleon set in motion the grand design which, but for its inherent flaws, was to have concentrated a Franco-Spanish fleet on the Channel to escort the invasion force. The Rochefort squadron had escaped at the same time as had Villeneuve from Toulon. They were to have met in the West Indies. Now Napoleon revised the plan, instructing Villeneuve to first call at Cadiz to drive off Orde's ships. Together, the Toulon and Cadiz squadrons were to rendezvous at Martinique. At the same time, Admiral Ganteaume was to break out of Brest, release the Franco-Spanish squadron at Ferrol, and also proceed to Martinique. If all these movements were successfully carried out, a fleet of forty-three French ships of the line would be assembled, plus whatever Spain chose to provide. Spain had committed itself to preparing thirty ships when it declared war, but they had great difficulty in manning so many ships and in fact only twenty were made fit for sea by the time of Trafalgar. The combined fleet was to sail back across the Atlantic, brush aside the Royal Navy Western Squadron, and make for Boulogne.

The fatal paradox was that the escapes from Toulon and Brest depended upon accidents of weather, and the odds of the Royal Navy making a bad guess at the enemy's intentions, yet Napoleon's plan depended on five squadrons all being able to make their moves on schedule. It was a dangerous game. Napoleon had little chance of succeeding in his gamble, and the implications of failure were open-ended. If any one of his squadrons were caught in the open sea by a British force and badly damaged or, worse, if more than one squadron should be defeated in detail, British forces would be released to take the offensive. They would be able to extend protection to British trade into every corner of Europe, and be able to support the deployment of soldiers to stiffen the resistance of Napoleon's enemies. British wealth from maritime trade was the backbone of re-sistance to Bonapartism. A free hand at sea, and the elimination of any danger of invasion, would increase the options for the British army being used offensively in support of the forces arrayed against France.

The first, and decisive, failure of Napoleon's plan occurred when Admiral Ganteaume failed to get out of Brest. He had had an unusually good opportunity when Cornwallis was away on sick leave, and the Western Squadron was reduced to fifteen ships of the line. Using the line of shutter telegraph towers that stretched from Brest to Paris, he advised Napoleon that he was confident of being able to fight his way out, but he was ordered to await a chance of getting away without a battle. This chance never materialised.

Villeneuve, however, was more fortunate. On 30 March he sailed in his 80-gun flagship *Bucentaure* accompanied by three other 80s, seven 74s, eight frigates and with more than 3,000 soldiers on board. A neutral merchant ship provided intelligence of Nelson's squadron south of Sardinia, and by changing course under cover of darkness, Villeneuve was able to shake off the shadowing British frigates. He passed Gibraltar on 9 April and arrived off Cadiz at dusk. Orde had had enough warning to avoid contact with the superior force, and, conforming with standard practice, fell back on the Western Squadron. Admiral Gravina was now in command of the squadron at Cadiz. On receipt of Villeneuve's signal he mustered all the ships which were fit for sea, only six, two of which were 64s, and all of which were short of men. In less than four hours, Villeneuve was on his way out into the Atlantic.

The most immediate threat posed by Villeneuve's sortie was to the troop convoy carrying Sir James Craig and the relief force for Malta which was now approaching the Portuguese coast under a very light escort. Reluctantly, because it endangered Portugal's tenuous hold on neutrality, it put into Lisbon until it was evident that Villeneuve was well

2. Rear Admiral Hercules Robinson, *Sea Drift*, Portsea: T Hinton, 1858, p208.

off the coast, and then proceeded for Gibraltar. Their expected arrival helped to persuade Nelson to remain in the western Mediterranean, laying out his screen to catch the French fleet if it sailed eastward. He waited a month in the greatest agitation of spirits before he received definite news that Villeneuve had passed Gibraltar. Then, when it was clear that his responsibilities in the Mediterranean had been fulfilled, he worked his own way to the westward, delayed by westerly gales. In a typical act of selfless tactical good sense, he detached a three-decker, *Royal Sovereign*, to join the escort of the troop convoy to ensure that it was able to stand up to the Spanish squadron at Cartagena.

The information that Villeneuve was bound for the West Indies was passed to Nelson in Gibraltar by a British officer in Portugese service, Commodore John Campbell, who was later dismissed by the Portugese for his actions. Rather than falling back on the Western Squadron, Nelson set off in hot pursuit with *Victory*, an 80 and seven 74s, after a force double his numbers. He was taking a risk of being defeated by superior force, but the same calculation that determined his tactics at Trafalgar, that Franco-Spanish morale and seamanship were inferior, no doubt affected his thoughts. If he caught up with them he could make it

difficult for them to do any harm to British interests, and he could shadow them until they fell in with other British ships. Should he fail to fall in with Villeneuve, the enemy would nonetheless have to assume the worst, and he could be back in European waters not long after the Franco-Spanish squadron itself returned.

This was how it fell out. Nelson failed to meet the Franco-Spanish force in the West Indies, but nonetheless succeeded by the rumour of his presence in preventing Villeneuve achieving much beyond the capture of 'HMS Diamond Rock', which was a small British outpost just off the coast of Martinique, and the capture of a convoy of fourteen merchantmen. It was at this point that Napoleon's orders reached Villeneuve, instructing him to sail to Ferrol and then to Brest so that all the available forces could concentrate to support the invasion attempt. When Villeneuve headed out once more into the Atlantic, Nelson was only four days behind. The brig *Curieux* was sent ahead with a warning for Cornwallis. Her captain, George Bettesworth, was able to count the Franco-Spanish squadron as it passed, and observe that it was headed for the Bay of Biscay. On 7 July he was in Plymouth, and at 11pm on the 8th the news was at the Admiralty.

Admiral Sir Robert Calder's Action off Cape Finisterre, 23 July 1805, by William Anderson (1757-1837). Calder's engagement with Vice Admiral Villeneuve on his return from the West Indies, fought in foggy weather and outnumbered, was a disappointment despite the fact that he took two prizes. (National Maritime Museum, London: BHC 0540)

Trafalgar Deployment

St Vincent had resigned when Pitt formed his second ministry in May 1804, and his successor, Lord Melville, was driven out a year later by allegations of financial irregularities. Pitt had to find a First Lord of the Admiralty who would be politically acceptable, and capable of exerting an effective strategic control. The office was not always given to an admiral, but in 1805 Pitt had the sense to do so, and chose Admiral Sir Charles Middleton, who had made a name for himself as a naval administrator. He was over eighty years old, but his experience was vast. Elevated to the peerage as Lord Barham, it was he who received the news brought by the *Curieux*. He ordered the Western Squadron to cast to the southwest to bar Villeneuve access to Brest or Rochefort, and detached the blockade force from off Rochefort to reinforce a squadron under Vice Admiral Sir Robert Calder watching Ferrol.

Napoleon thought that the Brest fleet might now be able to slip into the Channel and provide cover for the invasion force. Admiral Ganteaume, however, knew that the risk was unacceptable. Napoleon estimated that he only needed four days to complete the crossing, but Ganteaume knew that the problem was to get the right four days when the sea was calm. He estimated he would have to be able to hold the narrow seas for two weeks, which would be plenty of time for Cornwallis to find him. He wrote,

> [If we] venture into the Channel with no more than twenty-two vessels which compose our fleet, it would not be long before we were observed, or before the vessels we had eluded would get contact. To these they would not have failed to join the whole of the force at their disposal on the coasts and in the ports of England, and then it seems to me the chances would be against us.[3]

The Brest fleet remained in port, and Villeneuve was caught by a squadron under Sir Robert Calder off Finisterre.

Rear Admiral Sir Robert Calder (1745-1815), by Lemuel Francis Abbott (1760-1803). (National Maritime Museum, London: BHC 2593)

Calder's action on 22 July was a skilful manoeuvre battle in foggy weather. With an inferior force he engaged the enemy line, and captured two of them. However, he did not renew the action on the next two days, and Villeneuve was able to get his fleet into Vigo. Calder was eventually censured at a court martial for his failure to act more aggressively. His concern with the possibility that Villeneuve might be reinforced was judged to have been misplaced.[4] Nelson's reaction on hearing of the battle was to comment that Calder appeared

> to have had the ships at Ferrol more in his head than the squadron in sight . . . He lays stress upon other considerations than fighting the enemy's squadron, if he could have done it, which he denies to be possible.[5]

After the battle of Trafalgar, when Villeneuve fell into conversation with Captain Durham of the *Defiance* on the quarterdeck of Collingwood's flagship, he expressed a regret that he and Calder had not 'fought it out that day. He would not be in his present situation, nor I in mine.' Certainly, if Calder had missed a chance, so had Villeneuve. However, he was hampered by having as many as 1,700 sick, and being down to four days' water. The failure of

3. Ganteaume to Decrès, 14 July 1805, J S Corbett, *The Campaign of Trafalgar*, London, 1910, II pp208–10.

4. Nicholas Tracy, 'Sir Robert Calder's Action', *Mariner's Mirror*, vol 77 no 3 (August 1991), pp259-270; *Blackwood's Magazine*, vol 187 no 993 March 1910, Edinburgh: William Blackwood, pp318–342.

5. J S Corbett, *Trafalgar*, II p196.

HMS Windsor Castle
*firing, by Nicholas
Pocock. Windsor Castle
was badly damaged
during Sir Robert
Calder's action, and the
need to protect her from
attack was a factor in
limiting the scale of
Calder's victory.*
(British Museum:
BM 870.12.10.234)

the French and Spanish fleets to copy the British introduction of an issue of lemon juice to prevent scurvy, which St Vincent had pioneered in the British Mediterranean fleet, was having its inevitable tactical consequences.

On 3 August Napoleon visited Boulogne again, to witness another embarkation rehearsal. The report given out was that everything went so well that he was able to repeat the operation in the afternoon. The whole affair was probably a propaganda effort: little over half the soldiers were available, and it was discovered that the landing craft could never be got out of harbour on a single tide. All the same, the Admiralty was sufficiently alarmed that it warned Cornwallis on the 9th that invasion was an immediate threat.[6]

In reality, however, Napoleon's always slender chance of effecting a decisive naval concentration in the Channel was now diminished beyond recall. Villeneuve had had to sail from Vigo because it was not defended against naval attack, and did not have facilities for resupplying and repairing the fleet. He took

his fleet to sea and made for Corunna and Ferrol. Gravina's ships had already passed into the defended harbour with no chance of getting out again against the wind, when a message reached Villeneuve from Napoleon that he was to proceed immediately to release the ships at Brest. He could only order the French ships to anchor in Corunna Bay. Even had he been able to continue, however, it is doubtful whether the Brest squadron would have been able to get out, and Napoleon would have been little better off if Villeneuve had succeeded only in getting into Brest himself. Gravina, who had spent nearly two years trapped at Brest between 1799 and 1802 had no doubts about the question, and wrote Decrès politely indicating his conviction that the invasion attempt had been decisively defeated.[7] Villeneuve had come to respect Gravina's judgment, and doubtless was influenced by his argument.

On 13 August Napoleon learnt that Villeneuve was in Ferrol. Nine days later he learnt that Villeneuve had sailed, and he hastily ordered Ganteaume to sail the Brest squadron when Villeneuve arrived. The Franco-Spanish combined fleet, however, was headed south to Cadiz where it was hoped that it would be easier to obtain supplies. According to General Lauriston, commanding the embarked soldiers, the fleet knew it was beaten:

> Sire, I am only on board temporarily but I have the honour to be Your Majesty's aide-de-camp; I am truly humiliated at finding myself present at so many ignominious manoeuvres, powerless to do the slightest thing for the honour of Your Majesty's flag. We sail like a fleet of merchantmen who fear the attack of 4 or 5 of the line and it is a single man [Nelson] who is the cause of all this. . . . The captains have no heart left to do well. Attention is no longer paid to signals, which are kept flying on the masts two or three hours. Discipline is completely gone.[8]

Lauriston's vicious and sycophantic account was doubtless influenced by his ambitions, but Villeneuve's command was in a poor condition. Two of Gravina's ships, and one French had had to be left behind at Vigo with the sick. In compensation, nine Spanish ships had been collected at Ferrol, but these had had no sea training. Inevitably their station-keeping was poor.

Whatever chance there might have been for the invasion was at an end, at least for that year. In fact, even before the news reached Paris that Villeneuve had gone south, the Minister of the Marine, Admiral Denise, Duc Decrès, urged Napoleon to look on that possibility 'as a decree of destiny, which is reserving you for other operations. . . . It is grievous to me,' he added, 'to know the naval profession, since this knowledge wins no confidence nor produces any result on your Majesty's combinations.'[9] He begged him to form a naval staff that might be able to advise him more effectively. Three days later, on 25 August, still before Villeneuve's movements were known in Paris, Napoleon told Talleyrand that he had given up his invasion plan and would concen-

Almirante Don Frederico Gravina (1756-1806). (Musée de la Marine, Paris: 75172)

trate on the problem of dealing with Austria which had mobilised to cooperate with Russia and Britain. The next day Marshal Berthier, the Emperor's chief of staff, received orders to break up the camp at Boulogne. The Army of England became the Grand Army, and Napoleon turned to face the crisis in central Europe that his ambitious policies in Italy had brought about.

The *Marine Français* had been spared a tragedy in the Channel, but Napoleon was not content with maintaining a fleet in being. Ten days before he departed to join the army, on 15 September, he sent Villeneuve orders to employ the forces under his command to carry troops to Naples to meet the threat posed by Sir James Craig's army and the Russian army from Corfu. The Anglo-Russian deployment proved to be the catalyst which finally led to the general action off Trafalgar.

In strategic terms, the invasion campaign was over, and attention could be entirely focused on the Mediterranean. In operational terms, there was no changing of gears in the Royal Navy. The objective remained, as it had always been, to defeat the Franco-Spanish fleet in detail before it could do any harm, and so that British resources would be set free for offensive purposes. Because Napoleon had given so little attention to the possible counter-moves of the British, his orders to Villeneuve played into their hands.

6. Barham to Cornwallis, 10 August 1805, *Historic Manuscripts Commission, Various Collections*, IV p410.

7. Gravina to Decrès, 3 August 1805, Archives Nationales, Paris (Marine); quoted by Alacalà Galiano, 1909.

8. General Alexander Lauriston to Napoleon, 21 August 1805, Desbrière, II pp113–117.

9. Decrès to Napoleon, 22 August 1805, Desbrière, II pp7–8.

Nelson Takes Command

On leaving the West Indies, Nelson had headed for Gibraltar, thinking it to be the most likely destination for the ships from Toulon and Cadiz, and being concerned for the security of British interests in the Mediterranean. At Gibraltar he learnt the news the *Curieux* had brought, and steered for the northward in accordance with the standing instructions for commanders to concentrate on the Western Squadron once it was clear that there was no immediate threat on their own stations. Calder, unfortunately, had not found any means of informing him that Villeneuve was sheltering in Ferrol, and a northerly wind drove Nelson's ships so far to seaward that they did not pass within sight of Calder's. Leaving most of his ships with Cornwallis, Nelson brought to at Spithead on 18 August.

After an absence of over two years, Nelson went home for what turned out to be his last and not very protracted leave. Barham called for his journal, but when he had read it found no fault with Nelson's conduct, and came to respect his judgments. The populace, who vilified Calder, gave Nelson a rapturous welcome. Lord Minto wrote:

I met Nelson today in a mob in Piccadilly

Lord Collingwood (1750-1810), Nelson's second-in-command at Trafalgar. Artist unknown. (National Maritime Museum, London: PAD 3140)

and got hold of his arm, so that I was mobbed too. It is really quite affecting to see the wonder and admiration, and love and respect, of the whole world; and the genuine expression of all these sentiments at once, from gentle and simple, the moment he is seen. It is beyond anything represented in a play or in a poem of fame.[10]

The orders Napoleon had given Villeneuve, and Villeneuve's actual movements, were of course matters of intense interest in London. Nelson believed that the West Indies were not the intended object, and that Villeneuve was likely to make for Cadiz, and thence to Toulon. He called on Castlereagh, the Foreign Secretary, where he met General Wellesley, and on Pitt. He complained to Captain Keats that he was 'set up for a conjurer'. Only reluctantly had he expressed his opinion because if he made any mistake, as he said, 'the charm will be broken'.[11]

Vice Admiral Cuthbert Collingwood, Nelson's old friend and soon to be his second-in-command, was convinced that Napoleon intended a renewed attempt against Ireland, but Barham agreed with Nelson, and ordered Cornwallis to detach a squadron to look for Villeneuve at Ferrol.[12] He had already done so, sending Calder with eighteen ships. This left an inferior force before Brest, but the danger of it being surprised by Villeneuve, had he in fact headed north, was remote. Cornwallis would have been faced with the necessity of refusing action and keeping to windward, but he would still have posed an unacceptable threat to any Franco-Spanish fleet which entered the Channel. The detachment south was essential if Villeneuve were not to be given a free run in the Mediterranean. There was also a need to provide escort for the West Indian convoy expected within the next few weeks. With the ships stationed at Cadiz added to the force, it numbered thirty-six of the line. As Captain Codrington wrote shortly before Trafalgar, had Cornwallis not detached

Calder, and had Calder not continued south to reinforce Collingwood, 'this immense force would probably by this time have been already in Toulon to co-operate with the French army in Italy'.[13]

Collingwood had been forced to retreat from his station with the arrival of Villeneuve, but had avoided being drawn into the Gibraltar current. When Calder did not find Villeneuve in Ferrol, he continued south to Cadiz. Although still heavily outnumbered by the combined fleet, Collingwood was strong enough after Calder's ships had joined him to resume the blockade because he would always be able to attack the van of the combined fleet before the main body could leave harbour. A little over two weeks after Nelson reached

Merton, Captain Henry Blackwood of the frigate *Euryalus* called there at 5am on his way to London to report the news.[14]

The nation had reason to be grateful for Emma's sympathetic understanding that Nelson must be set free to offer his services. On Friday 13 September he said his goodbyes to her and to Horatia and set off from Merton on the road to Portsmouth.

At half-past ten drove from dear, dear Merton, where I left all I hold dear in this world, to go to serve my King and Country. May the Great God whom I adore enable me to fulfill the expectations of my Country, and if it is His good pleasure that I should return, my thanks will never cease being

10. Elliot to his wife, 26 August 1805, *Minto* III p363.

11. Nelson to Keats, 24 August 1805, DLN VII pp15–16.

12. Collingwood to Nelson, 21 July 1805, Newnham Collingwood, pp93–4.

13. To his wife, 16 October 1805, *Codrington* I p56.

14. 'Memoirs of Vice-Admiral . . . Blackwood', *Blackwood's Edinburgh Magazine*, vol 34 (July 1833) no 210 pp7–8; DLN VII p26.

Single and Battle Recognition Pendants, issued and signed by Nelson & Bronte on the 29th of September to the fleet off Cadiz. Ten pendants could be used to identify 100 ships because they could be flown from different positions in the rigging, as indicated in the right-hand column. In battle, when there was a danger that a ship might lose a spar and be unable to show its pendant in its proper position, a different recognition code was used. Each ship would fly its own pendant wherever it could, along with a second pendant shown in the column on the left. The two-pendant code could also make up 100 combinations. (British Museum Add MS 21506 f.155)

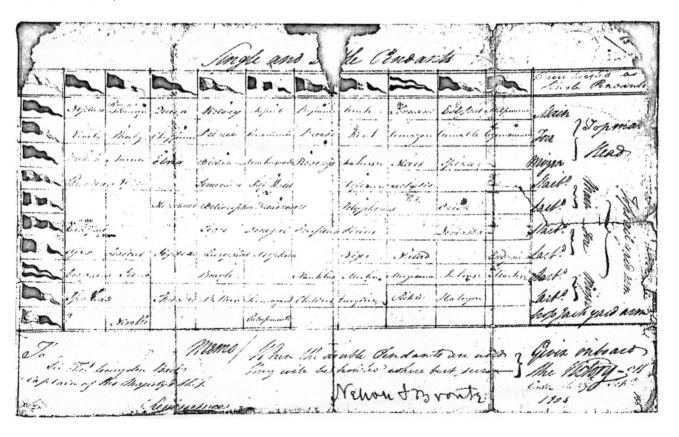

Sir Thomas Masterman Hardy (1769-1839), by Richard Evans (1784-1871). The picture was painted when Hardy was a Rear Admiral. (National Maritime Museum, London: BHC 2746)

15. Nelson's Private Diary, DLN VII pp33–35.

16. Southey, pp332–33.

17. ADM 3/154, 3, 9, 11 September, 5 October 1805.

18. Nelson to Lieut-General the Hon Henry Fox, 30 September 1805, DLN VII p55.

19. Midshipman Henry Walker to Mrs R Walker, 22 November 1805, *Logs*, II p322.

20. A T Mahan, *The Life of Nelson, The Embodiment of the Sea Power of Great Britain*, London: Sampson Low & Marston, 1898, vol 2 p333.

21. Duff to his wife, Sophia, 10 October 1805, DLN VII p71. See also Fremantle to ?, 28 September 1805, mm vol 16 (1930) pp409-10.

22. Codrington to his wife, 5 November 1805, *Codrington*, I pp68–69.

23. Collingwood to Spencer-Stanhope, 2 November 1805, Add MS 52780.

24. Collingwood to Blackett, 2 November 1805, Newnham Collingwood, p136.

25. Fraser, *Sailors*, pp259–60.

26. *Blackwood's Edinburgh Magazine*, vol 187 no 933, March 1910, p341.

offered up to the Throne of His Mercy. If it is His good providence to cut short my days upon earth, I bow with the greatest submission, relying that He will protect those so dear to me, that I may leave behind. His Will be done: Amen, Amen, Amen.[15]

According to the contemporary biography of Nelson by Robert Southey, at Portsmouth he tried to elude the populace but they found him out and followed him to his barge. The officer of the guard who tried to drive them away, was himself forced to back off.[16] Never has a commander found so deep an affection amongst the people, and amongst his officers and men. He boarded the *Victory* at St Helens, taking with him copies of Popham's telegraphic signal book to issue to the fleet.[17] On 28 September he joined the fleet watching Villeneuve and the Franco-Spanish fleet in Cadiz.

He had sent orders ahead that his flag was not to be saluted, so that the enemy would not be given notice of his arrival. To the governor of Gibraltar he wrote requesting him to avoid publicising his arrival, and to downplay the number of ships he had.[18] With his joining he brought the British force up to twenty-nine ships of the line. Five more joined him later, but on the day of the battle five ships were away resupplying at Gibraltar, and one was returning to England. At least as important as were the reinforcements was the reputation he brought with him. Midshipman Henry Walker was to write his mother after the battle:

Lord Nelson took the command of our fleet on the 29th of September, and though we had before that no doubt of success in the event of an action, yet the presence of such a man could not but inspire every individual in the fleet with additional confidence. Every one felt himself more than a match for any enemy that there was any probability of being opposed to.[19]

Barham had asked Nelson to select his own subordinate officers, but he had replied: 'Choose yourself, my lord, the same spirit actuates the whole profession; you cannot choose wrong.'[20] Only five of the captains had commanded their ships for more than two years, and only five had commanded a ship of the line in battle. But Nelson's superb qualities of leadership were adequate to the task. Captain Duff of the *Mars* was not alone in regarding Nelson as a man he would follow 'without any kind of orders'.[21]

As flag captain, Nelson wanted Sir Thomas Foley who had fought with him at the Nile and Copenhagen, but Foley was ill and declined the offer. In his place, Nelson's old friend but relatively junior captain Thomas Masterman Hardy was appointed. Captain Edward Codrington of *Orion* was impressed by Hardy. He wrote in a letter to his wife after Trafalgar that

From the first day that I saw him on board the *Victory* I was captivated by his manner, so unusual and yet so becoming to his situation as confidant of Lord Nelson; and I gave in to the general good opinion of the fleet. He has not beauty or those accomplishments which attract sometimes on shore above all other qualities; but he is very superior in his situation, and I feel for him more, perhaps, than our short acquaintance justifies.[22]

Nelson's second-in-command, Colling-wood, was an older man than Nelson by ten years, but Nelson had served with him as a lieutenant in the West Indies, and it was Collingwood along with Troubridge who had been so prompt to provide Nelson with desperately-needed support at the Battle of Cape St Vincent. 'Since the year '73,' he wrote to a friend after Trafalgar, 'we have been on the terms of the greatest intimacy; chance has thrown us very much together in service, and on many occasions we have acted in concert; there is scarce a naval subject that has not been the subject of our discussion, so that his opinions were familiar to me.'[23] He was a much crustier man than Nelson, but a thorough professional, and greatly admired by most of his officers, with the exception apparently of Codrington. He had been in general actions at the Glorious First of June and at Cape St Vincent, was experienced with blockade duty on the coast of Spain, and was a man whom Nelson could trust. Collingwood told Blackwood that Nelson 'did nothing without my counsel'. 'We made our line of Battle together, and concerted the mode of attack, which was put in execution in the most admirable style.'[24]

An officer of the *Royal Sovereign* described Collingwood, when he called on him a year after Trafalgar, as

> thin and spare in person, which was then slightly bent, and in height above five feet ten inches. His head was small, with a pale, smooth, round face, the features of which would pass without notice, were it not for the eyes, which were blue, clear, penetrating; and the mouth, the lips of which were thin and compressed, indicating firmness and decision of character. . . . On entering his presence, he took a rapid, searching survey of me from head to foot; then . . . in a quiet tone, amounting almost to gentleness, he put a few questions to me.[25]

Even before Trafalgar he had been longing for home and his family, but the Admiralty considered him indispensable. Five years later he died at his post, worn out by constant service, and never having seen his family again.

Nelson brought with him an order for Calder to return home to face the court martial he had requested. He urged him to stay for the battle which he felt to be imminent, but Calder disagreed, and asked to be allowed to return home in his three-decker *Prince of Wales*. Showing more compassion than judgment, Nelson did so. Calder let himself down badly, once he reached Portsmouth and learned that the battle had been fought and won, by applying for a share of the prize money. His brother officers responded at the court martial to this selfishness and insensitive greed by censuring his conduct, leading to his early retirement. The higher standards Nelson had set for the navy made Calder's condemnation inevitable, but later the Admiralty relented and in 1810 he was appointed to fly his flag as C-in-C Portsmouth.[26]

Rear Admiral Louis was a particular friend of Nelson's. He was to miss the battle, however, because it was necessary to begin the rotation of ships into Gibraltar for repairs and supplies. Louis was given command of the first detachment to go. Rear Admiral the Earl of Northesk thus became third in command. He was not well known by Nelson, or by Collingwood, but there seems to have been established a good working relationship.

William Carnegie, Rear Admiral the 7th Earl of Northesk (1758-1831), by Thomas Phillips (1770-1845). (National Maritime Museum, London: BHC 4224)

Contact

Past experience suggested that Calder's estimation that the blockade would have to be extended through the winter was all too probable. The effect of the long pursuit from Toulon, followed by orders to take dreadful risks while endeavoring always to avoid battle, was demoralising for Villeneuve. General Lauriston's report to Napoleon, that he had become obsessed with 'the fear of Nelson', need not be taken as unimpeachable, but clearly Villeneuve did not consider the odds were in favour of the Franco-Spanish force.[27] He was not alone in his reluctance to risk battle.

He summoned a council of war on 8 October, after the arrival of *Victory* and two 74s had been observed and when it was rumoured that Nelson had assumed command. The Spanish commanders, Gravina, Vice Admiral Alava, Rear Admiral Cisneros who had taken part in the Battle of Cape St Vincent, and Rear Admiral Escaño who served as Gravina's chief of staff, all advised against risking battle with inexperienced crews, and counselled waiting until bad weather or the shortage of supplies might have driven off the blockaders. Gravina was also most unwilling to act against Naples, which was the land of his birth, and protested that Spain could not

act against King Ferdinand who was brother to Charles IV.[28]

Nelson changed Collingwood's dispositions, moving the inshore ships of the line further away from the coast where they were safer from onshore winds, and could form a link between the frigates watching the harbour, and the battlefleet. They could also support the frigates in the event that the combined fleet sortied. A schooner and a cutter were stationed with the frigates to carry dispatches. Duff was put in command of the heavy screen, and instructed to

> keep, with *Mars*, *Defence*, and *Colossus*, from three to four leagues between the Fleet and Cadiz, in order that I may get the information from the Frigates stationed off that Port, as expeditiously as possible. Distant Signals to be used, when Flags, from the state of the weather, may not readily be distinguished in their colours. If the Enemy be out, or coming out, fire guns by day or night, in order to draw my attention. In thick weather the Ships are to close within signal of the *Victory*; one of the Ships to be placed to windward, or rather to the Eastward of the other two, to extend the distance of seeing; and I have desired Captain Blackwood to throw a Frigate to the Westward of Cadiz, for the purpose of an easy and early communication.[29]

Nelson moved the main fleet well to seaward with the hope that they would be out of sight to watchers ashore. It was feared that Villeneuve would not move if he thought there would be a battle. The distant watch was also made necessary by the current into the Mediterranean. If Nelson had chosen a position near the Trafalgar shoals there was a danger that a westerly gale would oblige the fleet to pass through the Straits of Gibraltar, from whence it would have difficulty returning. This would have left open the route to the English Channel. To guard against that 'worst

27. Lauriston to the Emperor, 21 August 1805, Desbrière, II pp113–117.

28. Minutes of the Council of War, 8 October 1805, (untitled document), Archives Nationales, Paris (Marine) BB4/230; and Gravina to Godoy, 28 September 1805, quoted by Alcalà Galiano, 1909.

29. Nelson to Duff, and to Blackwood, 4 October 1805, DLN VII pp70-73; and *Naval Miscellany* I p437.

case', the lesser danger had to be accepted that the enemy would sail on a night land breeze and get into the Mediterranean while the British were becalmed off shore.

When he was furnished with a copy of General Craig's instructions for the Naples operation, and when Blackwood informed him that troops were being embarked in the combined fleet, Nelson's belief that Villeneuve would be heading for the Mediterranean was reinforced. He was able to relax his anxiety that the combined fleet might be joined by the Cartagena squadron on an easterly Levanter wind and make for the West Indies.

The British believed that the combined fleet would eventually be forced out of Cadiz because of the impossibility of finding provisions for so many men from the resources available locally. These could not be supplemented by sea because Collingwood, independent of London which was concerned about neutral reactions, had instituted a blockade of Andalusian ports. Plans were also afoot to drive the combined fleet to sea by attacking it with the new Congreve rockets, 'the soul of

artillery without the body'. For fear of such an attack, the combined fleet was crowded into the inner harbour, and Franco-Spanish efforts at storing ship were hampered by men being employed in boat patrols at the harbour mouth.

In fact, however, Villeneuve was only driven out of harbour by the fear of being removed from his command. Napoleon was ready to believe Lauriston's accounts, and decided on 18 September to replace Villeneuve with Vice Admiral Rosily, who reached Madrid on 12 October but was unable to proceed because the roads were unsafe. Somehow, Villeneuve got word on the 17th of his successor's imminent arrival. Earlier, he had received an exhortation from Napoleon that he was no longer to regard the preservation of his ships as important 'if they are lost with glory'. His honour was at stake, and he determined with Gravina's support to carry out the movement into the Mediterranean even if that necessitated a battle. The next day, he ordered Magon to sea with seven ships of the line and a frigate to try and capture the screening force. He then

1804 Chart of the South Coast of Spain and the Strait of Gibraltar.– View of the approaches to Cadiz. (British Museum: BL 18212 (7))

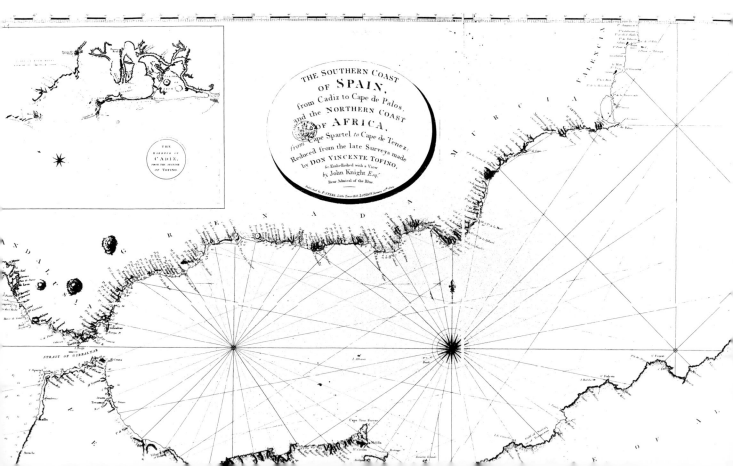

Blackwood (1770-1832), by John Hoppner (1758-1810). Blackwood commanded the frigates which kept Nelson informed of the sailing and deployment of the combined Franco-Spanish fleet before the battle of Trafalgar. (National Maritime Museum, London: BHC 2557)

received intelligence that Rear Admiral Louis's force was at Gibraltar, and, concluding that now was the time to take the fleet to sea when the blockaders were at their lowest number, ordered it to be ready for immediate departure.[30]

Light airs made it a slow business moving ships out of the harbour into Cadiz bay, and it was on the morning of 19 October by the naval calendar that ran from noon to noon, or 20 October by the civil calendar, that the *Sirius* used Admiral Popham's telegraphic signals to inform the commander of the inshore squadron, Blackwood, 'Enemy have their topsails hoisted.' An hour later *Sirius* signalled, 'The enemy ships are coming out of port or getting under sail', number 370 by Popham's telegraphic signals. Midshipman Hercules Robinson later recalled that the

in-shore squadron [was] so close to Cadiz as to see the ripple of the beach and catch the morning fragrance which came off the land; and then as the sun rose over the Trocadero, with what joy we saw the fleet inside let fall and hoist their topsails, and one after another slowly emerge from the harbour's mouth. Before noon they had formed a long line of nearly six miles in length, standing under easy sail to the Westward, the wind at S.S.W.[31]

30. Villeneuve to the Minister of the Marine, 18-20 October 1805, Desbrière, II pp111-112.

31. Hercules Robinson, *Sea Drift*, p209.

32. Captain Cumby's Letter, *The Nineteenth Century, A Monthly Review*, ed. James Knowles, London: Sampson Low, Marston, 1899, vol 46, July-December 1899 pp718-728.

Blackwood passed the message to *Phoebe* which he had stationed to the westward, she to the 74-gun *Mars*, and Captain Duff passed the message to Nelson at 9:30am. Lieutenant William Pryce Cumby, First Lieutenant in *Bellerophon*, was mortified that Captain Cook, whose eyesight was not as good as his, would not repeat the signal until he was certain.

> Soon afterwards the *Mars* hauled down the flags, and I said, 'Now she will make the *distant signal* 370' which distant signals were made with a flag, a ball, and a pendant differently disposed at different mastheads by a combination totally unconnected with the colour of the flag or pendant used. She did make the distant signal No. 370 as I had predicted; this could not be mistaken, and as we were preparing to repeat it, the *Mars* signal was answered from the *Victory*.[32]

Blackwood also sent sloops to Gibraltar and Cape Spartel at the southern side of the Strait, but they failed to find Rear Admiral Louis.

The fleet was then 50 miles from Cadiz. Nelson ordered 'General chase, south-east.'. At 8am on the 20th the *Victory* was hove too. Collingwood, and the captains of the screening ships of the line, came on board for a conference. Then Nelson signalled the fleet to form order of sailing in two columns (No. 72). This movement brought the fleet into the mouth of the Straits of Gibraltar, and to avoid the danger of being forced through them by the current Nelson now put the fleet on a north-westerly course. There was intense disappointment because it was feared that Villeneuve had put back into Cadiz.

The ships that *Sirius* had sighted were Rear Admiral Magon's. The rest of the Franco-Spanish fleet had been unable to sail because of the calm, and Magon's ships had been unable to make their sweep because of light airs until the late afternoon, when they stood to the northward. Their mission had been hopeless from the start, but the wind did not permit their return to Cadiz. In consequence, Villeneuve felt he had no choice but to renew the effort to sail the rest of the fleet, which he was able to do when a light wind came from the south about the time that the British fleet hove-to off Cape Trafalgar. During the late morning the wind began to strengthen, coming around to the southwestward with rain squalls, foul for the Straits. Villeneuve ordered the fleet to reef and make course to the west-northwest, and tried to make as much westing as possible so that they could safely clear the shoals off Cape Trafalgar. About noon he ordered the Franco-Spanish fleet to form order of sailing in three columns, Gravina's squadron of observation, which was both a scouting force and a tactical unit, sailing as the third column. Together, there were eighteen French ships of the line and fifteen Spanish, with five French frigates and two brigs. About 4pm a shift of the wind obliged Villeneuve to tack, and lay on a course to the south-south-west.

Blackwood had brought *Euryalus* to within signalling distance of the *Victory* at 3pm on the 20th, and informed Nelson that 'The enemy

Distance Signals from the 1799 Admiralty Signal Book for Ships of War. This system of signalling depended on the shape of the signal alone and could be used at distances which made it impossible to distinguish the colours of signal flags. As only one number at a time could be flown, it was a slower system and quite unsuited to transmitting complicated signals such as Popham's Telegraphic Signals.
(© Crown Copyright/MOD)

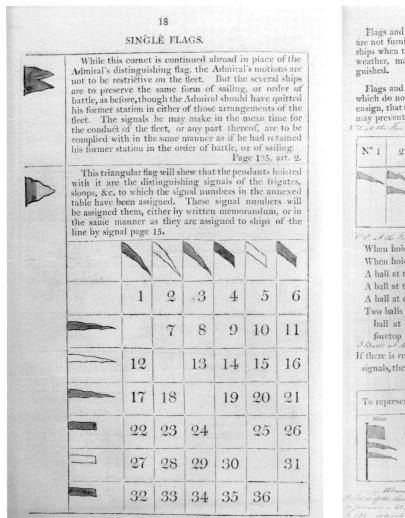

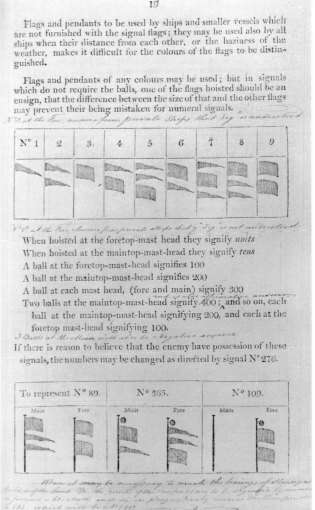

Movement of the British Fleet from midnight 20-21 October until the action opened before noon.

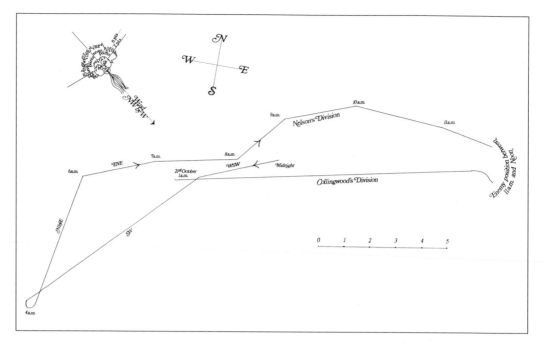

appears determined to push to the westward'. That, Nelson wrote in his diary, 'they shall *not* do if in the power of Nelson & Bronte to prevent them. At 5 telegraphed Captain B., that I relied upon his keeping sight of the enemy.'[33]

Until 4am on the 20th/21st, when Nelson ordered a course north by east, the fleets were diverging. Villeneuve's scouts sighted the main British fleet and signalled with guns and rockets. A brig found the flagship in the dark, and reported sighting eighteen British ships of the line. Villeneuve, remembering Nelson's precipitous attack at the Nile, feared there might be a night action, when the order of sailing would have risked friend firing into friend. He signalled the fleet to form line of battle, taking their bearing from the leewardmost ship, and without seeking to conform to their proper order. This was simpler than forming the 'ordre naturel', but nonetheless difficult in the dark. The failure of the leewardmost ship to exhibit the lights which it ought to have done created confusion, caused the squadrons to become mixed up, and to form into several different lines on whatever ships they were able to find. At 5:50am it was light enough for the Franco-Spanish fleet to see the British silhouetted against the dawn.

Blackwood had followed the Franco-Spanish fleet and kept Nelson informed of its movement by night signals. 'Enemy standing to the southward' was signalled by exhibiting two blue lights at hourly intervals, and 'enemy standing to the westward' was signalled by three guns fired in quick succession, every hour.[34] Robinson recalled that

> When we had brought the two fleets fairly together we took our place between the lines of lights, as a cab might in Regent Street, the watch was called, and Blackwood turned in quietly to wait for the morning.[35]

At 4am Nelson ordered the fleet to sail North by East, which placed them 9 miles to windward of the enemy when they were sighted from the *Victory* at 6am. The sea was flat, and the sun shone. The wind was light, but to the experienced seaman it was evident that there was a hard blow coming. Nelson immediately signalled the fleet a reminder to form order of sailing in two columns (No. 72) and ordered it to sail large East-Northeast (No. 76) so as to retain the weather gage, and cut off the combined fleet from Cadiz. The British fleet was somewhat scattered, but the columns started to form, and to set all sail. Everyone knew that battle was imminent.

33. Nelson's diary, DLN VII p137.

34. Memorandum, 20 October 1805, DLN VII p136.

35. Hercules Robinson, *Sea Drift*, p209.

Nelson's Tactics

Nelson's tactics at the Battle of Trafalgar were consistent with the developing practice since the Battle of the Saintes, and especially with Lord Howe's method of securing decisive results by closing with the enemy rapidly from windward, and then preventing its further manoeuvre by cutting through its line and engaging from the leeward. Central to this conception was the belief that close mutual support, efficient ship handling and good gunnery were more important than good station-keeping and fleet manoeuvre. Nelson rammed his fleet, in two columns, into the enemy line with precisely the same dependence on momentum and morale as was seen in the infantry tactics of the French Revolutionary army under the command of Napoleon's marshals. Napoleon won battle after battle in this way, until his columns came up against a well-disciplined line of British regular infantry. Nelson's tactics would similarly have been defeated by a skillful French admiral commanding a fleet of the pre-revolutionary Marine, but that was not the enemy Nelson faced at Trafalgar. His tactics were suited to the occasion; to his knowledge of the professional abilities and morale of his fleet and that of his enemy. Had he realised, however, that Villeneuve was determined to fight if he could not get clean away, he might have given his fleet more time to get into order for mutual support.

Our understanding of Nelson's tactical ideas are based on a plan of attack he drew up, probably in 1803; a conversation he had with Sir Richard Keats in August or September 1805; a memorandum written on the *Victory* off Cadiz 9 October 1805; and an additional tactical signal issued by Nelson to the fleet. None of these presented exactly the tactical plan used at Trafalgar, but they represent the line of thought Nelson was pursuing, and which he discussed with his officers.

The most important passages of the 1803 memorandum are those which express his confidence in the ability and will of his fleet to defeat the enemy if only he can bring them

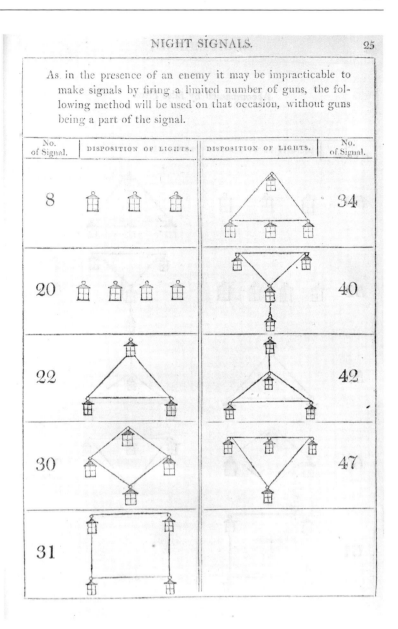

Night Signals from the 1799 Admiralty Signal Book for Ships of War. The signals shown indicate: #8 Having passed by an enemy's ship without taking possession of her (to be accompanied by a rocket); #20 To make sail after lying-by, the van first (2 guns); #22 Tack, the headmost and weathermost ships first (2 guns); #30 Haul the wind on the larboard tack (3 guns); #34 Bring to on the starboard tack (3 guns); #40 Alter course to starboard (4 guns); #42 The fleet is to tack together (4 guns); #47 Bear-up and sail large, or before the wind (4 guns and a rocket). (© Crown Copyright/MOD)

into close action. 'A day is soon lost' if an admiral tries too hard to manoeuvre so as to provide his fleet with a clear tactical advantage. Instead, Nelson was prepared to take calculated risks, such as wearing his fleet while in the act of cutting the enemy line, a manoeuvre

Captain Sir R G Keats, published by J Stratford, 1 March 1810. (National Maritime Museum, London: PAD 3466)

which would expose the sterns of his rearmost ships to the guns of the enemy van, and his own van to the undamaged ships of the enemy rear. Only a pronounced advantage in ship-handling, gunnery and morale could justify such action.

In fact Nelson did not attempt at Trafalgar either tactical manoeuvre which had interested him in 1803. His conversation with Sir Richard Keats shows that he had continued to simplify his thinking, leaving even more to the initiative of his subordinates. He did not have the opportunity to read Von Clausewitz's study *On War,* which was not published until 1832, but he would have approved of Clausewitz's observation that 'Everything in war is very simple, but the simplest thing is difficult.'[36] The 'friction' which impedes any military operation defeats complexity. Keats reported that

One morning, walking with Lord Nelson in the grounds of Merton, talking on Naval matters, he said to me, 'No day can be long enough to arrange a couple of Fleets and fight a decisive Battle according to the old system. When we meet them,' (I was to have been with him), 'for meet them we shall, I'll

tell you how I shall fight them. I shall form the Fleet into three Divisions in three Lines. One Division shall be composed of twelve or fourteen of the fastest two-decked Ships, which I shall keep always to windward or in a situation of advantage, and I shall put them under an Officer who, I am sure, will employ them in the manner I wish, if possible. I consider it will always be in my power to throw them into Battle in any part I may choose; but if circumstances prevent their being carried against the Enemy where I desire, I shall feel certain he will employ them effectually, and, perhaps, in a more advantageous manner than if he could have followed my orders.' (He never mentioned, or gave any hint by which I could understand who it was he intended for this distinguished service.) He continued–'With the remaining part of the Fleet formed in two Lines, I shall go at them at once, if I can, about one third of their Line from their leading Ship.' He then said, 'What do you think of it?'. Such a question I felt required consideration. I paused. Seeing it he said, 'But I will tell you what *I* think of it. I think it will surprise and confound the Enemy. They won't know what I am about. It will bring forward a pell-mell battle, and that is what I want.'[37]

This was the first recent mention of the separation of the fleet into divisions but he had discussed a similar plan with his officers before the Nile. He does not specifically indicate that they were to be deployed in column to attack the enemy line, but it is not unreasonable to read that into his conversation because it is evident that he was thinking of a highly flexible battle plan, and because of his opinion that the enemy would find it hard 'to know what I am about'. There would have been no tactical surprise in using three squadrons in line ahead.

The value of attacking in several columns did not lie in the dispersal of enemy fire against more than one column, because the enemy gunners would not all have been able to concentrate on one column in any event because of the limitations of range. The enemy

36. Clausewitz, p119.
37. DLN VII p241 n.
38. TUN/61. See Tunstall/Tracy, pp250–251.

was being permitted to cross the British 'T'. This was a very dangerous manoeuvre for the fleet Nelson commanded, but technical limitations prevented it being the disaster it was to be a hundred years later when the Japanese fleet brought the Russian line under fire at the Battle of Tsushima. Nelson's purpose was not to reduce the danger of the approach, but to strengthen the shock once the approach had been made. The use of three columns would serve to engage more of the enemy ships, and presumably increase the scale of the victory.

His main effort was to be against the enemy rear, and he would entrust his subordinate flag officer to see that the job was well done. His own responsibility was to contain the enemy van so that it could not interfere with the attack on the rear, and to add to his own laurels, and to the enemy's loss, by capturing or destroying as many as possible of the ships in the centre. He counted on the surprise which his courting of risks would occasion to confound the enemy.

Nelson had continued to develop his idea, or perhaps it would be more accurate to say that he continued to simplify it. He tightened the conception in the Cadiz memorandum by establishing that the order of sailing should also be the order of battle, except that the flagships should move back from the exposed position at the head of the column. He also broke with convention by indicating that the attack should be made under full sail, which risked collisions, and would prevent the slower sailers keeping their station, but which would reduce the time of the approach.

The manoeuvre anticipated for the leeward column when attacking the enemy line to windward resembled Lord Howe's intent at the Glorious First of June. The approach at Trafalgar was from the windward, but Vice Admiral Collingwood did order his division to deploy in line of bearing so that the enemy line would be cut in many places, and engaged from the other side, or both sides. Had Nelson done so as well, contact with the enemy might have resembled Duncan's tactics at Camperdown. He did not do so, however, probably because until close to the enemy line he continued to think that Villeneuve was trying to avoid action. Because of the speed of the approach, the leeward column was unable to fully execute Collingwood's order. Nelson did not employ an advanced squadron at Trafalgar, perhaps because his numbers were inadequate. Instead, the Earl of Northesk's ships formed the rear of Collingwood's division.

The signal which Nelson issued to his fleet required it 'To cut through the enemy's line and engage them on the other side.' The place where the enemy line was to be cut would be indicated by another signal. Ships were to make all possible sail, and when they reached the enemy line they were to cut away the studding sails so as to reduce speed quickly, and reduce the risk of the sails catching fire.[38] This signal was not used at Trafalgar, but in fact the fleet acted as though it had been.

The essential component of the plan was that of morale. The head-on attack exposed the leading ships to injury they could not im-

Nelson's order of battle issued on 10 October 1805. When the battle was fought, however, the order was not strictly adhered to. The memorandum which followed has been printed at the end of this chapter. (British Museum: Add MS 33,963)

mediately return, and then placed them in the heart of the enemy fleet where they either had to fight with a skill and courage based on confidence in Nelson and themselves, or perish. Much depended on the certainty that the captains in the rear would not hesitate to come with all speed to support the leaders. Perhaps only Nelson could have persuaded his captains that they could brave these dangers and win. When he joined the fleet off Cadiz his reception, as he wrote to Emma Hamilton, 'caused the sweetest sensation of my life'.

> I believe my arrival was most welcome not only to the Commander of the Fleet, but also to every individual in it; and when I came to explain to them the *'Nelson touch'* it was like an electric shock. Some shed tears, all approved. 'It was new–it was singular–it

was simple!' and, from Admirals downwards, it was repeated–'It must succeed, if ever they will allow us to get at them! You are, my Lord, surrounded by friends whom you inspire with confidence.'[39]

The Cadiz memorandum probably did no more than state in writing what he had previously described to his 'friends' in the great cabin of the *Victory*.

In retrospect, not all the captains were entirely convinced of the merits of Nelson's tactics, and some either failed to understand his intention, or were confused by his subsequent changes of mind. Captain Robert Moorsom of the *Revenge* believed that 'a regular plan was laid down by Lord Nelson some time before the action, but not acted upon'. He may not have understood the subtleties of Nelson's

39. Nelson to Emma
Hamilton, 1 October 1805,
DLN VII p60.

Engraving of Nelson's conference with his captains on board Victory *before the battle of Trafalgar, by Marshall Craig, artist, James Godby, engraver, and published by Edward Orme. (National Maritime Museum, London: PAD 4050)*

LIST OF SHIPS PRESENT AT TRAFALGAR

(Note: All three national fleets had ships named Neptune or Neptuno, and both the British and French had ships named Swiftsure. Téméraire and Tonnant in the British fleet were prizes taken from the French.)

BRITISH Van–Weather Line

Ship	Guns	Commander
Victory	100	Vice Admiral Viscount Nelson, KB, Captain Thomas Masterman Hardy
Téméraire	98	Captain Eliab Harvey
Neptune	98	Captain Thomas Francis Fremantle
Britannia	100	Rear Admiral the Earl of Northesk, Captain Charles Bullen
Leviathan	74	Captain Henry William Bayntun
Conqueror	74	Captain Israel Pellew
Agamemnon	64	Captain Sir Edward Berry
Ajax	74	Lieutenant John Pilfold (acting)
Orion	74	Captain Edward Codrington
Minotaur	74	Captain Charles John Moore Mansfield
Spartiate	74	Captain Sir Francis Laforey, Baronet
Defiance	74	Captain Phillip Charles Durham
Prince	98	Captain Richard Grindall
Dreadnought	98	Captain John Conn
Africa	64	Captain Henry Digby

BRITISH Rear–Lee Line

Ship	Guns	Commander
Royal Sovereign	100	Vice Admiral Cuthbert Collingwood, Captain Edward Rotheram
Belleisle	74	Captain William Hargood
Colossus	74	Captain James Nicoll Morris
Mars	74	Captain George Duff
Tonnant	80	Captain Charles Tyler
Bellerophon	74	Captain John Cooke
Achille	74	Captain Richard King
Polyphemus	64	Captain Richard Redmill
Revenge	74	Captain Robert Moorsom
Swiftsure	74	Captain William Gordon Rutherford
Defence	74	Captain George Hope
Thunderer	74	Lieutenant John Stockham (acting)

Frigates

Euryalus	Captain the Hon Henry Blackwood
Naiad	Captain Thomas Dundas
Phoebe	Captain the Hon Thomas Bladen Capel
Sirius	Captain William Prowse

Schooner

Pickle	Lieutenant John Richard Lapenotière

Cutter

Entreprenante	Lieutenant Robert Young

SPANISH

Ship	Guns	Commander
Santissima Trinidad	130	Rear Admiral Don Baltaser Cisneros, Brigadier Don F Uriarte
Principe de Asturias	112	Admiral Don F Gravina, Rear Admiral Don Antonio Escaño Brigadier Rafael de Hore
Argonauta	80	Captain Don Antonio Pareja
Neptuno	80	Brigadier Don C Valdes
Santa Ana	112	Vice Admiral Don Ignacio de Alava Captain José Gardoqui
Rayo	100	Brigadier Don Enrique Macdonnell
Montanes	74	Captain Don J Alcedo
Monarca	74	Captain Don T Argumosa
San Juan Nepomuceno	74	Brigadier Don C Churruca
San Francisco de Asis	74	Captain Don Luis de Flores
Bahama	74	Brigadier Don D Galiano
San Justo	74	Captain Don Gaston
San Leandro	64	Captain Don José Quevedo
San Augustin	74	Brigadier Don F X Cajigal
San Ildefonso	74	Brigadier Don José de Vargas

FRENCH

Ship	Guns	Commander
Bucentaure	80	Vice Admiral P C J B S Villeneuve, Captain J J Magendie
Formidable	80	Rear Admiral P R M E Dumanoir le Pelley Captain J M Letellier
Algésiras	74	Rear Admiral C Magon de Médine, Captain Le Tourneur
Indomptable	80	Captain J J Hubert
Neptune	80	Captain E T Maistral
Pluton	74	Captain J M Cosmao-Kerjulien
Mont Blanc	74	Captain J G N La Villegris
Swiftsure	74	Captain C E l'Hôpitalier-Villemadrin
Scipion	74	Captain C Bellenger
Berwick	74	Captain J G Filhol-Camas
Intrépide	74	Captain L A C Infernet
Aigle	74	Captain P P Gourrège
Héros	74	Captain J B J R Poulain
Fougueux	74	Captain L A Baudoin
Duguay Trouin	74	Captain C Touffet
Argonaute	74	Captain J Epron
Redoutable	74	Captain J J E Lucas
Achille	74	Captain G Deniéport

Frigates

Ship	Guns	Commander
Hermione	40	Captain Mahé
Hortense	40	Captain La Marre La Meillerie
Cornelie	40	Captain de Martinenq
Thémis	40	Captain Jugan
Rhin	40	Captain Chesneau
Argus (brig)	10	Lieutenant Taillard
Furet (brig)	18	Lieutenant Dumay

thinking, but at least he did appreciate that 'his great anxiety' was 'to get to leeward of them, lest they should make off to Cadiz before he could get near'.[40] An unknown officer who probably served on *Conqueror* later wrote a critique of Nelson's tactics which indicate that he, despite the actual wording of the Cadiz memorandum, was expecting a more conventional and safer plan of attack.

> If the regulated plan of attack had been adhered to, the English fleet should have borne up together, and have sailed in a line abreast in their respective divisions until they arrived up with the enemy. Thus the plan which consideration had matured would have been executed, than which perhaps nothing could be better; the victory would have been more speedily decided, and the brunt of the action would have been more equally felt, &c.[41]

On at least one ship, *Bellerophon*, the first lieutenant and master were given the Cadiz memorandum to read so that they would understand Nelson's intentions should the captain be killed.[42] It was not, however, regarded by Nelson as more than a general statement of intention. Unlike the battle of Copenhagen, when Nelson had been able to issue his captains with detailed instructions, at Trafalgar he

had to plan for a greater degree of improvisation, if he was to get the annihilating victory he wanted. Collingwood was sure that the results were 'the effect of system and nice combination, not of chance', but Nelson's calculations went on right down to the wire and not all his captains agreed that he made the right decisions.[43]

In the final analysis, Nelson's personal rapport with his command outweighed in importance his tactical ideas. When sending the memorandum to Collingwood Nelson wrote,

> I send you my plan of attack, as far as a man dare venture to guess at the very uncertain position the enemy may be found in: but, my dear friend, it is to place you perfectly at ease respecting my intentions, and to give full scope to your judgment for carrying them into effect. We can, my dear Coll, have no little jealousies: we have only one great object in view, – that of annihilating our enemies, and getting a glorious peace for our Country. No man has more confidence in another than I have in you; and no man will render your services more justice than your very old friend.[44]

Nothing could have been more different from the service jealousies which defeated British hopes at the battle of Toulon.

Villeneuve's Tactics

Although there is no evidence that Nelson's ideas had in any direct way been betrayed to the enemy, it is certain that Admiral Villeneuve did in fact have a fair understanding of how Nelson would go about his business. In August he had written that he would be sorry to meet twenty British ships of the line: 'Our naval tactics are antiquated. We know nothing but how to place ourselves in line, and that is just what the enemy wants'.[45] In his final instructions to the Allied fleet on 21 October he wrote that

> The enemy will not confine himself to forming on a line of battle with our own and engaging us in an artillery duel, in which success is frequently with the more skillful but always with the more fortunate; he will endeavour to envelope our rear, to break through our line and to direct his ships in groups upon such of ours as he shall have cut off, so as to surround them and defeat them.[46]

This estimation must largely have been based

on his experience of Nelson's methods at the Nile, on a manuscript signal book which was captured when the schooner *Redbridge* was taken in 1804, and possibly from reading Clerk of Eldin, and studying the battle of Camperdown.

Surprisingly, Villeneuve did not give his subordinates any tactical plan for meeting the expected attack, beyond recommending that they read the general introductory section of the French signal book. His only innovation had been the formation of a squadron of observation, of twelve ships organised in two divisions under the overall command of Admiral Gravina in the 112-gun *Principe de Asturias*. This force might have proved a highly effective instrument if it had been used to attack the leeward line on its flank, or had been deployed to leeward of the main fleet to engage British ships which passed through the line. In fact, however, the squadron of observation was simply used to extend the Franco-Spanish line. Either Villeneuve was more concerned by the discovery that the British fleet was larger than he had expected, or he had not adequately discussed with Gravina how his force should be employed.

As soon as he saw the British fleet, and had light enough to signal, Villeneuve ordered his command to form the proper line-of-battle, or 'ordre naturel' on the starboard tack. This obliged individual ships to wear out of the *ad hoc* lines which had been formed, and try and reach their proper stations. To Nelson it looked as though they were wearing in succession, and the British were puzzled to discover what was the Franco-Spanish formation. What was in fact taking place was the sort of disorder which in St Vincent's elegant phrase, amounted to 'bitching it'. The confusion was compounded when sometime between 7:15 and 8:30am, and before the line had been drawn up, Villeneuve ordered his fleet to wear together and form in reverse order. Commodore Cosmo de Churruca, who commanded the *San Juan Nepomuceno* and was to die in the action, was believed to have regarded Villeneuve's decision as disastrous. Admiral Escaño, on the other hand, only re-

gretted that Villeneuve had not made the signal a hour earlier so as to give the inexperienced officers and seamen more time to get in station.

In the light wind, ships which had been separated from their squadrons in the night could only be moved into their proper stations if those at the van all but stopped their way. Inevitably, those in the new rear found the line becoming congested ahead of them, and had to bear away to leeward, or even wear back onto their old course to avoid collision. The manoeuvre was never fully carried out, and the combined fleet, with Gravina's division forming the rear, took up a rough crescent formation sagging away to leeward and with a large gap in the centre.

The advantage which Villeneuve might have made of the position of the squadron of observation somewhat to windward was lost when Gravina ordered it to conform to the movements of the main fleet. Villeneuve, at 11:30am, ordered him to keep the wind so as to be able to support the centre and double any ships attacking it, but Gravina did not do so, perhaps because it was by then too late. On the other hand, the involuntary doubling of the line due to the difficulty of taking up station properly in the light wind did reinforce it against the assault Nelson was making.

Commodore Churruca perceived that the effect of Nelson's attack would be to isolate the Franco-Spanish van, rendering it incapable of playing a useful part. He thought that Villeneuve should have ordered the van to wear together to threaten the British rear. When no signal was made, he muttered that all was lost, and ordered the chaplain to absolve the souls of the crew. He promised them eternal happiness if they died doing their duty, but threatened that shirkers would be shot.

Had Villeneuve stood on to the southeastward he might have got away through the Straits of Gibraltar, but evidently he did not consider that the odds would have been better. Nelson would of course have pursued him, and the Franco-Spanish fleet would have had to pass Gibraltar where Vice Admiral Louis was taking on supplies.

40. Robert Moorsom to Richard Moorsom, 4 December 1805, *Logs*, II p244.

41. Sir Charles Ekins, *Naval Battles from 1744 to the Peace of 1814*, London: Baldwin, Cradock and Joy, 1828, p271; and *Fighting Instructions*, pp351–358.

42. Captain Cumby's letter.

43. Collingwood to Sir Thomas Pasley, 16 December 1805, *Collingwood* #97 p168.

44. 9 October 1805, Newnham Collingwood, p100.

45. Villeneuve to Decrès, 13 August 1805, Louis Adolphe Thiers, *History of the Consulate and Empire of France under Napoleon*, 12 volumes, London: Chatto and Windus, 1893, III pp394–395.

46. Villeneuve's Final Instructions, reissue of those of 21 December 1804, Desbrière, II pp129–132.

Deployment

Nelson had signalled 'Prepare for Battle' shortly after 6am, but the light wind meant that it would be another six hours before the fleets were engaged. In late October that left only a comparatively short afternoon to get the results he wanted. Accompanying the fitful wind was a heavy swell, and a falling barometer. There was every prospect that the heavy sultry day would end in a gale, as indeed it did. Nelson was especially concerned that the Franco-Spanish fleet would succeed in getting back into Cadiz, and supposed that Villeneuve's decision to reverse order was made with that intention. In fact, however, it ensured that an engagement could not be avoided.

Villeneuve's commitment to battle only became evident to Nelson in the last minutes before the ships opened fire. The years of patrol and the long chase had effected him as much as it had Villeneuve, and perhaps made him more reckless than a cooler calculation would have advised. Nelson's reminder to the fleet to form order of sailing in two columns (No. 72), and then to 'bear up and sail large' (No. 76), was consistent with his usual way of controlling an unformed fleet. The order was carried out in succession so that the lee and weather columns formed in Collingwood's and Nelson's wakes.[47] Neither he nor Collingwood were willing to delay the attack so that slower ships could gain their proper stations.

As soon as Collingwood saw the northward movement of the Franco-Spanish line he had steered to close the *Santa Ana*, the last ship in what was now the allied third division, and Vice Admiral Alava's flagship. At about 8:45am Collingwood exercised his authority

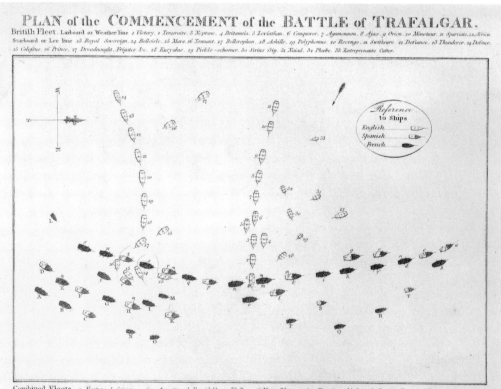

Plan of the commencement of the battle of Trafalgar. (National Maritime Museum, London: PAD 4051)

over the leeward column by signalling it to deploy into 'the larboard line of bearing' [No. 42] and to 'make more sail' [No. 88].[48] This rather fundamental order in effect over-rode Nelson's tactical signals to attack in the order of sailing. Collingwood may have thought that Nelson would eventually deploy the windward column into line of bearing so that the fleet could bear away in a single line of battle parallel to the Franco-Spanish fleet. Nelson, however, was taking no chance of Villeneuve being able to fight a defensive action and withdraw in good order. His determination to annihilate the enemy even at great risk was driven not only by his two years of blockade and pursuit, but also by the hundred years of experience the navy had had of the skill with which French fleets broke off action when it seemed best to them.

When Nelson kept a press of sail, Collingwood ordered two ships in his columns, *Belleisle* and *Achille,* to alter course together one point to starboard, and *Revenge* was ordered to take station on an unspecified compass bearing. In effect he was acknowledging that the lee line could only deploy one point off line ahead. Because the speed of the flagship was not reduced to permit deployment to take place, the signal served primarily to inform his captains that they were to seek to engage the whole of the Franco-Spanish rear.[49] Neither British division ever gained a more coherent formation than did the Franco-Spanish line. *Victory* and *Royal Sovereign* had both been cleaned recently, and could not be outsailed.

Dr Beatty wrote in his narrative of Nelson's death that as the morning wore on it was 'plainly perceived by all on board the *Victory,* that from the very compact line which the enemy had formed, they were determined to make one great effort to recover in some measure their long-lost naval reputation.'[50] Blackwood reported that Nelson was struck by the 'good face' the enemy were putting on.[51] Lieutenant Browne remarked to his parents that 'whatever may have been the cause of their temerity, they appeared to seek the action with as much confidence as ourselves.'[52]

Sir William Beatty (d 1842), by Arthur William Devis (1763-1822). (National Maritime Museum, London: BHC 2538)

Had he anticipated it, perhaps Nelson would have taken more care to get his fleet into better order for mutual support. Neither Nelson nor Collingwood, however, was prepared to reduce sail so that the ships which were supposed to lead the assault could move forward. Nelson's formal order of battle is not known, largely because he attached no importance to it.

Blackwood took it upon himself to suggest to Nelson that the flagships were being unduly exposed, and Nelson, seeing that *Royal Sovereign* was drawing ahead, signalled Duff in the *Mars* to take its position at the head of the leeward line. Collingwood would not slow down for the purpose. Later, when it was pointed out that *Téméraire* ought to be leading the windward column, Nelson agreed to order her to take up station. When she tried to do so, however, he signalled, or hailed, her with the cheerful demand that she respect Nelson's place as leader of the attack. Three times he signalled ships in his own and in Collingwood's squadrons which were unable to keep up because they were slow sailers, indicating that they should take whatever place they could. Nelson was obviously pleased by Collingwood's refusal to reduce sail: 'See how that noble fellow Collingwood carries his ship into action.' This piece of theatre left no doubt but that the admirals were ready to subject themselves to the same dangers which awaited their subordinates.

47. Sir Julian Corbett, *The Campaign of Trafalgar,* Longman's 1910, pp362–363 nn.

48. Collingwood's Journal, *Logs,* II p202.

49. Corbett, *Trafalgar,* p368n.

50. Sir William Beatty, *Authentic Narrative of the Death of Lord Nelson,* 1807, p18.

51. DLN VII p147.

52. George Browne, 4 December 1805, *Logs,* ii p195.

Into Battle

The headlong rush was in fact no more than a walking pace. There was a long morning to be got through. Nelson had come on deck dressed as usual with his four stars sewn on his admiral's frockcoat, but he had forgotten to put on his sword. He displayed the euphoria which he usually felt in battle, and he remarked that 21 October was his family's 'lucky day' as that was the day in 1757 on which his uncle Maurice Suckling had distinguished himself in an action of three British against seven French ships, and said to Blackwood that he would not be satisfied by the capture of less than twenty enemy sail of the line. He was never content to leave the working of the ship to the flag captain, Hardy, and now he went through the gun decks, talking to the men at their stations. He had brought the captains of the four frigates now present with the fleet onboard *Victory*, so that they could be given any last minute orders to carry through the fleet, and he asked Blackwood to witness the codicil of the will in which Nelson left Emma to the care of the nation.[53] On his knees in his cabin he penned his last prayer:

> May the Great God whom I worship, grant to my Country, and for the benefit of Europe in general, a great and glorious victory; and may no misconduct in anyone tarnish it; and may humanity after Victory be the predominant feature in the British Fleet. For myself individually, I commit my life to Him who made me, and may His blessing light upon my endeavors for serving my Country faithfully. To Him I resign myself, and the just cause which is entrusted to me to defend. Amen, Amen, Amen.[54]

Second Lieutenant Samuel Burdon Ellis of the Marines in the *Ajax* 74, sixth in the windward line, wrote:

The battle of Trafalgar, 21 October 1805, by Samuel Drummond (1765-1844). (National Maritime Museum, London: BHC 0550)

Oblique drawing of the battle of Trafalgar showing the approach of the British fleet at noon; by P M Nicolas, artist. (National Maritime Museum, London: PAD 8607)

I was sent below with orders and was much struck with the preparations made by the bluejackets, the majority of whom were stripped to the waist; a handkerchief was tightly bound round their heads and over the ears, to deaden the noise of the cannon, many men being deaf for days after an action. The men were variously occupied – some were sharpening their cutlasses, others polishing the guns, as though an inspection were about to take place instead of a mortal combat, whilst three or four, as if in mere bravado, were dancing a hornpipe; but all seemed deeply anxious to come to close quarters with the enemy. Occasionally they would look out of the ports and speculate as to the various ships of the enemy, may of which had been on former occasions engaged by our vessels.[55]

William Robinson, one of the seamen in the *Revenge* during this time, who was known 'politely by the officers of the navy' as Jack Nasty-Face, wrote that

each ship was making the usual preparations, such as breaking the captain's and officers cabins, and sending all lumber below – the doctors, parsons, purser, and loblolly men, were also busy, getting the medicine chests and bandages out; and sails prepared for the wounded to be placed on, that they might be dressed in rotation, as they were taken down to the after cockpit.[56]

On *Bellerophon*, recalled Lieutenant Cumby, at 11:00am,

finding we should not be in action for an hour or more, we piped to dinner, which we had ordered to be in readiness for the ships company at that hour, thinking that Englishmen would fight all the better for having a comfortable meal, and at the same time Captain Cooke joined us in partaking of some cold meat &c on the rudder head, all our bulkheads, tables, &c being necessarily taken down and carried below.[57]

At 11:40am Nelson signalled to Collingwood his intention to pass through the head of the enemy line, to prevent them getting into Cadiz. He then made the general signal to 'make all sail with safety to the masts.' Finally, according to the account of Captain Blackwood, he asked his signal Lieutenant, John Pasco, to 'amuse the Fleet with a signal': 'England Confides that Every Man will do his Duty.' Pasco suggested that 'Confides' be replaced with 'Expects' as that was one of the words in Popham's dictionary, and would not have to be spelled out. Nelson was delighted, and the famous signal was run up, covering *Victory*'s rigging with bunting.[58] Its reception was mixed. Collingwood affected to be irritated, and the lower deck on *Ajax* could not see any need for it, but apparently the men on some of the ships cheered. Lieutenant Barclay recorded that the signal 'was joyfully wel-

53. Beatty, p13; DLN VII pp137–138.

54. Beatty, p13; DLN VII pp139–140.

55. *Ellis*, p4.

56. Jack Nasty-Face [pseud.] William Robinson, *Nautical Economy or Forecastle Recollections of Events during the Last War Dedicated to the Brave Tars of Old England by a Sailor politely called by the Officers of the Navy, Jack Nasty-Face*, London: William Robinson, 1836, p15.

57. Cumby, p722.

58. DLN VII pp149–150.

The battle of Trafalgar, 21 October 1805, by William John Huggins. (National Maritime Museum, London: BHC 0542)

comed by the ship's company' of *Britannia*, and Midshipman Walker on *Bellerophon* that it was 'received on board our ship with three cheers and a general shout of, "No fear of that!"'.[59] At any rate, Nelson was pleased. 'Now,' he said, 'I can do no more. We must trust to the great Disposer of all events, and the justice of our cause'. His last signal was for 'Close Action' which he ordered hoisted and left flying.

All the ships of both divisions were flying the white ensign which had been adopted as the usual battle ensign after 1797 so as to avoid confusion with the flags of France and Spain. Bands were playing 'Hearts of Oak' and 'Britons Strike Home'. When the enemy's ranging shots were falling alongside Nelson advised his frigate captains to return to their ships, and entrusted them with going amongst the fleet to urge their captains to 'adopt whatever course they thought best, provided it led them quickly and closely alongside an enemy'.

Hardy had asked Nelson whether he thought his uniform coat with stars did not make him too obvious a target, and Nelson replied that it was too late to change it. The evidence that he had a premonition of his death is strong, but that he knew his duty too well to take steps to avert it. Once the disposition of the fleet had been made which ensured that there would be close action, the role of the admiral was to set an inspiring example, particularly for one such as Nelson who made a point of giving his captains as much tactical responsibility as possible. Unlike armies ashore where generals usually posted themselves where they could see the enemy's movements, there was no tradition of admirals commanding from the rear. Above all, admirals must appear calm when all about them is carnage. Blackwood suggested to Nelson that he should transfer his flag to a frigate where he could exercise tactical control more effectively, and be out of the firing line, but Nelson refused. When Blackwood bade farewell with the words 'I trust, my Lord, that on my return to the *Victory*, which will be as soon as possible, I shall find your Lordship well and in possession of twenty prizes', Nelson replied: 'God bless you Blackwood. I shall never speak to you again.'[60]

The Leeward Column

Collingwood's style was very different from Nelson's, but he too was doing his duty. In the morning he had impressed his servant with the calm way he shaved himself while talking about the action in prospect. He advised Lieutenant Clavell, a favourite, to change his boots for shoes, because it could be such a nuisance for the surgeon should he be shot in the leg. Midshipman Thomas Aikenhead, who died in the action, said in his last letter to his family that Collingwood was 'quite young' at the thought of battle.[61] In his victory dispatch Collingwood wrote that

> As the mode of our attack had been previously determined on, and communicated to the Flag-officers and Captains, few signals were necessary, and none were made except to direct close order as the line bore down.[62]

Except for indicating to Flag-Captain Edward Rotheram where *Royal Sovereign* should make her attack, Collingwood had no task to perform. According to Southey, only the day before, when Collingwood had admitted that he was not on the best of terms with Rotheram Nelson had asked them to shake hands, and pointing over the bulwark said, 'Look; yonder are the enemy!' Now they paced the deck together as the shot began to reach; 'Rotheram', said Collingwood, 'what would Nelson give to be here?'[63] When the fighting was heaviest, he and Lieutenant Clavell calmly rolled up a top-gallant studding-sail which had fallen across the deck, and stowed it carefully in a boat.[64]

The leeward column had been ordered to 'cut through beginning from the twelfth ship from the enemy's rear', and Collingwood reported that he carried out this order precisely. In fact, the *Royal Sovereign* appears to have cut through the Franco-Spanish rear fifteen ships from its end, passing through their line immediately astern of Vice Admiral d'Alava's flagship, the *Santa Ana*, which she engaged. Perhaps Collingwood did not see three of the allied ships which were to the leeward of their line, and if visible at all, might not have been distinguishable from the frigates and small craft. He may also have varied from his instructions because he felt that he should engage the 120-gun flagship. As the other ships in the leeward division came up they proceeded to make the twelve windward ships astern of the *Santa Ana* the object of their attack, breaking through the line wherever they came to it.[65]

Royal Sovereign was the only three-decker at the head of the leeward column. This was consistent with the intent to cut the enemy rear in line of bearing at as many places as possible. For that duty it was appropriate that the other three-deckers, *Prince* and *Dreadnought* should be near the end of the line. However, had Villeneuve not worn the fleet to form a close-hauled line in reverse order it would have been Nelson's column which would have undertaken the attack on the rear. This suggests that the order of the ships in the lee line was determined entirely by the decision to use the Earl of Northesk's squadron simply as an extension of the line, and by the accident that some ships had cleaner bottoms and so outran the others.

The pace of the attack did not permit the lee line to fully deploy on line of bearing. In consequence, its head was under fire long before its tail. Collingwood later wrote that the enemy held their fire until the British themselves commenced the action, which does not appear to have been the case, but his main intent was to emphasise the discipline with which they awaited the assault. In fact, *Royal Sovereign* took a heavy beating before she could open fire. Collingwood was to remark that 'it seemed a very long time before he found his friends around him'.[66] This was the inevitable consequence of Nelson's concern to prevent the enemy getting away.

The *Fougueux* tried to prevent Alava's flagship being raked by working up until her bowsprit closed the gap astern of the *Santa*

59. Lieutenant John Barclay's Journal, *Britannia*; Midshipman Henry Walker, *Bellerophon*, to Mrs R Walker, 22 November 1805; *Logs*, II pp213, 322.

60. DLN VII p150.

61. *NC* 15 p119.

62. Collingwood to William Marsden, Esq., 6 November 1805, DLN VII p213.

63. Southey, p348.

64. Newnham Collingwood, p108.

65. *Evidence*.

66. Collingwood to Sir Thomas Pasley, 16 December 1805, *Collingwood* #97 p168.

Ana, but Collingwood ordered Rotheram to ram her if necessary. *Fougueux* backed her main topsail on seeing what was happening, and *Royal Sovereign* passed through the gap raking the *Santa Ana* and bringing to on her leeward side. Midshipman Hercules Robinson later wrote:

I see at this moment glorious old Collingwood, a quarter of a mile ahead of his next astern and opening the battle with the magnificent black *Santa Ana*, cutting the tacks and sheets and halyards of his studding sails as he reached her, and letting them drop in the water (grieving, I have no doubt, at the loss of so much beautiful canvas), and as his main yard caught the mizzen vangs of his opponent discharging his double-shotted broadside into her stern.[67]

'She towered over the *Royal Sovereign* like a castle', was Collingwood's own memory, 'you have no conception how completely she was ruined.'[68] The first broadsides killed hundreds, but it was to take more than two hours hard fighting before the Spaniard surrendered. By then, *Royal Sovereign* was herself a wreck with nearly 150 casualties. Having outrun her companions, there was no support to prevent her own quarter being raked with a broadside from *Fougueux*, or to disrupt the gunnery of three other ships on her bows and quarter. Midshipman George Castle, having described with enthusiasm his part in firing a carronade into the Spaniards, added that 'It was shocking to see the many brave seamen mangled so; some with their heads half shot away, others with their entrails mashed, lying panting on the deck'.[69]

To tell you the truth of it, [Sam, one of the seamen, later wrote his father,] when the game began, I wished myself at Warnborough with my plough again; but when they had given us one duster, and I found myself snug and tight, I . . . set to in good earnest, and thought no more about being killed than if I were at Murrell Green Fair, and I was presently as black as a collier.

How my fingers got knocked overboard I don't know, but off they are, and I never missed them till I wanted them.'[70]

When eventually the arrival of support followed by hard fighting secured the position around the *Royal Sovereign*, Collingwood had her taken in tow by *Euryalus*. He sent Blackwood to board the *Santa Ana* and bring back Vice Admiral Alava, but he found him dying of wounds. Later, when Collingwood learnt of Nelson's death, he transferred his flag to Blackwood's frigate so that he could control the fleet better.

Belleisle, 74, third in line, took a similar beating before being able to reply. Years later, Colonel Owen, Royal Marines, whose battle station was on the quarterdeck, described the scene:

Captain Hargood had taken his station on the forepart of the quarter deck on the starboard side, occasionally standing on a carronade slide, whence he issued his orders for the men to lie down at their quarters, and with the utmost coolness directed the steering of the ship.

The silence on board was almost awful, broken only by the firm voice of the captain, 'Steady!' or 'Starboard a little!' which was repeated by the master to the quartermaster at the helm; and occasionally by an officer calling to the now impatient men: 'Lie down there, you, sir!' As we got nearer and nearer to the enemy the silence was, however, broken frequently by the sadly stirring shrieks of the wounded, for of them, and killed, we had more than fifty before we fired a shot; and our colours were three times shot away and rehoisted during the time.

Seeing our men were fast falling, the first lieutenant ventured to ask Captain Hargood if he had not better show his broadside to the enemy and fire, if only to cover the ship with smoke. The gallant man's reply was somewhat stern, but emphatic: 'No, We are ordered to go through the line, and go through she shall, by God!'[71]

67. Hercules Robinson, *Sea Drift*, p206.

68. Newnham Collingwood, p165.

69. Fraser, *Sailors*, p256.

70. Fraser, *Sailors*, p258.

71. Colonel Owen to ?, 21 October 1840, *Hargood*, p14.

72. Lt Paul Harris's account, *Hargood*, p281.

73. *Hargood*, p282.

74. *Logs*, II p245.

Lieutenant Paul Harris, Royal Marines, wrote that

> My eyes were horror-struck at the bloody corpses around me, and my ears rang with the shrieks of the wounded and the moans of the dying. At this moment, seeing that almost every one was lying down, I was half disposed to follow the example, and several times stooped for the purpose; but—and I remember the impression well—a certain monitor seemed to whisper 'Stand up and do not shrink from your duty!'

The firm example of the older Owen helped keep him from panic, but the relief was intense when finally the order was given to 'Stand to your guns'.[72]

Belleisle was engaged successively by at least five of the Franco-Spanish rear, and was eventually totally dismasted and unable to fire most of her guns for fear of igniting the wreckage. Lieutenant Harris recalled that

> At this hour a two-decked ship was seen, apparently steering towards us. It can easily be imagined with what anxiety every eye turned towards this formidable object which would either relieve us from our un-welcome neighbours or render our situation desperate. We had scarcely seen British colours since one o'clock—it was now half-past three—and it is impossible to express our emotion as an alteration of the stranger's course displayed the white ensign to our sight.[73]

Swiftsure, later joined by *Polyphemus*, took up positions covering *Belleisle*, and engaged the enemy.

Gradually all the ships of the lee line got into action. As it impacted on the enemy line, it lost all formation. In the melée both sides inflicted very heavy punishment, as ships sought to manoeuvre to place themselves in an advantageous position, and to provide support for their fellows. The next into action, Duff's 74-gun *Mars*, was beaten into a wreck by the *Pluton* and *Fougueux*, Captain Duff and twenty-nine others killed, and sixty-nine wounded. Her log recorded that

> the poop and quarter-deck [were] almost left destitute, the carnage was so great; having every one of our braces and running rigging shot away, which made the ship entirely ungovernable, and was frequently raked by different ships of the enemy.[74]

The battle of Trafalgar and the victory of Lord Nelson over the Combined French and Spanish Fleets, October 21 1805, by Clarkson Stanfield. (National Maritime Museum, London: BHC 0544)

Every ship sought to fire a raking broadside into an enemy, and once subjected to such devastation, it required superb management of the gun-decks to recover a rate of fire adequate to subdue the enemy gunnery. Once a ship's fire began to slacken, its casualties quickly mounted. Fire could be directed alternatively straight into the hull, and with the quoins under the breeches of the guns removed to give full elevation, up through the enemy deck.

The 80-gun *Tonnant*, which had been captured at the Nile and been taken into the British fleet, was hard engaged by the French *Algéciras*, which was Magon's flagship. The firing was so heavy, at such close range, that *Tonnant* played its fire pump on the broadside of the French ship to stop the flame of discharge setting both ships alight. Sharpshooters in the rigging of the *Algéciras* cleared *Tonnant*'s quarterdeck, but eventually her assailant's masts were brought down by shot and the sharpshooters were thrown into the sea. *Algéciras* was taken by boarding, and Magon was found dead along with seventy-seven of the crew, with another 142 wounded.

Bellerophon came under a heavy fire from four French and Spanish ships, and was twice nearly boarded by the *Aigle*. Grenades thrown through the gunports set fire to powder on

Captain John Cooke (1763-1805), by Lemuel Francis Abbott (1760-1803). Captain Cooke commanded Bellerophon *at Trafalgar and was killed in action.* (National Maritime Museum, London: BHC 2629)

Bellerophon's lower deck, killed or wounded over a hundred men, and blew open the door of the passage to the magazine. It also, however, blew closed the door into the magazine itself. One of those burned by the grenades 'instead of going down to the surgeon, ran aft and threw himself out of one of the stern ports'. Captain Cooke and all but four of the fifty-eight men stationed on the quarterdeck were killed or wounded. Lieutenant Cumby, who had been below giving orders that *Bellerophon*'s gunners should fire up through the decks, took command. He later recalled that he had avoided speaking to any of his wounded messmates 'not wishing to trust my private feelings at a time when all my energies were called for in the discharge of my public duty'. Circumstances later forced him to notice that a friend of his was injured, Captain Wemyss of the Marines, who was waiting to have his arm amputated. The latter replied 'Tis only a mere scratch, and I shall have to apologise to you by and by for having left the deck on so trifling an occasion.' Eventually a heavy cannonade drove the French from their lower-deck guns, and killed or injured two-thirds of the crew. *Aigle* drifted away, but *Bellerophon*, her rigging devastated and still heavily engaged on her other side, was unable to follow.[75] *Aigle* was later engaged by *Defiance*, and, although her company drove back a boarding party, so many were killed or wounded, including her captain and commander, that she had to strike.

Collingwood's old ship, the 98-gun three-decker *Dreadnought* which he had drilled to the point where it could fire three carefully directed broadsides every three and a half minutes, made a good account of herself against Admiral Gravina's *Principe de Asturias* and the *San Juan de Nepomuceno*. The latter had been manoeuvering to rake *Bellerophon* when *Dreadnought* caught her with broadsides which wreaked such destruction that, Admiral Churruca having been killed and her crew demoralised, she struck within ten minutes. *Dreadnought* then shifted her fire to the *Principe de Asturias*. Gravina was mortally wounded, but because *Dreadnought* was such a slow sailer, his second-in-command, Escaño, was able to get *Principe de Asturias* off towards Cadiz, signalling the fleet to rally around her.

The critique of Nelson's tactics by the unknown officer of the *Conqueror* remarked that the difficulty the combined fleet had experienced in getting into line meant that at places in the rear it was in effect a double or triple line, well suited to resist the shock of Collingwood's attack.

> In the rear, the line was in some places trebled; and this particularly happened where the *Colossus* was, who, after passing the stern of the French *Swiftsure*, and luffing up under the lee of the *Bahama*, supposing herself to leeward of the enemy's line, unexpectedly ran alongside of the French *Achille* under cover of the smoke. The *Colossus* was then placed between the *Achille* and the *Bahama*, being on board of the latter; and was also exposed to the fire of the *Swiftsure*'s after-guns. All these positions I believe to have been merely accidental; and to accident alone I attribute the concave circle of the fleet, or crescent line of battle.[76]

Gradually good gunnery and good luck gave the British the upper hand. *Bahama* and the French *Swiftsure* eventually both struck to *Colossus*; *Achille* reduced the Spanish *Montanes* to a wreck, and then heavily engaged the Spanish *Argonauta*, before the French *Berwick* relieved her by laying to on *Achille*'s other side. But *Achille* soon forced the French *Berwick* to strike, after fifty-one men had been killed and nearly 200 wounded. The French *Achille* was engaged by the last ship in the British lee line, the three-decked *Prince* which set her on fire with her broadsides.

The Windward Column

Nelson's division was in action ten to twenty-five minutes after the *Royal Sovereign* opened fire, the uncertainties produced by each ship's time being somewhat different confusing the record. The master of the *Victory*, Thomas Atkinson, recorded that 'At 11:50 the enemy began firing upon us. At 4 minutes past 12, opened our larboard guns at the enemy's van'. Immediately astern of the *Victory* was the *Téméraire*. Her master, F Price, recorded in his log that: 'At 18 minutes past noon the enemy began to fire. At 25 minutes past noon the *Victory* opened her fire. Immediately put our helm a port to steer clear of the *Victory* and opened our fire on the *Santisima Trinidad* and two ships ahead of her, when the action became general.'[77]

Midshipman Badcock of the *Neptune* described the scene:

> Some of [the enemy's ships] were painted like ourselves—with double yellow sides, some with a broad single red or yellow streak, others all black, and the noble *Santissima Trinidada* (138) [sic] with four distinct lines of red, with a white ribbon between them, made her seem to be a superb man-of-war, which, indeed, she was. Her appearance was imposing, her head splendidly ornamented with a colossal group of figures, painted white, representing the Holy Trinity, from which she took her name. This magnificent ship was destined to be our opponent. She was lying-to under topsails, top-gallant-sails, royals, jib, and spanker; her courses were hauled up, and her lofty, towering sails looked beautiful, peering through the smoke as she awaited the onset. The flags of France and Spain, both handsome, chequered the line, waving defiance to that of Britain.
>
> Then in our own fleet, union jacks and ensigns were made fast to the fore and fore-topmast-stays, as well as to the mizzen-

75. DLN VII pp170-173; Cumby, p723. See also letter from a Midshipman in the *Defence* (28 October 1805) and from Midshipman Colin Campbell in the *Defiance*. *Mariner's Mirror* vol 9 (1923) pp59–60, 119–120.

76. Ekins, *Naval Battles*, p352. See Edward Fraser, 'The Journal of Commander Thomas Colby. nn.-1797-1815' *Mariner's Mirror* vol 13 (1927) pp259–271.

77. *Logs*, II pp183, 219.

rigging, besides one at the peak, in order that we might not mistake each other in the smoke, and to show the enemy our determination to conquer. Towards eleven, our two lines were better formed, but still there existed long gaps in Vice Admiral Collingwood's division. Lord Nelson's van was strong: three three-deckers (*Victory*, *Téméraire* and *Neptune*) and four seventy-fours, their jibbooms nearly over the other's taffrails, the bands playing 'God Save the King', 'Rule Britannia', and 'Britons Strike Home'; the crews stationed on the forecastles of the different ships, cheering the ship ahead of them when the enemy began to fire, sent those feelings to our hearts that insured victory.[78]

The windward column had retained the form of a somewhat irregular line-ahead formation, but the competition to get into action was so great that the line had bunched. Captain Codrington of the *Orion*, which was the eighth ship in the line, told his wife that some of the ships had in effect been in a bow and quarter line.[79] This compact force had the shock necessary for effecting the purpose of isolating Collingwood's attack on the rear, and the resources to contain any movement by the Franco-Spanish van. It was thought by some that Nelson feinted to port, threatening the Franco-Spanish van before steering for the centre. His signal to Collingwood that he intended to cut the end of the enemy line has led some to think he was aiming to attack the enemy van, but this does not appear to have been the case. It was the tail of the windward column, at right angles to the Franco-Spanish line, which really served to isolate its van.

According to Dr Beatty, the Franco-Spanish fleet very coolly opened fire with single guns until they had the range. 'A minute or two of awful silence ensued' wrote William James in his nearly contemporary *Naval History*, 'and then, as if by signal from the French admiral, the whole van, or at least seven or eight of the weathermost ships, opened a fire upon the *Victory*, such a fire as had scarcely before been directed at a single

ship'.[80] With the first broadside Admiral Villeneuve's flag was broken out on the *Bucentaure*. Nelson had apparently been steering for the four-decker *Santisima Trinidad*. Collingwood had signalled that he believed Villeneuve was commanding from a frigate, and Nelson appears to have been uncertain as to where he should direct his attack. When the flags were broken out and he saw that the ship he should be engaging was somewhat to starboard, Nelson ordered the *Victory* to pass astern of the *Bucentaure* so that she could engage her on the leeward side.[81] The discovery of where Villeneuve was flying his flag made it clear where was the decisive point.

Victory had to bear away to starboard, and run down under heavy fire before she could pass across the stern of the *Bucentaure*. The *Victory*'s wheel was smashed and steering had to be done by hands at the tiller in the gunroom. Nelson's public secretary, John Scott, was one of the first killed, being nearly cut in half by a roundshot. The marines drawn up at the poop suffered heavily until Nelson ordered them moved.

In a few minutes afterwards a shot struck the fore-brace-bits on the quarter-deck, and passed between Lord Nelson and Captain Hardy; [recalled Dr Beatty] a splinter from the bits bruising Captain Hardy's foot and tearing the buckle from his shoe. They both stopped; and were observed by the Officers on deck to survey each other with inquiring looks, each supposing the other to be wounded. His Lordship then smiled, and said: 'This is too warm work, Hardy, to last long' and declared that 'through all the battles he had been in, he had never witnessed more cool courage than was displayed by the *Victory*'s crew on this occasion.'[82]

The double-shotted broadsides which *Victory* fired into the stern of *Bucentaure* as she slowly moved past were so effective that she all but ceased to be a fighting machine. For some time, however, she continued to be hammered by the ships as they came up, taking the first double-shotted broadside from the

78. Vice Admiral W S Lovell K H (formerly Midshipman William Stanhope Badcock) *Personal Narrative of Events, 1799-1815* (second edition) London pp46–47 (1879) 8807 24; *English Historical Review* 1890 p769; and Fraser, *Sailors*, p218.

79. Codrington to his wife, 30 October 1805, *Codrington*, I p64.

80. William James, *The Naval History of Great Britain from the Declaration of War by France, in February 1793, to the Accession of George IV, in January 1820*, 6 volumes, London: Harding, Lepard and Co., 1826 (Second Edition), IV pp53–54.

81. Signal log of *Euryalus* 11:40, *Logs* II p149.

82. Beatty, pp28–29.

83. Fraser, *Sailors* p302.

Two sketches of HMS Victory, *by J M W Turner, who travelled down to Sheerness to take notes before undertaking his great canvas of the battle of Trafalgar. Unlike De Loutherbourg, Turner did not attach a great importance to single point perspective or technical detail.* (The Tate Gallery)

British *Neptune* and *Britannia*. Marine Captain James Atcherley of the *Conqueror*, who went to secure the magazine when later she surrendered, reported a scene of horror:

The dead, thrown back as they fell, lay along the middle of the decks in heaps, and the shot, passing through, had frightfully mangled the bodies. . . . An extraordinary proportion had lost their heads. A raking shot, which entered the lower deck, had glanced along the beams and through the thickest of the people, and a French officer declared that this shot alone had killed or disabled nearly forty men.[83]

Captain Hardy did not bring *Victory* around to engage her lee side, as Nelson had

BATTLE OF TRAFALGAR

by J M W Turner. Commissioned by George IV for the Painted Hall at Greenwich in 1824, this masterpiece did not find favour with the sailors who wanted all the strings to be in the right place. William James, in his contemporary *Naval History*, wrote

a picture was required, representing the *Victory* engaged in the battle of Trafalgar. The first marine painter of the day undertook the task; and, in due time, the large area of canvas, which . . . became necessary for this, was covered with all the varied tints which Mr Turner knows so well how to mingle and combine, to give effect to his pictures and excite the admiration of the beholder.

Unfortunately for the subject which this splendid picture is meant to represent, scarcely a line of truth, beyond perhaps the broadside view of the *Victory*'s hull, is to be seen upon it. To say what time of the day, or what particular incident in the *Victory*'s proceedings, is meant to be referred to, we do not pretend; for the telegraphic message is going up, which was hoisted at about 11h 40m A.M., the mizzen topmast is falling, which went about 1 P.M., a strong light is reflected upon the *Victory*'s bow and sides from the burning *Achille*, which ship did not catch fire until 4h 40m, nor explode until 5h 45m P.M., the fore topmast, or rather, if our memory is correct, the foremast, of the British three-decker is falling, which never fell at all, and the *Redoutable* is sinking under the bows of the *Victory*, although the French ship did not sink until the night of the 22d, and then under the stern of the *Swiftsure*.

We are sorry to be obliged to add that, with all these glaring falsehoods and palpable inconsistencies upon it, the picture stands, or until very lately did stand, in that room of the king's palace, for which it was originally designed. The principal reason urged for giving to this very costly and highly honoured performance so preposterous an appearance, is that an adherence to truth would have destroyed the pictorial effect. Here is a ship, shattered in her hull, and stripped of the best part of her sails, pushing into a cluster of enemy's ships without a grazed plank or a torn piece of canvas, to fire her first gun. Here is symbolized the first of naval heroes, with chivalric valour, devoting himself to his country's cause; and yet, says an artist of high repute, 'there is a lack of pictorial materials'. We hope some public-spirited individual, if not the state itself, will show whether this is really the case; for it is almost a national disgrace that there should yet be wanted a picture which, in accuracy of representation, no less than in strength and brilliancy of execution, is calculated to illustrate, and to stand as a lasting memorial of, one of the greatest sea-battles that ever has been, or that perhaps ever will be fought: a battle to the success of which England at this time owes, if not her political existence, her prosperity, happiness, and exalted station.

James ends by giving a 'hint' to how a painter 'who may consider it worth his while, or within his powers' should go about the business. (National Maritime Museum, London: BHC 0565)

intended, because the *Redoutable*, the French *Neptune*, and *Santisima Trinidad* were closely seconding the flagship. Instead of cutting the enemy line, the British column was impacting on it, and lost tactical formation. Seeing the effect of her first broadside, Nelson said to him that it did not 'signify' which ship he put *Victory* alongside, 'Take your choice'.[84] Hardy chose to engage the best-manned and worked up ship in the French fleet, the 74-gun *Redoutable*. Marine Second Lieutenant Lewis Rotely wrote:

> We were engaging on both sides; every gun was going off. A man should witness a battle in a three-decker from the middle deck, for it beggars all description: it bewilders the senses of sight and hearing. There was the fire from above, the fire from below, besides the fire from the deck I was upon, the guns recoiling with violence, reports louder than thunder, the decks heaving and the sides straining. I fancied myself in the infernal regions, where every man appeared a devil. Lips might move, but orders and hearing were out of the question; everything was done by signs.[85]

The ships were so close together that there was fear the gun blasts would set *Redoutable* on fire, consuming both ships. *Victory*'s firemen threw buckets of water onto the sides of the enemy after every discharge.

The chaplain, Dr Scott, was horrified by the scene:

> The carnage on the deck of the *Victory* became terrific. Dr Scott's duties confined him entirely to the cockpit, which was soon crowded with wounded and dying men; and such was the horror that filled his mind at this scene of suffering, that it haunted him like a shocking dream for years afterwards.

The injured were treated in strict sequence, unlike modern battlefield medical practice which gives priority to those who are severely wounded, but who can be expected to live if treated quickly. After witnessing a young lieutenant who had been badly wounded tear off his bandages so as to bleed quickly to death, Dr Scott

rushed up the companion-ladder, now slippery with gore—the scene above was all noise, confusion, and smoke—but he had hardly time to breathe there, when Lord Nelson himself fell, and this event at once sobered his disordered mind. He followed his Chief to the cockpit.[86]

Jean Lucas, captain of the *Redoutable*, had made a thorough study of boarding, and had equipped and trained his men to perfection. The ships were lashed together at the bow by grapples, and, having observed that the *Victory*'s upper deck guns were almost silent, he thought from losses amongst the crews, he ordered his own lower gun-ports closed so that he could mass his crew. At the sound of a trumpet, the men poured up from below, and those armed with carbines and grenades climbed the shrouds. Their fire swept the deck of the *Victory*, but it was impossible to get the boarders across the gap to the three-decker. The main yard was ordered cut down to form a bridge, but Captain Adair of the *Victory*'s marines brought up men from below who repulsed the attempt, although he himself was killed. *Victory*'s quarter-deck carronade cut a swath in the men awaiting to board. At this point *Redoutable* drifted up against *Téméraire* on her disengaged side, she was grappled, and a broadside was fired into her which killed more than 200 of the French crew, beat in her stern, and started such leaks that she appeared bound to sink. Dr Beatty wrote that *Victory*'s guns were fired at maximum depression and with reduced charges to prevent the shot passing right through *Redoutable* and into the *Téméraire*. James, however, believed that *Victory* had stopped firing by the time *Téméraire* came alongside *Redoutable*.[87] 'He who has not seen the *Redoutable* in this state can never have any conception of her destruction. I do not know of anything on board which was not cut up by the shot; in the midst of this horrible carnage the brave lads who had

84. Beatty p30; DLN VIII p157.

85. Kenneth Fenwick, *HMS Victory*, London: Cassel & Co., 1959, p274.

86. Dr Scott's account, DLN VII p245.

87. Beatty p31 DLN VII pp139–40; William James, *Naval History*, IV p80.

Captain Sir Edward Codrington (1770-1851), by George Frederick Clarke. (National Maritime Museum, London: BHC 2620)

not yet succumbed and those who were wounded, with whom the orlop-deck was thronged, still cried: 'Vive L'Empereur!' 'We're not taken yet!' 'Is the Captain still alive?'[88] When finally Lucas ordered *Redoutable* surrendered, 490 men had been killed and a further eighty-one wounded. By then, her company had not only killed Nelson, but with the help of the French *Neptune* had done such damage to *Victory* and *Téméraire* that neither were able to bring the weight of their batteries into the closing stages of the action. The *Fougueux* had fallen alongside *Téméraire*, and the four ships lay abreast of each other without steerage way.

Villeneuve, like Nelson and Collingwood, had set a high standard of courage, pacing the quarterdeck of the *Bucentaure*. When she was dismasted and unable to train her remaining guns, he decided that it was time to move his flag to another ship. None of the ship's boats, however, had survived the cannonade and fall of spars, and when he hailed the *Santisima Trinidad* for them to send a boat he received no answer. The French frigates did not provide much support to the fleet during the melée, unlike their British counterparts. In despair, but unwilling further to subject the ships' people to useless suffering, he let the *Bucentaure*'s captain lower the colours.

According to Lieutenant Atcherley's account, Villeneuve enquired to whom he had the honour of surrendering. When he was told that it was Captain Pellew of the *Conqueror*, he replied 'It is a satisfaction to me that it is to one so fortunate as Sir Edward Pellew I have lowered my flag.' Atcherley corrected him: 'It is his brother, Sir.' 'His brother,' exclaimed Villeneuve, 'What, are there two of them? Hélas!' *Conqueror* had by then sailed on, and, after he secured the magazine and posted sentries, Atcherley conveyed Villeneuve, Captain Magendie and the Flag Captain Prigny to the *Mars* where they surrendered their swords to Lieutenant Hennah who had assumed command after Captain Duff had been killed.[89]

Nelson had been right that it would be difficult for the Franco-Spanish van to come about and play a part in the melée in the centre and rear. The rear of the British windward column as it advanced into battle was well placed to react to any movement towards the centre on the part of the Franco-Spanish van, and in addition, each ship in it was engaged in succession by the 64-gun *Africa* which had become detached from the British fleet during the night and chose to take the shortest route towards the action round the *Victory*.[90] Rear Admiral Dumanoir was slow to respond to the crises in the centre and rear, and at 1:30pm Villeneuve signalled to the ships of the van to wear together. This manoeuvre was carried out with great difficulty. It was widely believed that the concussion of thousands of heavy guns could, and did, stop an already light breeze altogether.[91] Four French and a Spanish ship from the van came down the windward side of the British fleet, while Captain Infernet brought *Intrépide* directly down towards the *Bucentaure*, followed by the Spanish *Neptuno*. When finally they were able to open fire on the British weather line, it was about 3pm, by which time the outcome of the battle was no longer in any kind of doubt. In his report the Emperor, Villeneuve refrained from any criticism of Dumanoir. The minister of the Marine, Vice Admiral Decrès, was less restrained, but a Court of Enquiry cleared him of any default.[92]

88. Desbrière II pp211–221.

89. Fraser, *Sailors* pp301–302.

90. Captain Henry Digby's Log, *Africa*; and Captain Robert Moorsom to his father, Richard, 1 November 1805, *Logs*, II pp243, 297.

91. Jack Nasty-Face, pp36–37.

92. Desbrière II, pp134–142 and 334–38.

93. Master Cass Halliday's Log, *Orion*; Captain Henry Digby's Log, *Africa*, *Logs*, II p279, 298.

94. Codrington to his wife, 31 October 1805, *Codrington*, I p65.

Collingwood had seen the movement to the north, and had ordered the weather line to come to windward on the port tack. Only a few ships saw the signal, and were able to respond, but they formed a rough line-of-battle which kept Dumanoir at a distance. *Minotaur* and *Spartiate* which were just coming into action at the rear of the windward column brushed pass the *Formidable* and then lay to to leeward, preventing any relief of the centre. They were the obvious target of Dumanoir's action, but in fact they contained the threat from the Franco-Spanish van. They were reinforced by longer range fire from the ships around *Victory*, and by *Thunderer* from the lee line.

Codrington thought the *L'Intrépide* 'was the only one which wore and came to action gallantly, keeping a very good fire both on *Leviathan* and the Spaniard, of whom she was taking possession'. The 64-gun *Africa* was closely engaged, and appeared to Cass Halliday, Master of *Orion*, to have almost ceased firing'.[93] Codrington managed to bear down sufficiently to get *Orion*'s starboard guns to bear on

> *Intrépide*'s starboard quarter, and then to turn gradually round from thence under his stern, pass his broadside, and bring to on his larboard bow. He had said he would not strike till his masts and rudder were shot away; and this we did for him in so handsome a way that he had no time to do us much injury.[94]

The ships of the leeward line were able to present enough of a battle line to the threat from Dumanoir's ships that at 4:30pm they gave up the attempt to support Gravina and set a course for the Straits.

Nelson's Death

The Death of Nelson, by Arthur William Devis (1763-1822). (National Maritime Museum, London: BHC 2894)

It was a shot from the *Redoutable* which killed Horatio Nelson. According to Dr Beatty, Nelson did not post sharpshooters in the rigging of his ships because there was a danger that they would set fire to the sails, and because the men they killed on the upper deck of an enemy ship could not effect the outcome of the gunnery battle. Captain Lucas's concentration on boarding, on the other hand, made possession of the enemy upper deck all-important. A musket ball fired from *Redoutable*'s rigging passed through Nelson's chest and lodged in his spine. He was carried below, holding a handkerchief over his face and decorations so that the men in the gun-decks should not see him and become discouraged. There was nothing that could be done, except to make his last hours as comfortable as possible. Hardy sent a lieutenant to inform Collingwood of the situation, but Nelson had no intention of resigning his authority so long

The battle of Trafalgar, 21 October 1805, fall of Nelson, by Denis Dighton (1792-1827). (National Maritime Museum, London: BHC 0552)

as he lived. Below, listening to the sound of the guns and knowing he had little time left to make any necessary orders, his attention focused on the need to ensure the fleet was safe in the storm which he knew to be coming. Just before *Victory* had come under fire, he had made a general signal ordering the fleet 'To be prepared to anchor at close of day'.[95] Now as he lay dying in *Victory*'s orlop deck, he urged Hardy to anchor and would not be put off by assurances that Collingwood would see that the necessary orders were given. The sickly light airs and heavy swell which, with the falling barometer presaged the gale, were also driving the drifting mass of ships towards the shoals off Cape Trafalgar.

Nelson's other concern was for the welfare of Emma and little Horatia. He repeatedly reminded his personal chaplain, the better-known Dr Scott who had been Hyde Parker's chaplain at Copenhagen: 'Doctor, I have not

been a *great* sinner,' he said, and '*Remember,* that I leave Lady Hamilton and my Daughter Horatia as a legacy to my Country.'[96] Hardy had not been able to leave the deck for an hour and a half after Nelson was carried below, and Nelson was very concerned that he had been killed, but in the end he was able to visit his old friend and chief twice before he died. He was able to tell him of Dumanoir's defeat, and that fourteen or fifteen of the enemy had surrendered. Nelson's last words were: 'Thank God, I have done my duty. God and my Country.' These have a histrionic ring, and became a symbol of what was best about nineteenth century Britain: there is no question but they were spoken with candor by a man who had made duty his philosophy. The *Victory*'s log recorded that 'partial firing continued until 4:30pm, when a Victory having been reported to the Right Hon Lord Viscount Nelson, KB, and Commander-in-chief, he then died of his wound.'[97]

The battle of Trafalgar, 21 October 1805: death of Nelson, by George Chambers (1803-1840). (National Maritime Museum, London: BHC 0545)

Victory Followed by Storm

Only eleven ships of the Franco-Spanish fleet returned safely to Cadiz. Dumanoir's four escaped capture only a short time, until they ran into a squadron of four ships of the line and four frigates under Sir Richard Strachan in the Bay of Biscay. Eighteen were left to windward of the Trafalgar shoals, seventeen of which were dismasted, and thirteen in the possession of British prize crews. One, the French *Achille* was on fire. As many men and women as possible were saved from her, and at sunset she blew up. 'It was a sight the most awful and grand that can be conceived', wrote an officer in the *Defence*.

In a moment the hull burst into a cloud of smoke and fire. A column of vivid flame shot up to an enormous height in the atmosphere and terminated by expanding into an immense globe, representing, for a few seconds, a prodigious tree in flames, specked with many dark spots, which the pieces of timber and bodies of men occasioned while they were suspended in the clouds.[98]

Amongst the people rescued naked from the sea was a woman, Jeanette, who was the wife of a topman and had disguised herself as a man in order to accompany him. Transferred from

95. Collingwood's Journal; Master William Kirby's Log, *Defiance*; Captain John Cooke's Log, *Bellerophon*, etc., *Logs*, II pp202, 253, 272.

96. Dr Beatty's and Dr Scott's accounts, DLN VII pp244–252.

97. Thomas Atkinson's log, Master of the *Victory*, *Logs* II p185.

98. Fraser, *Enemy*, pp220–2.

Sketchwork for a painting of Sir Richard J Strachan's action off Rochefort, 2 November 1805, during which he captured the four French ships under Rear Admiral Dumanoir which had escaped at the end of the battle of Trafalgar. Artist unknown. (National Maritime Museum, London: PAD 8532)

Pickle to *Revenge*, she was supplied with seaman's clothing, needle and thread, and soon provided herself with woman's attire. Four days later, according to Captain Moorsom of the *Revenge,* she found that her husband had also survived.

Years later, after the asperity of his memories had softened, Midshipman Robinson recalled how boats from the *Euryalus* were employed

> getting hold of a dozen of her men who were hoisted into the air out of the exploding ship, cursing their fate, *sacré*ing, tearing their hair, and wiping the gunpowder and salt water from their faces; and how in the evening these same fellows, having got their supper and grog and dry clothes, [danced] for the amusement of our men under the half-deck.[99]

At the time, there was little levity in the British fleet. Depressed reactions to the intense emotions of battle were inevitable.

Robinson, 'Jack Nast-Face', wrote that

> Orders were now given to fetch the dead

bodies from the after cockpit, and throw them overboard; these were the bodies of men who were taken down to the doctor during the battle, badly wounded, and who by the time the engagement ended were dead. Some of them, perhaps, could not have recovered, while others might, had timely assistance been rendered, which was impossible; for the rule is, as order is requisite, that every person shall be dressed in rotation as they are brought down wounded, and in many instances some have bled to death.[100]

British casualties had been remarkably small: 449 officers and men had been killed and 1,214 wounded, only 10 per cent of the deaths in the Franco-Spanish fleet, but quite enough. Nelson's death was mourned on every ship.

Only four prizes were to be taken into Gibraltar. By the morning of the 22nd the heavy gale Nelson had expected was blowing. Those ships which still had anchors and cables were glad enough to anchor, but many did not, and the prizes were in such a beaten condition that it was more than the combined efforts of their crews and their British captors to keep them all safe and afloat. One, the French *Algéciras*, was lost to the British when the prize crew had to release the captives in order to erect a jury rig. The *Santa Ana* was recaptured when Captain Cosmao made a sortie from Cadiz with three French and two Spanish ships of the line and a few frigates. But three of the rescuers were themselves wrecked, along with six others, either sunk or wrecked.

The exertion of keeping the remainder afloat could not be kept up.

A midshipman of the *Bellerophon* who was part of the prize crew on board the *Monarca* found the experience more dreadful than the battle itself:

> I felt not the least fear of death during the action, which I attribute to the general confidence of victory which I saw all around

---

'An Anecdote of Trafalger'

by William Heath, artist, M Dubourg, engraver, and Edward Orme, publisher. After the battle of Trafalgar Captain Robert Moorsom of the *Revenge* wrote to his father:

> I must tell you an anecdote of a Frenchwoman. The *Pickle* schooner sent to me about fifty people saved from the *Achille*, which was burnt and blew up. Amongst them was a young Frenchwoman of about twenty-five, the wife of one of the main topmen. When the *Achille* was burning, she got out of the gunroom port and sat on the rudder-chains till some melted lead ran down upon her and forced her to strip and leap off. She swam to a spar where several men were, but one of them bit and kicked her till she was obliged to quit and get to another which

supported her. She was taken up by the *Pickle* and sent on board the *Revenge*, and amongst the men she was lucky enough to find her husband. We were not wanting in civility to the lady. I ordered her two purser's shirts to make a petticoat; and most of the officers found something to clothe her. In a few hours Jeannette was perfectly happy and hard at work on her petticoat.

The seaman who was 'politely' known by the officers of the *Revenge* as Jack Nasty-Face reported the same story, but was unaware that Jennette had found her husband alive. *Logs* ii p244-45; Jack Nasty-Face; and see also a longer but unattributed account in Fraser, *Enemy*, pp221-226. (National Maritime Museum, London: PAD 4092)

99. Hercules Robinson, *Sea Drift*, p207.

100. Jack Nasty-Face, pp33–36.

A. *El C? Trafalgar al E. 34.° N. à ¾ de legua por la mañana buen tiempo.*   B. *Altos de Meca.*

A. *El C? Trafalgar al N. 33.° O. à 2. leguas despues de medio dia buen tiempo.*

Views of Cape Trafalgar from an Admiralty Chart of 1800. In the 1795 translation of Henry Michelott's Directions for the Mediterranean Pilot (John Adams ed.) is the warning that

> You must not come near the point of Trafalgar, because of a great many rocks that lie above and under water, which stretch about half a mile into the sea. Over-against this point of Trafalgar, directly SE half E at about 5 miles distance, there is a very dangerous rock under water, called the Seiterre of Trafalgar, on which you only have five feet water, and the sea always breaks over it; from that rock there stretches towards the NW a great ledge of rocks under water, which continues all along the coast.

Joseph Conrad, in his memoir Mirror of the Sea *(London, 1975 pp191-92), warns that*

> in that corner of the ocean, once the wind has got to the northward of west (as it did on the 20th, taking the British fleet aback), appearances of westerly weather go for nothing, and that it is infinitely more likely to veer right round to the east than to shift back again. It is in those conditions that, at seven on the morning of the 21st, the signal for the fleet to bear up and steer east was made. . . . The mere idea [he adds] of these baffling easterly airs, coming on at any time within half an hour or so, after the firing of the first shot, is enough to take one's breath away, with the image of the rearmost ships of both divisions falling off, unmanageable, broadside on to the westerly swell, and of two British Admirals in desperate jeopardy.

(British Museum: BL D DE H SEC 10 (E))

me; but in the prize, when I was in danger of, and had time to reflect upon the approach of death, either from the rising of the Spaniards upon so small a number as we were composed of, or what latterly appeared inevitable from the violence of the storm, I was most certainly afraid; and at one time, when the ship made three feet of water in ten minutes, when our people were almost all lying drunk upon deck, when the Spaniards, completely worn out with fatigue, would no longer work at the only chain pump left serviceable; when I saw the fear of death so strongly depicted on the countenances of all around me, I wrapped myself up in a Union Jack and lay down upon deck.[101]

Collingwood's feelings were little different.

The condition of our own ships was such that it was very doubtful what would be their fate. Many a time I would have given the whole group of our capture, to have ensured our own. . . . I can only say that in my life I never saw such efforts as were made to save these ships [the prizes]; and would rather fight another battle than pass through such a week as followed it.[102]

Unaware that there remained only two ships at Cadiz which were capable of making another sortie, in fact only the *Neptune* and *Montañés* were fit for service, he finally ordered the prizes sunk after the men had been removed.

Codrington described *Orion*'s experience.

For an hour and a half or two hours we dare

101. Henry Walker? NC 15 pp206–208.

102. Collingwood to William Marsden, Esq., 6 November 1805, DLN VII p213.

103. Codrington to his wife, 31 October 1805, Codrington, I p67.

104. Hargood, p147.

not attempt to set even a storm stay-sail, although within about six miles of a lee shore where we must have been lost; and we therefore prepared to trust to our anchors, and cut away the masts; but the wind abating sufficiently for us to set our reef fore and main sail, after unwillingly making up my mind to cut the tow-rope, and sacrifice the unfortunate people in the prize, the *Bahama*, in spite of their signals of distress, I wore round, took advantage of the wind veering a little to the westward, and clawed off shore. It is a great comfort to me that the people in the prize were taken out by my launch, after all, on the 26th, and the vessel burned on the strand yesterday.[103]

Colonel Owen recalled that *Belleisle*, her tow-line broken,

being without masts, rolled excessively in the trough of the sea, taking in the water over each gangway; in this state we drifted on towards a lee shore, and during the middle watch the breakers were seen on our lee bow. At this time our fate appeared inevitable: two guns on the maindeck had broken loose, and were with difficulty chocked up by the seamen's hammocks; the ship was altogether unmanageable, and gradually drifting towards the surf, the roar of which added to the horrors of the scene. At this juncture a few gallant men, under the superintendence of the second lieutenant–Thomas Coleman,–with uncommon exertion and perseverance, erected a small spar on the forecastle, on which they hoisted a boat's sail, by aid of which the ship was wore.[104]

Lieutenant John Edwards of the *Prince*, which had *Santisima Trinidad* in tow, wrote:

'Tis impossible to describe the horrors the morning presented, nothing but signals of distress flying in every direction. The signal was made to destroy the prizes. We had no time before to remove the prisoners; but what a sight when we came to remove the wounded, of which there were between three and four hundred. We had to tie the poor mangled wretches round their waists,

HMS Endymion *rescuing a French two-decker, 1803, by Ebenezer Colls. Although the subject of this picture is an event two years before Trafalgar, the picture gives a good impression of the storm which followed the battle. (National Maritime Museum, London: BHC 0532)*

and lower them down into a tumbling boat, some without arms, others no legs, and lacerated all over in the most dreadful manner.[105]

But not all the wounded could be got out in time. Many drowned in the orlop decks of their ships, unable to move or be saved. A few were rescued from the sea. A total of nine ships were driven ashore and wrecked.[106]

Those of the British prize crews who were wrecked met with extraordinary kindness from the Spaniards ashore, who had watched their fleet sacrificed by their atheistic and republican ally.[107] The wounded prisoners who survived the storm were landed at Cadiz, in terrible pain. The gentry helped in this work of mercy, but to one witness there was a degree of ostentation in their clothes and manner.[108]

Ironically, the heavy gale following the battle of Trafalgar might have provided Villeneuve with the looked-for opportunity of getting clear of Cadiz without fighting. Now he was a captive, and a guest of Captain Blackwood in the *Euryalus*. Twenty-six of the flag officers and captains of the Franco-Spanish fleet were killed or wounded. Approximately 3,370 French officers and men had been killed or drowned and 1,160 wounded; and the Spanish casualties were 1,038 killed or drowned and 1,385 wounded.

Frigate in a Storm, by W Clarkson Stanfield. (British Museum: BM 1906.8.24.536)

Battle Reports

Eleven days after the battle, Collingwood wrote to his old friend, Admiral of the Fleet Sir Peter Parker, who had been an early patron of Nelson and Collingwood.

You will have seen from the public accounts that we have fought a great Battle, and had it not been for the fall of our noble friend, who was indeed the glory of England and the admiration of all who ever saw him in battle, your pleasure would have been perfect—that two of your own pupils, raised under your eye, and cherished by your kindness, should render such service to their Country as I hope this Battle, in its effect, will be.

. . . It was a severe Action, no dodging or manoeuvering. They formed their line with nicety, and waited our attack with great composure, nor did they fire a gun until we were close to them and we began first. Our ships were fought with a degree of gallantry that would have warmed your heart. Everybody exerted themselves and a glorious day was made of it.

People who cannot comprehend how complicated an affair a Battle at sea is, and judge of an Officer's conduct by the number of sufferers in his Ship, often do him a wrong. Though there will appear great differences in the loss of men, all did admirably well; and the conclusion was grand beyond description; eighteen hulks of the enemy lying among the British Fleet without a stick standing, and the French *Achille* burning. But we were close to the rocks of Trafalgar, and when I made the signal for anchoring, many Ships had their cables shot, and not an anchor ready. Providence did for us what no human effort could have done, the wind shifted a few points and we drifted off the land.

105. Fraser, *Enemy*, p316.

106. Master George Forbes's Log, *Swiftsure*; Midshipman Henry Walker, *Bellerophon*; Logs, II pp283–284, 326; Jack Nasty-Face, pp33–36.

107. Collingwood to Blackwood, 2 November 1805, Newnham Collingwood, pp137-138.

108. NC 18 pp466–467.

W Clarkson Stanfield (1793-1867), by John Simpson (1782-1847). Clarkson Stanfield was the only artist of marine subjects to have served in the Royal Navy as a pressed man. He left the navy in 1818 but made good use of his memories in his subsequent paintings. (National Maritime Museum, London: BHC 2339)

Sketch for a painting of a Shipwreck, by J M W Turner. Turner's work with the representation of light and energy gave him a capacity to express storm which was entirely new. (The Tate Gallery: LXXXVII-9)

The storm being violent, and many of our ships in most perilous situations, I found it necessary to order the captures, all without masts, some without rudders, and many half full of water, to be destroyed, except such as were in better plight; for my object was their ruin and not what might be made of them.[109]

Blackwood's letter to his wife the day following the battle was written in more impassioned words, and perhaps reflected the mood of the fleet most accurately:

The first hour since yesterday morning that I could call my own is now before me, to be devoted to my dearest wife, who, thank God, is not a husband out of pocket. My heart, however, is sad, and penetrated with the deepest anguish. A Victory, such a one as has never been achieved, yesterday took place in the course of five hours; but at such an expense, in the loss of the most gallant of men, and best of friends, as renders it to me a Victory I never wished to have witnessed - at least, on such terms. After performing wonders by his example and coolness, Lord Nelson was wounded by a French Sharpshooter, and died three hours after,

beloved and regretted in a way not to find example. To any other person, my Harriet, but yourself, I could not and would not enter so much into the detail, particularly of what I feel at this moment. But to you, who know and enter into all my feelings, I do not, even at the risk of distressing you, hesitate to say that in my life, I never was so shocked or so completely upset as upon my flying to the *Victory*, even before the Action was over, to find Lord Nelson was then at the gasp of death. Thank God, he lived to know that such a Victory, and under circumstances so disadvantageous to the attempt, never was before gained. Almost all seemed as if inspired by the one common sentiment of conquer or die. The Enemy, to do them justice, were not less so. They waited the attack of the British with a coolness I was sorry to witness, and they fought in a way that must do them honour. As a spectator, who saw the faults, or rather mistakes, on both sides, I shall ever do them the justice to say so. They are, however, beat, and I hope and trust that it may be the means of hastening a Peace. Buonaparte, I firmly believe, forced them to sea to try his luck, and what it might procure him in a pitched battle. They had the flower of the combined Fleet, and I hope it will convince Europe at large that he has not yet learnt enough to cope with the English at sea.[110]

A seaman of the *Victory*, James Bayley, wrote to his sister that Nelson's last words were that he was 'going to Heaven' but that Hardy should 'never haul down your colours to France, for your men will stick to you'.

These words was to Captain Hardy, and so we did, for we came off victorious, and they have behaved well to us, for they wanted to take Nelson from us, but we told captain as we brought him out we would bring him

---

NELSON'S 1803 TACTICAL MEMORANDUM:

The business of an English commander-in-chief being first to bring the Enemy's fleet to battle on the most advantageous terms to himself (I mean that of laying his ships close on board the enemy as expeditiously as possible and secondly to continue them there without separating until the business is decided), I am sensible beyond this object it is not necessary that I should say a word, being fully sensible that the admirals and captains of the fleet I have the honour to command will, knowing my precise object, that of a close and decisive battle, supply any deficiency in my not making signals, which may, if extended beyond those objects, either be misunderstood, or if waited for very probably from various causes be impossible for the commander-in-chief to make. Therefore it will only be necessary for me to state in as few words as possible the various modes in which it may be necessary for me to obtain my object; on which depends not only the honour and glory of our country, but possibly its safety, and with it that of all Europe, from French tyranny and oppression.

If the two fleets are both willing to fight, but little manoeuvering is necessary, the less the better. A day is soon lost in that business. Therefore I will only suppose that the enemy's fleet being to leeward standing close upon a wind on the starboard tack and that I am nearly ahead of them standing on the larboard tack. Of course I should weather them. The weather must be supposed to be moderate, for if it be a gale of wind the manoeuvering of both fleets is but of little avail, and probably no decisive action would take place with the whole fleet.

Two modes present themselves, one to stand on just out of gun-shot, until the van ship of my line would be about the centre ship of the enemy; then make the signal to wear together; then bear up [and] engage with all our force the six or five van ships of the enemy, passing, certainly if opportunity offered, through their line. This would prevent their bearing up, and the action, from the known bravery and conduct of the admirals [and] captains, would certainly be decisive. The second or third rear ships of the enemy would act as they please, and our ships would give a good account of them, should they persist in mixing with our ships.

The other mode would be to stand under an easy but commanding sail directly for their headmost ship, so as to prevent the enemy from knowing whether I should pass to leeward or to windward of him. In that situation I would make the signal to engage the enemy to leeward, and cut through their fleet about the sixth ship from the van, passing very close. They being on a wind and you going large could cut their line when you please. The van ships of the enemy would, by the time our rear came abreast of the van ships, be severely cut up, and our van could not expect to escape damage. I would then have our rear ship and every ship in succession wear [and] continue the action with either the van ship or the second as it might appear most eligible from her crippled state; and this mode pursued I see nothing to prevent the capture of the five or six ships of the enemy's van. The two or three ships of the enemy's rear must either bear up or wear; and in either case, although they would be in a better plight probably than our two van ships (now the rear), yet they would be separated and at a distance to leeward, so as to give our ships time to refit. And by that time I believe the battle would, from the judgment of the admiral and captains, be over with the rest of them. Signals from these moments are useless when every man is disposed to do his duty. The great object is for us to support each other, and to keep close to the enemy and to leeward of him.

If the enemy are running away, then the only signals necessary will be to engage the enemy on arriving up with them; and the other ships to pass on for the second, third, &c., giving if possible a close fire into the enemy on passing, taking care to give our ships engaged notice of your intention.

(British Museum: Add MS 36,747 f.55)

109. Collingwood to Parker, 1 November 1805, Collingwood #94 pp164–165.

110. 'Memoirs of Vice-Admiral . . . Blackwood', Blackwood's Edinburgh Magazine, vol 34 (July 1833) no. 210 pp7–8; DLN VII.

1805 CADIZ MEMORANDUM:

Secret: Thinking it almost impossible to bring a Fleet of Forty Sail of the Line into a Line of Battle in variable winds, thick Weather, and other circumstances which must occur, without such a loss of time that the opportunity would probably be lost of bringing the Enemy to Battle in such a manner as to make the business decisive; I have therefore made up my mind to keep the Fleet in that position of sailing (with the exception of the First and Second in Command) that the Order of Sailing is to be the Order of Battle; placing the Fleet in two Lines of sixteen Ships each, with an Advanced Squadron of eight of the fastest sailing Two-decked Ships, *which* will always make, if wanted, a Line of twenty-four Sail, on whichever Line the Commander-in-Chief may direct.

The Second in Command will, after my intentions are made known to him, have the entire direction of his Line to make the attack upon the Enemy, and to follow up the blow until they are Captured or destroy'd.

If the Enemy's fleet should be seen to Windward in Line of Battle and [in such a position] that the two Lines and the Advanced Squadron can fetch them, they will probably be so extended that their Van could not succour their Rear.

I should therefore probably make the 2nd in Command's signal to Lead through, about their Twelfth Ship from the Rear (or wherever he could fetch, if not able to get as far advanced); my Line would lead through about their Centre, and the Advanced Squadron to cut two, three or four Ships Ahead of their Centre, so far as to ensure getting at their Commander-in-Chief, on whom every effort must be made to capture.

The whole impression of the British Fleet must be to overpower from two to three Ships ahead of their Commander-in-Chief, supposed to be in the Centre, to the Rear of their fleet. *I will suppose twenty Sail of the Enemy's Line to be untouched;* it must be some time before they could perform a manoeuvre to bring their force compact to attack any part of the British fleet engaged, or to succour their own Ships; which indeed would be impossible, without mixing with the ships engaged.

Something must be left to chance; nothing is sure in a Sea Fight beyond all others. Shots will carry away the masts and yards of friends as well as foes; but I look with confidence to a Victory before the Van of the Enemy could succour their Rear and then that the British Fleet would most of them be ready to receive their twenty Sail of the Line, or to pursue them, should they endeavour to make off.

If the Van of the Enemy tacks, the Captured Ships must run to leeward of the British fleet; if the Enemy wears, the British must place themselves between the Enemy and the Captured and disabled British Ships; and should the Enemy close, I have no fears as to the result.

The Second in Command will in all possible things direct the Movements of his Line, by keeping them as compact as the nature of the circumstances will admit. Captains are to look to their particular Line as their rallying point. But, in case Signals can neither be seen or perfectly understood, no Captain can do very wrong if he places his Ship alongside that of an Enemy.

Of the intended attack from to windward, the Enemy in Line of Battle ready to receive an attack,

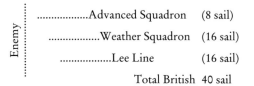

Enemy	.................Advanced Squadron	(8 sail)
	.................Weather Squadron	(16 sail)
	.................Lee Line	(16 sail)
	Total British	40 sail

The Divisions of the British fleet will be brought nearly within gun shot of the Enemy's Centre. The signal will most probably then be made for the Lee Line to bear up together, to set all their sails, even steering sails, in order to get as quickly as possible to the Enemy's Line and to Cut through, beginning from the twelfth Ship from the Enemy's Rear. Some Ships may not get through their exact place, but they will always be at hand to assist their friends; and if any are thrown round the Rear of the Enemy, they will effectually complete the business of twelve Sail of the Enemy.

Should the Enemy wear together, or bear up and sail large, still the twelve Ships composing, in the first position, the Enemy's Rear, are to be *the* object of the Commander-in-Chief; which is scarcely to be expected, as the entire management of the Lee Line, after the intentions of the Commander-in-Chief is [sic] signified, is intended to be left to the judgment of the Admiral Commanding that Line.

The Remainder of the Enemy's fleet, 34 Sail, are to be left to the Management of the Commander-in-Chief, who will endeavour to take care that the movements of the Second in Command are as little interrupted as possible.

(Sir William Beatty, *Authentic Narrative of the Death of Lord Nelson*, 1807, pp89-93. (with words in italics added by Mr Scott, Nelson's secretary); DLN vii p89)

home; so it was so, and he was put into a cask of spirits.[111]

The death and destruction were those of annihilation. Besides the 4,500 killed and 2,405 wounded in the Franco-Spanish fleet, there were another 7,000-odd taken prisoner. The high rate of mortality in the Franco-Spanish fleet is to some extent a reflection of the number of ships which sank in the storm. Only ten of the Franco-Spanish fleet of thirty-three ships survived destruction or capture, and of these only three were fit for service.

Villeneuve's own report to the Minister of the Marine was made with the reserve necessary because he knew his letter would be read by his British captors, but nonetheless he entered into a technical assessment of the reason for the Franco-Spanish defeat.

> The enemy owe their superiority to the power of their vessels (of which 7 were three-deckers, the least of these mounting not less than 114 guns); to the power of their artillery, all–owing to their carronades– being of heavy calibre; to the unity and speed of their movements; to the experience won by three uninterrupted years at sea, an experience entirely lacking to a large proportion of the Combined Fleet.

He was wrong about the number of guns in the British first-rates, but not about the superiority of their gunnery, partly because of their limited use of carronades. He, like Blackwood, made it clear that nothing had been lacking in morale in the combined fleet:

> The courage and devotion to their country and to the Emperor displayed by the executive and crews of HIM's ships could not be surpassed; it showed itself when the signals to set sail and to clear for action were made by the cheers and the shouts of 'Vive L'Empereur' with which these signals were greeted.[112]

Rear Admiral Escaño concluded his report of the battle:

Nothing is more seamanlike, or better tactics, than for a fleet which is well to windward of another to bear down upon it in two separate columns, and deploy into line at gunshot from the enemy. But Admiral Nelson did not deploy his columns at gunshot from our line, but ran up within pistol-shot and broke through it . . . It was a manner in which I do not think he will find many imitators.[113]

Captain Robert Moorsom was 'not certain that our mode of attack was the best', although, as he acknowledged, 'it succeeded'.[114] Joseph Conrad, from his personal experience of the winds around Cape Trafalgar, has written that Nelson was in greater danger during the approach than is generally realised. With the wind fitfully backing north-westerly, there was a grave danger that the heads of the columns would be becalmed, or even headed by a breath from the eastward, leaving them at the mercy of the Franco-Spanish line.[115] It is impossible to determine whether Nelson was in fact being rash, or whether he had such a fine understanding of the weather that he knew he could discount that risk. It has been suggested that Nelson might have made better use of his resources had he avoided the concentration of ships around the *Bucentaure*, cut through the gap which opened between the rear and centre of the combined fleet, and engaged in a close-ordered line ahead from leeward. Results as decisive as those Nelson had achieved, however, were exceedingly rare in the history of naval battle. The same riposte can be made to the idea that Nelson had wasted his three-deckers by exposing them at the head of the columns: he would never have obtained quite such whole-hearted support from his captains had it not been so entirely clear that he expected no one to expose themselves more than he did himself. In any case the three-deckers were needed at the head of the columns because they were more capable of withstanding the punishment the leaders inevitably attracted. Codrington, writing to a brother officer, put it simply: 'We all scrambled into battle as soon as we could, and I be-

111. NC 28 pp383–84.

112. Vice Admiral Villeneuve to His Excellency the Minister of the Marine and of the Colonies, 15 November 1805, Desbriere, II pp137–142.

113. Duro, VIII p353.

114. Robert Moorsom to Richard Moorsom, 4 December 1805, Logs, II p244.

115. Joseph Conrad, *The Mirror of the Sea*, London: J M Dent, 1975, pp189–192.

lieve have done our best in imitation of the noble example before us'.[116] Lieutenant George Browne of the *Victory*, when writing his parents six weeks after the battle, said

His Lordship duly appreciated the consequence and necessity of a decisive naval action, and determined so to place his fleet that a drawn battle or partial action should be entirely out of the question. Admiral Collingwood and himself led their separate divisions, well knowing that a British seaman will always follow and support his leader. This plan of attack was grand beyond example, and worthy of the great mind that formed it.[117]

Nelson's tactics had been focused on exploiting to the full the morale of the British fleet, which was a decisive instrument of war because of the intensive drilling of British gun crews. The attack in twin columns had at least ensured that the ships of the Franco-Spanish van could play little part in the action. The unknown officer of the *Conqueror* believed that

The mode of attack, adopted with such suc-

cess in the Trafalgar action, appears to me to have succeeded from the enthusiasm inspired throughout the British fleet from their being commanded by their beloved Nelson; from the gallant conduct of the leaders of the two divisions; from the individual exertions of each ship after the attack commenced, and the superior practice of the guns in the English fleet.

It was successful also from the consternation spread through the combined fleet on finding the British so much stronger than was expected; from the astonishing and rapid destruction which followed the attack of the leaders, witnessed by the whole of the hostile fleets, inspiring the one and dispiriting the other and from the loss of the admiral's ship early in the action.[118]

All the same, it is probable that the outcome would have been at least as satisfactory for the British fleet, and perhaps have yielded still better results at lower cost, if Nelson, when he saw that the combined fleet was prepared to fight, had taken in his studding sails to enable the columns to close up, and deploy on line of bearing.

116. Codrington to Lord Garlies, 28 October 1805, Codrington, I p60.

117. George Browne to his parents, 4 December 1805, Logs, II p193.

118. Ekins, *Naval Battles*, p355.

Manuscript copy of Nelson's Cadiz Memorandum, 1805. (British Museum: Add MS 33,963)

EPILOGUE

THE LETTER Lord Minto wrote to his wife when he heard the news of Trafalgar and of the death of Nelson stands as a fitting epitaph.

My sense of his irreparable loss, as well as my sincere and deep regret for so kind a friend, have hardly left room for other feelings which belong, however, hardly less naturally to this event. I was extremely shocked and hurt when I heard it, and it has kept me low and melancholy all day. One knows, on reflection, that such a death is the finest close, and the crown, as it were, of such a life; and possibly, if his friends were angels and not men, they would acknowledge it as the last favour Providence could bestow and a seal and security for all the rest. His glory is certainly at its summit, and could be raised no higher by any length of life; but he might have lived at least to enjoy it.[1]

The nation mourned Nelson, and gave him a state funeral in St Paul's cathedral. His undeserving elder brother was created an earl and given a grant of £99,000 to purchase the Trafalgar estate. Lady Nelson, Fanny, was provided with a pension of £2,000, Nelson's sisters each received a pension of £1,500, and a pension was paid to Earl Nelson and his heirs until 1946. Only Emma was ignored, both by the state and by Nelson's now wealthy brother. Never very effective at managing her finances, she was to die in poverty.

The officers and men who took part in the battle were generous with their hard-earned property. In the log of *Orion* it was entered, on 14 November 1805, that

1. Gilbert Elliot, Lord Minto, to his wife, 10 November 1805, Minto, III, pp373–374.

HMS Victory *carrying Nelson's body proceeding up the Channel, drawing by J M W Turner.* (The Tate Gallery: CXVIII 0)

Nelson's flagships at anchor, by Nicholas Pocock (1740-1821), dated 1807. (National Maritime Museum, London: BHC 1096)

The officers and ship's company being assembled, the captain read the proposal of the admiral to them that two thousand pounds should be deducted from the prize money for the action on the 21st of October, 1805, for the purpose of erecting a monument on Portsdown Hill to the memory of Lord Nelson, the late commander-

View of the cities of London and Westminster, accurately copied from the table of the Camera Obscura in the Royal Observatory at Greenwich, 1 March 1809 by Pugh, artist, and J Tomlinson, engraver. From Greenwich Nelson's body was taken by water up the Thames, to be buried at St Pauls which can be seen prominently on the horizon. (National Maritime Museum, London: PAD 2209)

Top left: Nelson's funeral barge. (National Maritime Museum, London: PAD 3935)

Lower left: 'Correct Representation of the Funeral Car which conveyed the Body of Lord Nelson from the Admiralty to St Pauls, 9 January 1806', published 1 February 1806 by W B Walker. (National Maritime Museum, London: PAF 4373)

in-chief, which the officers and ship's company all agreed to, and as much more if required.[2]

The figurehead of *Conqueror* had been destroyed in the battle; at the request of her ship's company it was replaced with a statue of Nelson on an heroic scale.

Admiral Gravina died a painful death from the wounds he had received. Villeneuve's fate was worse. Taken prisoner to England, where he was politely received and even attended Nelson's funeral, he was eventually exchanged for British prisoners of war. He crossed to France, but was killed before he could reach Paris. Possibly he committed suicide on Napoleon's orders. He was so patently an honest and loyal officer that his return to French society would have undermined the story of his incompetance and cowardice which Napoleon was fabricating to distract attention from his own responsibility for the disaster.

After 1805 Napoleon belatedly recognised the vital defensive importance of naval forces, and mobilized the ship-building resources of occupied Europe. Between 1806 and 1815 France built or acquired 306,000 tons of war-ships, with another 24,000 tons built in the Netherlands. However, command of the sea was too firmly held by the Royal Navy for history to be reversed. During that same period Britain built 375,000 tons of warships, and also added to the Royal Navy 135,000 tons of captured warships, most of which were taken from France. The result was that from 1805 to 1810 the Royal Navy increased its relative strength from 42 per cent of the world total of warships, to 50 per cent, dropping again to 44.4 per cent in 1815. France also increased its share of the world total, but never controlled more than 18 per cent of the world fleet. In 1810 the Royal Navy was up to 673,000 tons, the French Marine to 194,000 tons, and Napoleon also controlled 52,000 tons of ships

2. *Codrington*, I p69. See also Master Joseph Seymour's Log, *Conqueror*, 10 November 1805, *Logs* II p261.

'The Funeral Car', Nelson's funeral procession. Published by R Bowyer. (National Maritime Museum, London: PAF 4371)

THE Dying Request OF LORD NELSON;

ADDRESSED TO HIS

KING AND COUNTRY,

ON THE 21ST OCTOBER 1805, THE FATAL BUT GLORIOUS DAY OF THE BATTLE OF TRAFALGAR, WHEN HE SO NOBLY LOST HIS LIFE IN THEIR SERVICE.

PRAYER BEFORE THE BATTLE.

Written by Lord Nelson, at Seven o'Clock in the Morning, "the Enemy wearing "in Succession."

MAY the Great God whom I worship, grant to my Country, and for the benefit of Europe in general, a great and glorious Victory! and may no misconduct in any one tarnish it! and may humanity, after victory, be the predominant feature in the British Fleet! For myself, individually, I commend my life to Him who made me; and may his blessing light upon my endeavours for serving my Country faithfully! To Him I resign myself, and the just cause which is entrusted to me to defend. AMEN! AMEN! AMEN!

CODICIL.

2

CODICIL.

October the twenty-first, one thousand eight hundred and five, then in sight of the Combined Fleets of France and Spain, distant about ten miles.

WHEREAS the eminent Services of EMMA HAMILTON, Widow of the Right Honourable Sir WILLIAM HAMILTON, have been of the very greatest service to our King and Country, to my knowledge, without her receiving any reward from either our King or Country—

First, that she obtained the King of Spain's Letter, in 1796, to his Brother, the King of Naples, acquainting him of his intention to declare war against England; from which Letter the Ministry sent out orders to then Sir John Jervis, to strike a stroke, if opportunity offered, against either the Arsenals of Spain or her Fleets: that neither of these was done, is not the fault of Lady Hamilton; the opportunity might have been offered.

Secondly, the British Fleet under my command COULD NEVER HAVE RETURNED THE SECOND TIME TO EGYPT, had not Lady Hamilton's influence with the Queen of Naples caused letters to be wrote to the Governor of Syracuse, that he was to encourage the Fleet being supplied with every thing, should they put into any port in Sicily. We put into Syracuse, and received every supply; went to Egypt, and DESTROYED THE FRENCH FLEET.

Could I have rewarded these Services, I would not now call upon my Country; but, as that has not been in my power, I leave Emma Lady Hamilton, therefore, A LEGACY TO MY KING AND COUNTRY, that they will give her an AMPLE PROVISION to maintain her rank in life.

I also leave to the beneficence of my Country, my Adopted Daughter, HORATIA NELSON THOMPSON; and I desire she will use, in future, the name of NELSON only.

THESE

'A Tale of Trafalgar', by Sir David Wilkie. (National Maritime Museum, London: PAH 3984)

This expensively-printed copy of the last prayer Nelson wrote on his knees in the great cabin of HMS *Victory, and copy of the codicil Blackwood had witnessed leaving Emma and Horatia to the care of the nation, did not serve to soften the hard hearts of the British establishment. There is no evidence to support or refute the claim that Emma gave advance warning of the intention of Spain to declare war in 1796, but it is doubtful whether Maria Carolina, Queen of Naples, did in fact supply Nelson with letters opening the ports of the Sicilies to him before the Nile. Nelson certainly did not take any chances on his reception in Syracuse but sailed his fleet right in and purchased what he needed.*

3

THESE ARE THE ONLY FAVOURS I ASK OF MY KING AND COUNTRY, AT THIS MOMENT, WHEN I AM GOING TO FIGHT THEIR BATTLE.

May God bless my King and Country, and all those I hold dear! My relations it is needless to mention; they will, of course, be amply provided for.

NELSON & BRONTE.

Witness, HENRY BLACKWOOD.
T. M. HARDY.

Attestation.

30th *June* 1806.

APPEARED personally the Reverend ALEXANDER JOHN SCOTT, of St. John's College, in the university of Cambridge, and Vicar of South Minster, in the county of Essex, Doctor in Divinity; and made oath, that he, the deponent, on the 21st day of October, in the year 1805, and for some time preceding, was Chaplain on board his Majesty's ship Victory, one of the Squadron under the command of the late Right Honourable HORATIO Lord Viscount NELSON deceased; and the deponent says, that during an action, on the day aforesaid, between his said Majesty's Squadron and the Combined Fleets of France and Spain, off Trafalgar, the said Lord Viscount NELSON having been mortally wounded in the said action, soon after the same happened, addressed himself to this deponent, and said—" I am dying, Doctor; remember me to Lady HAMILTON, and remember me to HORATIA. Tell Lady HAMILTON, I have made a will, and left her and HORATIA a legacy to my Country." And this deponent says, that the said deceased, several times in the course of the same day, made declarations in the hearing of, and to this deponent, to the same effect; and having, on the same day, departed this life, he the deponent was present on board the said ship with Sir Thomas Masterman Hardy, Bart. then Thomas Masterman Hardy, Esq. Captain of the said ship, when they found, in the escrutoire of the said deceased, a book wherein, amongst other things, are the words following: to wit—" October " the twenty-first, one thousand eight hundred and five, then in sight of the Combined Fleets " of France and Spain, distant about ten miles." Also the words—" I leave EMMA Lady " HAMILTON, therefore, a legacy to my King and Country, that they will give her an " ample provision to maintain her rank in life. I also leave to the beneficence of my " Country, my Adopted Daughter, HORATIA NELSON THOMPSON." And ending—" My " relations it is needless to mention; they will, of course, be amply provided for." And thus subscribed—" NELSON & BRONTE." And this deponent says, that having viewed the book hereto annexed, marked A, wherein the several words before related appear, the same is the identical book found in the escrutoire aforesaid, in the hand-writing of the said deceased; and was, as he believes, meant and referred to by the said deceased, in his aforesaid declarations.

A. J. SCOTT.

Same day, the said ALEXANDER JOHN SCOTT,
Doctor in Divinity aforesaid, was duly sworn
to the truth hereof, before me—
GEORGE OGILVIE, *Surrogate.*
GEORGE SILK, *N.P.*

---

in the Dutch and Italian navies. Trafalgar, however, did discourage further development of the Spanish navy, and the Spanish revolt accelerated the decline. In 1810 the Spanish navy was down to 100,000 tons.[3]

The strategic consequences of Trafalgar were long-term ones. The immediate threat of invasion had already passed, once the conjunction of naval forces in the West Indies ordered by Napoleon had failed to take place. In the shorter term, the battle did little to impede Napoleon's continental conquests. The surrender of General Mack and 27,000 Austrian soldiers at Ulm occurred on the same day as Trafalgar, and Napoleon followed that triumph with another at Austerlitz on 2 December 1805 in which the armies of Austria and Russia were defeated. One of Collingwood's first acts after Trafalgar was to write a letter to Hugh Elliot, British envoy to the Kingdom of Naples. Trafalgar had frustrated Napoleon's plan to transport soldiers by sea to Naples, and it was important that King Ferdinand I be apprised at once of the continued power of the Royal Navy to secure his throne. After Austerlitz, however, Naples was overrun by a land invasion from the north.

In the longer term, on the other hand, Trafalgar was strategically important. Had Napoleon resisted the temptation to contest command of the sea from the Royal Navy, he might have been able to use detached squadrons to undermine Britain's maritime trade. British wealth was of vital importance to the campaign against Bonapartism. Between 1806 and 1816 the British economy generated £142 million in income tax alone, and three times that sum in customs duties. This revenue not only paid for the Royal Navy and the British Army, but also paid subsidies to conti-

3. Jan Glete, op. cit., Tables 23:35–41.

nental states which rose from about £2.6 million per annum to a peak of £20 million for the ten-month Waterloo campaign of 1814-15.[4] In 1806 Napoleon recognised the importance of weakening the British economy, but following Trafalgar he could expect to do little by naval means. Instead he committed vast human resources in drawing a customs frontier around Europe. That effort was wasted. Britain was the leader in the industrial revolution, and all Europe competed to find ways of circumventing Napoleon's 'Continental System'. Worse than futile; the irritant produced by the customs barrier led first to the revolt in Spain, and then to Tsar Alexander I's defiance.

Portugal, always sensitive to sea power, threw in its lot with Britain in 1807. This led to the invasion of Portugal by a Franco-Spanish army, but Spain rebelled against French control in 1808, and with the help of a British army commanded by General Arthur Wellesley, the future Duke of Wellington, Portugal recovered its independence. The Royal Navy was able to support Wellesley in the field, providing him with logistic supply by sea. The French army had to struggle to supply itself over mountain roads harassed by Spanish guerrilla forces. When Napoleon took the Grand Army into Russia in 1812, he had too few soldiers because of the resources squandered in enforcing the Continental System in Spain and on the coast of Germany, and was decisively defeated despite his capture of Moscow. In the final defeat of Napoleon at Waterloo, British money and the British army were decisive: neither might have been available but for the battle of Trafalgar.

Emperor Napoleon being transported in HMS Northumberland *to imprisonment at the island of St Helena in the south Atlantic. This watercolour is identified as having been painted by a Lieutenant A M Skene RN, who may be the Alexander Skene who died in 1823. The fleet with which Nelson defeated Napoleon's attempt to conquer Asia, and his threat to invade Britain, and which protected the maritime trade that paid for the armies that drove Napoleon from his empire, carried Napoleon on his final journey. When asked how he would spend his days in prison, Napoleon said that he would write his memoirs: 'Work' he said, 'is the scythe of time.'* (British Museum: BM 1884.11.8.13)

The Nelson Legacy

'Great and important as the victory is,' Lord Minto had continued, in his letter on receipt of the news of Trafalgar,

it is bought too dearly, even for our interest, by the loss of Nelson. We shall want more victories yet, and to whom can we look for them? The navy is certainly full of the bravest men, but they are mostly below the rank of admiral; and brave as they mostly all are, there was a sort of heroic cast about Nelson that I never saw in any other man, and which seems wanting to the achievement of impossible things which become easy to him, and on which the maintenance of our superiority at sea seems to depend against the growing navy of the enemy.

In fact, the nature of the naval war changed after Trafalgar. There was not to be another major fleet action before the end of the war in 1814, and during the rest of the nineteenth century the only general action the Royal Navy was to fight was that at Navarrino Bay in 1827. Codrington, by then an admiral, commanded a combined force of British, French, and Russian warships against an anchored Turkish and Egyptian fleet, thereby helping to establish Greek independence. That action was tactically uninteresting, and uninspiring. The navy in the nineteenth century was predominantly concerned with the problem of applying seapower to the needs of foreign policy, by shore bombardment, landing operations, and blockades, combined with the task of protecting trade by maintaining a naval presence in troubled areas. When the navy began to build ships of iron, propelled by steam, they were optimised for these tasks.

It is hardly surprising that the Royal Navy cherished the Nelson tradition. In doing so, however, it turned its back on Nelson's methods of command. Hercules Robinson, writing when he was himself a Vice Admiral, remarked that 'Sir Robert Calder told me once (after this brave man's own coup manqué),

that every officer should read two pages of the signal book every morning whilst the ship's barber powdered his side curls and tied his queue'. Had Nelson followed that advice, Robinson observed, he would have taken so long getting into action the British fleet would have been involved 'in a night's action, on a lee shore, whilst he [Villeneuve] was running for a friendly port'.[5] That was not the lesson which the Admiralty ultimately drew from the story. The Board, perhaps wisely, concluded that Nelsonian tactics were for men with Nelson's capacity to judge technical possibilities and to inspire the best from his captains. The unknown officer who witnessed the battle of Trafalgar probably from *Conqueror* concluded that

The *Victory, Téméraire, Sovereign, Belleisle, Mars, Colossus* and *Bellerophon* were placed in such situations in the onset, that nothing but the most heroic gallantry and practical skill at their guns could have extricated them. If the enemy's vessels had closed up as they ought to have done, *from van to rear*, and had possessed a nearer equality in active courage, it is my opinion that even British skill and British gallantry could not have availed. . . . A plan, to be entirely correct, must be suited to all cases. If its infallibility is not thus established, there can be no impropriety in pointing out the errors and dangers to which it is exposed, for the benefit of others.[6]

In 1807 Admiral Gambier issued instructions for a fleet of thirty ships for Baltic service, and the next year Collingwood issued a General Order for conduct of a fleet action. Both of these imitated the use of dual control and squadronal initative employed in Nelson's tactics at Trafalgar, both failed to satisfy the fundamentals of concentration of force, and neither made effective use of detached squadrons to contain parts of the enemy line. Collingwood's focus of attack on the enemy

4. Nicholas Tracy, *Attack on Maritime Trade*, p81. See: W K Hancock and M M Gowing, *British War Economy*, London, 1949, p4; François Crouzet, 'Wars, Blockade, and Economic Change in Europe, 1792-1815', *Journal of Economic History*, 24 pp567–588, 1964; and John M Sherwig, *Guineas and Gunpowder, British Foreign Aid in the Wars with France 1793-1815, passim.* Cambridge, Mass, 1969.

5. Hercules Robinson, *Sea Drift*, p214.

6. Ekins, *Naval Battles*, p357.

van was positively dangerous, and ignored two centuries of experience.[7] These flawed clones of Nelsonic tactics no doubt were part of the motive for the conservatism shown when in 1816 the Admiralty issued a revised *Book of Signals & Instructions*.[8]

The new book included a signal to 'cut through the enemy's line in the order of sailing in two columns'. This was clearly an attempt to regularise, and make less risky, Nelson's tactics at Trafalgar. Instead of simply depending on shock to burst through the enemy line, which might well have been reinforced to prevent that being carried out successfully, the new instruction called for each column to bear up on reaching the enemy line, and cut through it in succession in inverted order. Certainly, this would answer the criticism of Nelson's tactics at Trafalgar that too much of his fire-power became bogged down in a static action at the centre, where it could not affect the action at the ends, and where it was vulnerable to envelopment. The 1816 book also incorporated signals for anchoring by the stern when engaging an anchored enemy, which incorporated Nelson's experience at the Nile and Copenhagen.

Nelson's tactics enjoyed a revival when in the middle of the century navies began to acquire ironclad battleships. Although they were equipped with guns of ever-increasing weight, nineteenth-century naval gunnery was limited by rate of fire and by primitive fire control. Perversely, the ram staged a return, and Trafalgar appeared to be the model for a battle fought with ironclad rams. Only the battles of the Russo-Japanese war of 1904–05 made it clear that fighting would take place at longer ranges, and that tactics had to be designed to ensure effective gunnery. Not everyone was convinced, however, and it was to lay the ghost of Trafalgar that in 1913 the Admiralty authorised its study of Nelson's tactics.

Where the Royal Navy faltered was not in its recognition, against some service opposition, that Nelson's tactics at Trafalgar could not become a model for future battles, even in the age of the steam ram and certainly not in that of the Dreadnought battleship, but in its abandonment of Nelson's humane methods of command. The rigid formalism and strict adherance to manoeuvering signals which became a norm with the introduction of constant speed manoeuvering practice, made possible by steam propulsion, was at the expense of the two-way communication between the admiral and his officers such as had taken place in Nelson's great cabin around his dining table. The reversion to mid-eighteenth century methods of maximising tactical resources was not necessarily unsound, but the abandonment of Nelsonic humanity in Royal Navy command relationships, and savage repression of initiative, exacted a heavy price in the First World War. The navy which went to war in 1914 was not the Band of Brothers St Vincent had forged, and Nelson led, and its limitations were made evident at the Battle of Jutland. Churchill's apologia that in 1916 Admiral Jellicoe was the only man on either side who could have lost the war in an afternoon may have been true, but the same could have been said of Nelson in 1805.

Nelson's genius lay firstly in his command relationships with subordinates, and also with his superiors. Being sure of getting the best performance out of officers and men alike, he was able with confidence to assess the technical risks. Any mistake made by the enemy could and would be instantly exploited with overwhelming force.

---

7. Newnham Collingwood, 1828, pp313–314.

8. Ec/51.

APPENDICES

Further Reading

There are so many books relating to aspects of Nelson's life and to the navy during the period, that only a few of the best can be listed.

Julian Corbett, *The Campaign of Trafalgar*, London: Longmans, 1910.

Edouard Desbriere, translated by Constance Eastwick, *The Naval Campaign of 1805 – Trafalgar*, 2 vols, Oxford: Clarendon, 1933.

Robert Gardiner, *The Line of Battle, the Sailing Warship 1650 –1840*, Conway's History of the Ship, London: Conway Maritime Press, 1992.

Brian Lavery, *The Ship of the Line*, London: Conway Maritime Press, 1983.

T Sturges Jackson, editor, *Logs of the Great Sea Fights, 1794-1805*, 2 vols, London: Navy Records Society, 1900.

Piers Mackesy, *The War in the Mediterranean, 1803-1810*, London: Longmans, Green, 1957.

Sir Harris Nicolas, *The Letters and Despatches of Vice Admiral Lord Viscount Nelson*, 7 vols, London: Henry Colburn, 1844-1846.

Tom Pocock, *Horatio Nelson*, London: Bodley Head, 1987.

Dudley Pope, *The Great Gamble*, Weidenfeld & Nicolson, 1972.

Brian Tunstall and Nicholas Tracy, *Naval Warfare in the Age of Sail, The Evolution of Fighting Tactics, 1650-1815*, London: Conway Maritime Press, 1990.

A comprehensive bibliography of Nelson books is available: Leonard W Cowie, *Lord Nelson 1758-1805*, Bibliographies of British statesmen, No 7, Westport: Meckler, 1990.

Abbreviations used in footnotes

Add MS: British Library, Manuscript Collection, Additional Manuscripts

ADM 1: Admiralty Out Letters, Public Record Office

ADM 3: Admiralty Board Minutes, Public Record Office

Attack: Nicholas Tracy, *Attack on Maritime Trade*, London: Macmillan Press, Toronto: Toronto University Press, 1991

Barham: Sir J K Laughton, ed, *Letters and Papers of Charles, Lord Barham 1758-1813*, Navy Records Society Vols 32, 38 and 39, London, 1904-1911

Barrington: D Bonner-Smith, ed, *Letters and Papers of Admiral the Hon Charles Barrington*, Navy Records Society Vols 77 and 81, London, 1922-1927

Beatty: Sir William Beatty, *The Authentic Narrative of the Death of Lord Nelson*, London: Cadell and Davies, 1806

Browning: Oscar Browning, ed, *England and Napoleon in 1803: Being the Despatches of Lord Whitworth and Others*, London: Royal Historical Society, 1887

Clarke and M'Arthur: Clarke, James Stanier, and M'Arthur, John, *Life of Admiral Lord Nelson KB from his Lordship's Manuscripts*, (first published 1794-8), references are to the 3 vol, London edition of 1840

Cle: Clements Collection, National Maritime Museum, London

Clausewitz: Carl Marie von Clausewitz, *On War*, Peter Paret and Michael Howard, eds, Princeton: Princeton University Press, 1976

CO: Colonial Office Papers, Public Record Office

Codrington: Lady Bourchier, ed, *Memoir of the Life of Admiral Sir Edward Codrington*, London: Longman's Green, 1873

Coleridge: Barbara E Rooke, ed, *The Collected Works of Samuel Taylor Coleridge*, Princeton: Princeton University Press, 1969

Collingwood: Edward Hughes, ed, *The Private Correspondance of Admiral Lord Collingwood*, Navy Records Society Vol 98, London, 1957

Creswell: John Creswell, *British Admirals of the Eighteenth Century*, London, 1972

Croker: John Wilson Croker, ed, *The Croker Papers*, London: J Murray, 1884

Desbrière: Edouard Desbrière, *The Naval Campaign of 1805, Trafalgar*, translated by Constance Eastwick, 2 vols, Oxford; Clarendon, 1933

DLN: Sir Nicholas Harry Nicolas, *Dispatches and Letters of Vice Admiral Lord Viscount Nelson*, 7 vols, London, 1846

Drinkwater: J Drinkwater (Bethune), *Narrative of the Proceedings of the British Fleet*, London: Saunders and Otley, 1840

DUC: Duckworth Papers, National Maritime Museum, London

DUN: Duncan Papers, National Maritime Museum, London

Duro: Cesáreo Fernandez Duro, *Armada Espanola*, Museo Navale, Madrid, 1973 (facsimile of 1895-1903 edition)

Ec : Manuscript Collection, Admiralty Library

Ekins: C Ekins, *Naval Battles of Great Britain*, London, 1828

Ellis: Lady Ellis, ed, *Memoirs and Services of the Late Lieutenant-General Sir S B Ellis KCB, Royal Marines, from his own Memoranda*, London: Saunders, Otley, 1866

Enemy: Edward Fraser, *The Enemy at Trafalgar*, London, Hodder and Stoughton, 1906

Evidence: Evidence Relating to the Tactics Employed by Nelson at the Battle of Trafalgar, Report of a Committee Appointed by the Admiralty, Great Britain, Cd 7120, 1913

Fighting Instructions: Julian S Corbett, ed, *Fighting Instructions*, Navy Records Society Vol 29, London 1905

First Dutch War: S R Gardiner and C T Atkinson, eds, *Papers relating to the First Dutch War*, Navy Records Society, 6 vols, London, 1899-1930

Gardiner: Robert Gardiner, *The Line of Battle, the Sailing Warship 1650-1840,* London: Conway Maritime Press, 1992

Glete: Jan Glete, *Navies and Nations, Warships, Navies and State Building in Europe and America 1500-1860*, 2 vols, Stockholm: Almqvist & Wiskell International, 1993

Hargood: Joseph Allen, ed, *Memoirs of the Life and Services of Sir William Hargood*, Greenwich, Henry S Richardson, 1841

Hawke: Ruddock F Mackay, ed, *The Hawke Papers*, Navy Records Society Vol 129, 1990

HOL: Holland Collection, National Maritime Museum, London

Hood: David Hannay, ed, *Letters of Lord Hood 1781-82,* Navy Records Society Vols 3 and 20, London, 1895

HMC: Historical Manuscripts Collection, Various Collections

Jack Nasty-Face: 'Jack Nasty-Face' (pseud) William Robinson, *Nautical Economy or Forecastle Recollections of Events during the Last War Dedicated to the Brave Tars of Old England by a Sailor politely called by the Officers of the Navy, Jack Nasty-Face*, London: William Robinson, 1836

KEI: Keith Papers, National Maritime Museum, London

Keith: W G Perrin and C C Lloyd, eds, *Letters and Papers of Admiral Viscount Keith*, 3 vols, Navy Records Society Vols 62, 90 and 96, London, 1927-1955

Lavery: Brian Lavery, *The Ship of the Line*, London: Conway Maritime Press, 1983

Logs: T Sturges Jackson, ed, *Logs of the Great Sea Fights, 1794-1805*, 2 vols, London: Navy Records Society, 1900

Lovell: W S Lovell, *Personal Narrative of Events, 1799-1815,* London, 1879

Matcham: M Eyre Matcham, *The Nelsons of Burnham Thorpe*, London: John Lane, 1911

Macready: Frederick Pollock, ed, *Macready's Reminiscences, and Selections from His Diaries and Letters*, 2 vols, London: Macmillan, 1875

Minto: Emma Kynynmound, Countess of Minto, ed, *Life and Letters of Sir Gilbert Elliot, First Earl of Minto*, 1874

MKH: Hood Collection, National Maritime Museum, London

Morrison: A Morrison, ed, A W Thibaudeau, comp, *The Hamilton and Nelson Papers, 1798-1815*, London, 1894

Naish: George P B Naish, *Nelson's Letters to his Wife and other Documents, 1785-1831*, Navy Records Society, 1958

Naval Miscellany: Sir J K Laughton, *The Naval Miscellany*, 3 vols, Navy Records Society Vols 20 and 40, London, 1902-1928

Navies: Nicholas Tracy, *Navies, Deterrence and American Independence*, Vancouver: University of British Columbia Press, 1988

NC: Naval Chronicle, 41 vols, London: Joyce Gold, 1799-1819

Newnham Collingwood: G L Newnham Collingwood, ed, *A Selection from the Public and Private Correspondance of Vice Admiral Lord Collingwood*, London: James Ridgeway, 1828

NM: Naval Manuscripts, Admiralty Library

Otway: J Ralfe, *Historical Memoir of Sir Robert Otway, Bt, KCB, Vice Admiral of the Red* (extracted from *The Naval Biography of Great Britain*, 1828) London, 1840

Pocock: Tom Pocock, *Horatio Nelson*, London: Bodley Head, 1987

Pope: Dudley Pope, *The Great Gamble*, London: Ramage Company, 1972

PRO: Public Record Office, Indigenous collection

REC: Record Collection, National Maritime Museum, London

Rodney: Rodney Papers, London

Sailors: Edward Fraser, *The Sailors whom Nelson Led*, London, 1913

St Vincent: D B Smith, ed, *Letters of Admiral of the Fleet the Earl of St Vincent, 1801-1804*, Vol I, Navy Records Society Vol 55, 1912

SIG: Signal Books, National Maritime Museum, London

Signals and Instructions: Julian Corbett, ed, *Signals and Instructions 1776-1794*, Navy Records Society Vol 35, London, 1908

Sandwich: G R Barnes and J H Owen, *The Private Papers of John, Earl of Sandwich, First Lord of the Admiralty 1771-1782*, Navy Records Society Vols 69, 72, 75 and 78, London 1932-1938

Saumarez: Sir John Ross, ed, *Memoirs and Correspondence of Admiral Lord de Saumarez*, London, 1938

Sea Drift: Hercules Robinson, *Sea Drift*, Portsea: T Hinton, 1858

Sloan MS: Sloan Collection of Manuscripts, British Library, Manuscripts

Southey: Robert Southey, *Life of Nelson* (first published 1813), London: Constable & Co, 1916

Spencer: Julian Corbett, ed, *The Private Papers of George, Second Earl Spencer, First Lord of the Admiralty 1794-1801*, Navy Records Society Vols 46, 48, 58 and 59, London, 1913-1914

Thiers: Louis Adolphe Thiers, *History of the Consulate and Empire of France under Napoleon*, 12 vols, London: Chatto and Windus, 1893

Third Dutch War: R C Anderson, ed, *Journals and Narratives of the Third Dutch War*, Navy Records Society Vol 86, London, 1946

Tomlinson Papers: J G Bullock, ed, *Tomlinson Papers*, Navy Records Society Vol 74, London, 1935

Trafalgar: Julian Corbett, *The Campaign of Trafalgar*, 2 vols, London, 1910

Tucker: J S Tucker, *Memoirs of Admiral The Rt Hon the Earl St Vincent*, 2 vols, London, 1844

TUN: Tunstall Collection, National Maritime Museum, London

Tunstall/Tracy: Brian Tunstall and Nicholas Tracy, *Naval Warfare in the Age of Sail, The Evolution of Fighting Tactics, 1650-1815*, London: Conway Maritime Press, 1990

Vernon: Brian McL Ranft, ed, *The Vernon Papers (1739-1745)*, 99, London, 1958

Warner: Oliver Warner, *A Portrait of Lord Nelson*, London: Chatto and Windus, 1958

WYN: Wynne Collection, National Maritime Museum, London

Wynne: Anne Fremantle, *The Wynne Diaries 1789-1820*, Oxford University Press, 1982

INDEX